MERE THEOLOGY

A Guide to the Thought of C. S. Lewis

WILL VAUS

Foreword by Douglas Gresham

InterVarsity Press
Downers Grove, Illinois
Leicester, England

InterVarsity Press
P.O. Box 1400, Downers Grove, IL 60515-1426
World Wide Web: www.ivpress.com
E-mail: mail@ivpress.com

Inter-Varsity Press, England
38 De Montfort Street, Leicester LE1 7GP, England
World Wide Web: www.ivpbooks.com
E-mail: ivp@uccf.org.uk

InterVarsity Press®, U.S.A., is the book-publishing division of InterVarsity Christian Fellowship/USA®, a student movement active on campus at hundreds of universities, colleges and schools of nursing in the United States of America, and a member movement of the International Fellowship of Evangelical Students. For information about local and regional activities, write Public Relations Dept., InterVarsity Christian Fellowship/USA, 6400 Schroeder Rd., P.O. Box 7895, Madison, WI 53707-7895, or visit the IVCF website at <www.intervarsity.org>.

Inter-Varsity Press, England, is the book-publishing division of the Universities and Colleges Christian Fellowship (formerly the Inter-Varsity Fellowship), a student movement linking Christian Unions in universities and colleges throughout the United Kingdom and the Republic of Ireland, and a member movement of the International Fellowship of Evangelical Students. For information about local and national activities write to UCCF, 38 De Montfort Street, Leicester LE1 7GP.

All Scripture quotations, unless otherwise indicated, are taken from the Holy Bible, New International Version®. NIV®. Copyright © 1973, 1978, 1984 by International Bible Society. Used by permission of Zondervan Publishing House. Distributed in the U.K. by permission of Hodder and Stoughton Ltd. All rights reserved. "NIV" is a registered trademark of International Bible Society. UK trademark number 1448790.

Permission has been granted to reproduce material from a number of sources. See page 13 for a list of these sources.

Design: Cindy Kiple

Images: ©Arthur Strong / National Portrait Gallery, London

USA ISBN 0-8308-2782-X
UK ISBN 1-84474-026-9

Printed in the United States of America ∞

Library of Congress Cataloging-in-Publication Data

Vaus, Will, 1963-
    Mere theology: a guide to the thought of C.S. Lewis/Will Vaus.
        p. cm.
    Includes bibliographical references and index.
    ISBN 0-8308-2782-X (alk. paper)
    1. Lewis, C. S. (Clive Staples), 1898-1963—Religion. 2. Christian
literature, English—History and criticism. I. Title.
BX5199.L53V38 2004
230'.092—dc22
                                                              2003027942

British Library Cataloguing in Publication Data
A catalogue record for this book is available from the British Library.

| P | 20 | 19 | 18 | 17 | 16 | 15 | 14 | 13 | 12 | 11 | 10 | 9 | 8 | 7 | 6 | 5 | 4 | 3 |
| Y | 20 | 19 | 18 | 17 | 16 | 15 | 14 | 13 | 12 | 11 | 10 | 09 | 08 | 07 | 06 | 05 | 04 |

FOR DAD

I look forward to your embrace in the new Narnia,
just as Tirian was embraced by the good King Erlian.

CONTENTS

FOREWORD

FOR A LONG TIME I HAVE KNOWN that sooner or later, someone would write a book like this, and despite my acknowledgment of the need for such a book, it is an eventuality that I have anticipated with some anxiety. It has always worried me that some insufficient scholar or closed-minded religionist would come up with an attempt to translate Jack's (C. S. Lewis's) theology into the terms of his or her personal beliefs, lose sight of the real depths of Jack's thinking and thus leave readers enmired in a morass of misunderstood ideas and half-baked theories. With this book Will Vaus has allayed all my trepidation. Here we have a work of such scholarship and theological honesty that I find myself standing in awe of what Will has achieved.

Will is someone whom I have known for quite a while and have always been glad to regard as a friend. But now I will be able to tell people "I knew him before he was famous," for I believe that this book is going to propel him into a level of recognition that I can only hope he is ready for and prepared to accept and deal with. In this book Will has carefully and thoroughly examined all of Jack's published thinking and followed his train of thought through a lifetime of development, showing us how the theology that governed Jack's life grew and ripened through his letters, his books and his essays until we can understand not only what Jack believed but also why he believed it and how he arrived at that belief. We can follow the thinking along the same lines that Jack traveled, and if we have sufficient personal honesty and humility, no doubt many of us will come to the same conclusions that Jack did.

Often enough books about theology are hard to read, dry and flavorless, complicating the simple and glossing over the complex, but this book I have found easy to read (in difficult circumstances) and intriguing. Will is a writer of skill and one who exhibits a fine concern for his readers and a humility that allows him to present his material without pontification or any intrusion of his ideology or denominational leanings. If I have any bone to pick with him about this book it is that he has written something that may make the study of Jack's theology almost too easy for those studying C. S. Lewis at colleges and universities around the globe. Jack was a consummate teacher, and he was insistent on his pupils reading the original source material rather than lazily relying on what has been written about the writers they are studying. If you are reading this book as an aid to your C. S. Lewis studies, don't let yourself be beguiled by the excellence of this volume into neglecting to read the books that Will references here.

A chronological study of Jack's theological thinking is, I suppose, long overdue, and I can only be grateful that now that it is here, in this book, it has been written so well and with the integrity that Will has brought to the work. I am no theologian, having no training in the field and being very much an amateur, and thus I cannot approach this work with any professional authority. For me this is a very good book, and I have found it of value over the days it has taken me to read it while embroiled in complex business matters. I can only surmise how useful it will be to anyone with a serious scholarly interest in Jack and his life's work, but for those of us trying to grow in our faith and thus come closer to the Lord Jesus this is a valuable addition to our libraries. Read with joy and with a gentle comfort in the knowledge that this book will bring you closer to Jack and through him and his work, closer to Christ. After all, that is exactly what Jack would want, as he himself wrote only to bring us closer to the Lord Jesus whom he represented so well throughout his life and his works.

Douglas Gresham
Ireland, May 2003

ACKNOWLEDGMENTS

MY WHOLE LIFE HAS BEEN BLESSED BY having parents who made me believe that I could accomplish anything I set my mind to do. Thanks go to my mother, who stimulated in me a love for books at a very young age. And my undying gratitude follows my father to Heaven, for, among many gifts, making it possible for me to travel to England at the age of nineteen to see the sites associated with the life of C. S. Lewis and to read the Lewis books I had not yet explored.

This book never would have come to be were it not for my fourth-grade teacher, Mrs. Ewing, who first introduced me to the magical land of Narnia. The doors of imagination she opened for me by reading *The Lion, the Witch and the Wardrobe* to our class were more fantastic than the doors of Professor Kirke's wardrobe itself.

I want to acknowledge those who were influential in the genesis of this book without realizing it. Douglas Gresham's friendship and many shared conversations over the past several years have, I am sure, influenced this book indirectly in a number of ways. Discussion of Lewis and Lewis's theology with the late Sheldon Vanauken also stimulated my thinking on this subject, as did conversations with my friend Richard Burnett. I am thankful to the Columbia, South Carolina, Anglican Society, which invited me to give a Lenten lecture on C. S. Lewis in 1996. That invitation spurred me to write what eventually became the chapter of this book on God's sovereignty and human responsibility. My gratitude also goes to the New York C. S. Lewis Society, which originally published that chapter and the one on Scripture in its bulletin. I also appreciate Wheaton College for inviting me to give one of the lectures in their 1998 centenary celebration of Lewis's theology. The opportunity to spend time at Wheaton's Wade Center, perusing Lewis's old library, helped to further refine my chapter on God's sovereignty. Special thanks are due to Christopher Mitchell, director of the Wade Center, for encouraging me in my early desire to write this book, and to Sherwood Eliot Wirt for encouraging me to write at all.

I could not have written this book as easily were it not for the work of other Lewis scholars who have gone before me. In particular, I am indebted to Janine Goffar for *The C. S. Lewis Index*, to Wayne Martindale and Jerry Root for *The Quotable Lewis* and to Walter Hooper for his *C. S. Lewis Companion and Guide*. I referred to all three of these helpful volumes numerous times as I was searching for particular Lewis quotes and ideas.

I owe a great debt to those who read and commented on the early and late drafts of this work. I appreciate Walter Hooper for urging me to continue with this project and for giving helpful comments on the introduction. My thanks go to the Pittsburgh C. S. Lewis Society, especially Elaine Grimm and Lynn Word, who read portions of the book in its early stages. I could hardly have better literary friends than Lisa Beamer and Sharon Griffin, who read over my entire manuscript and gave many helpful comments. Brad Mercer, a colleague in ministry who I know only through e-mail, kept me going on this project many times by simply asking, "How's the book coming?" And I could not have found a better editor than Gary Deddo of InterVarsity Press, who gave me the gifts of encouragement and critique without which this book would not have seen the light of day.

Finally, the lion's share of my love goes to my family, who encouraged me in the long process of writing this book in countless ways. Thanks go to my wife, Becky, for believing in me and this project enough to allow me to spend countless days off and weeks on end, during multiple summers, cloistered away, reading, writing and editing. Thanks go to my boys, Jamie, Jon and Josh, for sharing my love for Narnia and understanding when Daddy needed quiet to think and work on this project. One day we will be able to give up merely writing and talking about Aslan, and we shall all go for a ride on his back, together forever.

PERMISSIONS

INTRODUCTION

C. S. LEWIS OFTEN GAVE DISCLAIMERS to the effect that he was not a real theologian. In his preface to *The Problem of Pain*, written in 1940, Lewis commented that if any real theologian were to read the book, he would very easily see that it was the work of a layman and an amateur.[1] By suggesting that he was not a real theologian Lewis meant that he did not have a degree in theology, nor was he a professor of theology. However, Lewis took a triple first at Oxford in the 1920s. He received first-class honors in philosophy, English literature and Greats (Greek and Roman classical literature). Then he worked as a tutor in English literature for thirty years at Oxford, as a Fellow of Magdalen College. And from 1954 until shortly before his death in 1963, he held the chair of medieval and Renaissance English literature at Cambridge.

Although Lewis was not a professional theologian, he did consider himself, and every Christian, to be an amateur theologian. At the beginning of *Beyond Personality*, Lewis's third installment of broadcast talks, published in 1945, he defined theology as "the science of God." He maintained that anyone who wants to think about God at all should like to have the clearest and most accurate ideas about him that are available. He believed that was what theology should provide, and therefore every Christian ought to be interested in it.[2]

In the same book, Lewis goes on to suggest that theology is like a map. If you want to get further in the Christian life, you must use that map. You won't get eternal life by just feeling the presence of God in flowers or music. He explains that theology started from people experiencing God and writing down their experimental knowledge of him. Thus theology is very helpful because it provides us with the combined knowledge of many Christians' experience of God over hundreds of years.

The goal of theology is practical. Lewis insists that there is no good in endlessly talking about God; God wants our talk about him to draw us into his life. That is the goal of theology and the goal of this book: to draw the reader more closely into the life of God, that life which Lewis, following St. Gregory of Nazianzus, called the Great Dance.

Lewis often talked about the difference between looking at something and looking along something. In this book we will be doing a lot of looking at C. S. Lewis and his writings, but I hope you won't stop there. What I want most for you is that you would look with me along Lewis's writings back up to the God of whom he writes.

At times I disagree with Lewis in some of his theological conclusions. However, one great value of Lewis's writings is that they make you think through issues in a creative way. With his illustrations he makes you see things you didn't see quite so clearly before. While I may disagree with Lewis at times, I am always grateful for what he has written. As you will see in the chapter on Scripture, Lewis accepted the Bible as the highest authority in the life of the Christian. He also valued older books more than modern ones, often saying that for every modern book a person reads, he should read one old one, like a book by Jane Austen, Milton or the Bible.[3] Therefore I don't think Lewis would mind us going back to the Bible and comparing his teaching with it. So that is what I would encourage you to do. Don't simply accept what Lewis teaches; compare it with Scripture to find out the truth.

My introduction to C. S. Lewis came in the fourth grade in public school. My teacher read to our class *The Lion, the Witch and the Wardrobe.* My parents immediately bought me the whole set of *The Chronicles of Narnia,* and I devoured each book. I have been fascinated with Narnia ever since. Years later I was challenged by my youth pastor to read some of Lewis's more directly theological works. Then at the age of nineteen I traveled to the British Isles one summer and read all of Lewis's explicitly Christian works while visiting the places where he lived, worked and worshiped. In more recent years I have led others on similar pilgrimages.

Over the years I have met many Lewis enthusiasts who have wondered, "What did Lewis believe about _____?" (You fill in the blank.) This book is written to answer those many questions about what Lewis believed.

It is important to note that this book, following Lewis's use of the term "mere christianity" is about "mere theology." Lewis used the word *mere* in its Middle English sense to mean "pure, unmixed, unadulterated." Of course, no theology will be completely pure until we see God "face to face." So what you have between the covers of this book is a representation of Lewis's attempt at "mere theology."

If you are picking up this book and have never read anything by C. S. Lewis, I hope that this introduction to his thought will serve as the beginning of a lifelong pilgrimage. And if you have been reading Lewis for some time, may the signposts in this guidebook provide helpful direction along the way. Here's to the journey!

Will Vaus
The Ivy Cottage, Twelfth Night, 2004

DEFENDING THE FAITH

C. S. LEWIS IS PERHAPS BEST KNOWN TODAY as the author of the children's books *The Chronicles of Narnia*. However, he has also been widely revered as the greatest Christian apologist of the twentieth century. Chad Walsh, in the first published study of the man and his work, called C. S. Lewis "the apostle to the skeptics." An apologist is one who gives a defense, in this case a defense of the Christian faith. There are four prongs to Lewis's defense of Christianity. We will examine each of them in turn: the argument from longing, the argument from morality, the argument from reason and the argument from Christ.

However, before we examine his arguments in defense of Christianity, we must recognize something that was quite clear to Lewis: we cannot prove the existence of God. C. S. Lewis once wrote about this in a letter to a young agnostic, Sheldon Vanauken. Lewis maintains that there is not a demonstrative proof of Christianity or of the existence of matter or of the good will and honesty of his best and oldest friends. He suggests that all three are (except perhaps the second) far more probable than the alternatives. He asks whether God is even interested in the kind of theism that would be a compelled logical assent to a conclusive argument. Are we interested in it in personal matters? We demand from our friends a trust in our good faith that is certain without demonstrative proof. It wouldn't be confidence if our friends waited for rigorous proof. He cites two examples from literature. Othello believed in Desdemona's innocence when it was proved, but that was too late. Lear believed in Cordelia's love when it was proved, but that was too late. The magnanimity, the generosity that will trust on a reasonable probability, is what God requires of us in our relationship to him.[1]

Lewis as an apologist never seeks to prove God. What he does seek to do is to demonstrate the reasonable probability of Christianity. As Lewis points out, the reasoning process is based upon intuition as well as logic. One cannot manufacture rational intuition by argument. There are certain things that must simply be "seen."[2] Furthermore, if Christianity is true, then there comes a time when "you are no longer faced with an argument which demands your assent, but with a Person who demands your confidence."[3] And Lewis knew quite well the importance for the apologist of falling back from the web of argument into the reality of Christ.[4] That being said, let us now examine Lewis's arguments for the reasonableness of the faith.

THE ARGUMENT FROM LONGING

Lewis's argument from longing appears in the first book he wrote after becoming a Christian: *The Pilgrim's Regress.* In that book he calls this longing romanticism. In the afterword to the third edition of *The Pilgrim's Regress* he defines terms. What he means by *romanticism* is a particular recurrent experience that dominated his childhood and adolescence, which he called *romantic* because inanimate nature and marvelous literature were among the things that evoked it. The experience was one of intense longing. It is distinguished from other longings by two things. First, though the sense of desire is acute and even painful, the mere wanting is felt to be somehow a delight. This hunger is better than any other fullness; this poverty is better than all other wealth. Second, there is a peculiar mystery about the object of this desire. Inexperienced people suppose they know what they want when they feel this longing. Thus if it comes to a child while he is looking at a far off hillside he at once thinks, "If only I were there." If it comes when he is remembering some event in the past, he thinks: "if only I could go back to those days." If it comes while a young man is reading a romantic tale or poem, he thinks he is wishing that such places really existed and that he could reach them. If it comes to an adolescent in a context with erotic suggestions, he believes he has a desire for the perfect beloved. If he discovers literature that treats of spirits and the like with some show of serious belief, he may think that he is desiring real magic and occultism. When it darts out upon him from his studies in history or science, he may confuse it with the intellectual craving for knowledge. But every one of these impressions is wrong. The only merit

Lewis claims for his book is that it is written by one who proved false all these ways of trying to satisfy the deepest longings of the heart.[5]

In *The Pilgrim's Regress*, John, the chief character, longs for an island in the west that he has seen in a vision. His longing for the island leads him on a journey far from his home in Puritania and far from the Landlord (God). However, when John reaches the island he finds out that it is merely the back side of the mountains of the Landlord and that he must retrace his steps in order to arrive once again at his real home.

Lewis communicates the power of longing in John's first vision of the island in *The Pilgrim's Regress*. There comes to John from behind him the sound of a musical instrument, very sweet and very short, and after it a full, clear voice—so high and strange that John thinks it is very far away, farther than a star. The voice says, "Come." Then John sees that there is a stone wall beside the road. However, this garden wall is unique in that it has a window in it. There is no glass in the window, and there are no bars; it is just a square hole in the wall. Through it he sees a green wood full of primroses, and he remembers suddenly how he went into another wood to pull primroses, as a child, very long ago—so long that even in the moment of remembering the memory seems still out of reach. While he strains to grasp it, there comes to him from beyond the wood a sweetness and a pang so piercing that instantly he forgets his father's house and his mother, and the fear of the Landlord, and the burden of the rules. "All the furniture of his mind is taken away." A moment later he finds himself sobbing. The sun has gone in. He cannot quite remember what has happened, whether it had happened in this wood or in the other wood when he was a child. It seems to him that through a mist he has seen a calm sea, and in the sea an island, where the smooth turf slopes down unbroken to the bays.[6]

There is probably no more dominant theme in all of Lewis's writings than this theme of longing, or what the Germans call *sehnsucht*, or what Lewis came to call joy. The theme appears in his sermons, like *The Weight of Glory*, where he says that he feels a certain shyness in regard to speaking of this longing. He says that he is trying to rip open the inconsolable secret in each of his listeners, a secret that pierces with such sweetness that when the mention of it becomes imminent, we grow awkward and affect to laugh at ourselves. It is a secret we cannot hide and cannot tell, though we desire to do both. We cannot tell it because it is a desire for something that has never appeared in our experience. Again, the books or the music in which we thought the beauty was located will betray us if we trust them. The beauty is not in them, it only comes through them, and what comes through them is longing. Beauty and the memory of our past are good images of what we really desire, but if they are mistaken for the thing itself, they turn into dumb idols, breaking the hearts of their worshipers. These images are not the thing itself; they are only the scent of a flower we have not picked, the echo of a tune we have not heard, news from a country we have not yet visited.[7]

The theme of longing also appears in Lewis's children's stories. The existence of the magical land of Narnia, and the fact that the children cannot get there whenever they want to, creates in them a longing. Within the stories, the experience of this joyful longing appears over and over again. In *The Lion, the Witch and the Wardrobe* Lewis describes what happens when the children from our world first hear the name of Aslan. Each one of the children feels something jump inside him or her. Edmund feels a sensation of mysterious horror. Peter feels suddenly brave and adventurous. Susan feels as if some delicious smell or delightful strain of music has just passed by her. Lucy gets the feeling you have when you wake up in the morning and realize that it is the first day of summer vacation.[8]

In his autobiography, *Surprised by Joy*, Lewis sums up the manner in which this longing led him to Christ. The longing started in childhood and came to him on various occasions. It came to him first as he was standing beside a flowering currant bush on a summer day, then when his brother brought a toy garden into the nursery, again while he was reading Beatrix Potter's *Squirrel Nutkin*, and later while he was reading Longfellow's *Saga of King Olaf*. Lewis asserts that the central story of his life is all about this unsatisfied desire, which is itself more desirable than any other satisfaction. He calls it joy, which is to be sharply distinguished from happiness and from pleasure. Joy (in Lewis's sense) has indeed only one characteristic in common with happiness and pleasure: the fact that anyone who has experienced it will want it again. Apart from that, Lewis's joy might almost equally be called a kind of unhappiness or grief. However, it is a kind we want. Anyone who has tasted it won't want to exchange it for all the pleasures in the world.[9]

In the end, however, Lewis concludes that this joy is valuable only as a pointer to something other and outer. It is valuable only insofar as it points us to God. While we are lost, joy naturally looms large in our thoughts, just as when we are lost in the woods the sight of a signpost is a great matter. But when we have found the main road and are passing signposts every few miles, we don't stop and stare anymore. The signposts encourage us, and we should be grateful to the authority that set them up, but we shouldn't get caught up in staring at signposts for the rest of our lives. Joy is a signpost to the new Jerusalem that should encourage us to continue on our way.[10]

After becoming a Christian, Lewis turned around and began using this joy, this longing, this experience of *sehnsucht* that led him to Christ, to lead others to Christ. In his afterword to *The Pilgrim's Regress*, he describes how longing is an argument for Christianity. According to Lewis, if a person diligently follows desire and resolutely abandons false sources when their falsity appears, that person will come out at last into the clear knowledge that the human soul was made to enjoy some object that is never fully given in our present mode of experience.[11] The longing that all human beings experience for something that cannot be had in this world suggests that we were made for another world, or for Someone outside of this world, namely, God.

Lewis uses this argument in a letter to Sheldon Vanauken. He asks Vanauken what the existence of a wish suggests. Lewis comments about how he was once impressed by Arnold's line "Nor does the being hungry prove that we have bread," but then he takes issue with the statement. Though being hungry doesn't prove that one particular person will get food, it does prove that there is such a thing as food! If we were a species that didn't normally eat, weren't designed to eat, would we feel hungry? If we are really the products of a materialistic universe, how is it we don't feel at home in it? Do fish complain about being wet? If they did, wouldn't that suggest that they had not always been, or would not always be, purely aquatic creatures? Lewis calls attention to how we are perpetually surprised at time. "How time flies! Fancy John being grown-up and married! I can hardly believe it!" Why can't we believe it? The reason is because there is something in us that is *not* temporal.[12]

The fact that we have a desire for something or someone that cannot be satisfied by anything or anyone in this world suggests that there is something or someone outside of this world who can satisfy our desire. As Blaise Pascal said, there is a God-shaped vacuum in the heart of every person. The existence of this vacuum, and the experience of intense longing for something that cannot be had in this world, both suggest that there is a God. Ecclesiastes 3:11 says that God "has also set eternity in the hearts of men." We all have a desire for timelessness. The argument from longing is one of the most powerful arguments for the existence of the supernatural realm, and Lewis is perhaps the best conveyor of this argument in modern fiction and nonfiction.

THE ARGUMENT FROM MORALITY

The second prong of Lewis's defense of Christianity consists of the argument from morality. This is the first argument that Lewis uses to defend the existence of God in his *Broadcast Talks*, later reprinted as the first two books of *Mere Christianity*.

The first book of *Mere Christianity* is entitled "Right and Wrong as a Clue to the Meaning of the Universe." The first thing Lewis does in this book is demonstrate from everyday experience the existence of ultimate right and wrong.

First, Lewis argues, the fact that there is ultimate right and wrong is seen in the way people quarrel with each other. When people quarrel with each other they always appeal to some sense of ultimate right and wrong. We can see this even with children. One of their favorite phrases is, "That's not fair!" Children have a sense of ultimate fairness, of ultimate right and wrong that is imprinted on their minds.

People who quarrel say things like, "I was there first. What gives you the right to push your way in?" Or they say, "I gave you one of my cookies, so you should share one of your crackers with me." Or else, "Honey, you promised that you would get the car washed! Now you better live up to your promise." The point of quarreling is to determine who is at fault, and you can't determine who is at fault unless there is right and wrong.

Second, Lewis points out that at some stage in the quarrel someone may offer an excuse for their behavior, but that in no way eliminates ultimate right and wrong. The person offering the excuse tries to show why his or her behavior was not in the wrong. People try to establish why they had a right to take the first person's place or why they shouldn't share their crackers, or they introduce an intervening event that relieves them from keeping their promise. Seldom does the person offering the excuse disagree with the other person's standard. Both of them know there is a right way to behave and a wrong way to behave. If we do not believe in ultimate right and wrong, then why do we spend so much time trying to prove that our behavior is right? Isn't it because we do believe there is ultimate right and wrong, and we desperately want to be found in the right?

Next Lewis answers the objection of those who claim that this sense of ultimate right and wrong is merely instinct. They say, "Isn't our sense of right and wrong just our herd instinct?" The answer is no; we have something more than instinct operating here.

Suppose you see someone in danger, or someone who is drowning and no one else is around to help. Your first instinct may be to help the person who is in danger or who is drowning because that person is a human being just like you, and that's what you would want if the situation were reversed. That is your herd instinct coming into play. In the next second, however, you will be thinking that you don't want to get involved because you don't want to get hurt. That is your instinct of self-preservation. Our instincts are often in conflict with one another, and over and above our instincts we often hear another voice, the voice of conscience, telling us what we should do. As in the situation above, our conscience would tell us that we should help the person who is in trouble. Interestingly enough, often our conscience will tell us to obey the weaker of our instincts, as in the case above. This shows that the sense of ultimate right and wrong is more than just instinct.

Furthermore, Lewis posits, if ultimate right and wrong were merely matters of instinct, then we ought to be able to point to some instincts that are always right and some that are always wrong. We cannot do that. Sometimes it is right to follow certain instincts in certain situations, while it is wrong to follow those same instincts in other situations. Take our instinct to fight. We would all recognize that sometimes it is right to fight to defend self or family, but someone who fights all the time we call a bully. Arguably, in this instance, there is a sense of ultimate right and wrong impinging upon our instincts. Lewis suggests that our instincts are like keys on a piano, neither right nor wrong in and of themselves. However, there is a right or wrong time to hit a certain key depending upon the piece of music you are playing. The moral law is like the sheet music that tells us which notes to play at what time.

Lewis goes on to answer the objection of those who claim that morality is merely a social contract. They say that societies have decided for themselves what is healthy for maintaining that society, but there is no ultimate right and wrong. It is all a matter of social convention. However, if you really want to maintain that morality is merely a social contract, then you have to be willing to accept the end result: if morality is merely a social contract, then what Hitler did was acceptable. If there is no ultimate right and wrong, then we have no means by which we can say that what Hitler did, by gassing six million Jews, was wrong. Most, if not all people, find this conclusion unacceptable. Why? Because a sense of ultimate right and wrong is ingrained in our very being.

Lewis also notes that the existence of ultimate right and wrong is evidenced by the great similarity between the moral codes of numerous cultures. Some people try to say that different cultures and civilizations have had different moralities, but this is not true. In the appendix to *The Abolition of Man*, Lewis shows the similarities between the moral codes of the major cultures of human history.

Lewis invites us to imagine a country where people are admired for running away in battle, or where a person feels proud of double-crossing all the people who have been kindest to him or her. He asserts you might as well try to imagine a country where two and two make five. People have differed with regard to which people you ought to be unselfish: should you be unselfish just to your family, or your fellow citizens, or everyone? But human beings have always agreed that you ought not to put yourself first. Selfishness has never been admired. Men have disagreed as to whether you should have one wife or four, but they have always agreed that you must not simply have any woman you want.[13]

Lewis maintains that there is a law of human nature, which transcends all cultures and points to the validity of the religious worldview vs. the materialist worldview. By "the Law of Human Nature" Lewis means the law of right and wrong. The existence of this law of human nature suggests that there is a Mind behind the universe, a Lawgiver who wants us to behave in a certain way. The existence of the moral law suggests a Mind behind the universe that is very interested in right conduct. In that sense, we can agree with the account given by Christianity, and some other religions, that God is good. But, Lewis says, we must not go too fast here. The moral law does not give us any ground for thinking that God is good in the sense of being indulgent, soft or sympathetic. There is nothing soft about the moral law. It is as hard as nails. It is no use, at this point, saying that a good God is a God who can forgive. You are going too quickly. Only a Person can forgive. And we have not gotten as far as a personal God—only as far as a power behind the moral law and more like a mind than it is like anything else. However, this Mind may still be very unlike a Person.[14]

This is as far as Lewis's argument from morality will take us in our search for ultimate reality. First, we know from history, experience and conscience that there is ultimate right and wrong. Second, we know that we have all done wrong. Third, the existence of ultimate right and wrong points to a Mind that is behind the moral law. That is all that the moral law can tell us.

THE ARGUMENT FROM REASON

The third prong of Lewis's defense of Christianity is his argument from reason. His primary work containing this argument is *Miracles*. His central argument in the book is that naturalism contains a great self-contradiction. He quotes Professor Haldane in support of his view: "If my mental processes are determined wholly by the motions of atoms in my brain, I have no reason to suppose that my beliefs are true . . . and hence I have no reason for supposing my brain to be composed of atoms."[15] If the naturalists are right and nature is all there is, then this begs the question, from where does reason come? Lewis posits that reason can only come from outside of nature. If nature is all there is, then there is no purpose behind the existence of the universe. If there is no purpose, then there is no reason. If there is no reason, then all arguments for or against naturalism are nonsensical and thus invalid.

Lewis's argument for the self-contradiction inherent in naturalism received criticism from Elizabeth Anscombe, later professor of philosophy at Cambridge. The criticism came in the form of a debate during a Socratic Club meeting in Oxford on February 2, 1948.[16] The particular statement in the first edition of *Miracles* to which Anscombe objected was Lewis's statement that "we may in fact state as a rule that no thought is valid if it can be fully explained as the result of irrational causes."[17] Anscombe insisted that a distinction should be made between irrational causes (such as passion, self-interest, obstinacy and prejudice) and nonrational causes (such things as brain tumors, tuberculosis and mental fatigue). She asked Lewis to clarify what he meant by the word *valid*. Anscombe also distinguished between the ground of a conclusion (the reasons a person would give if asked to explain why one thinks such and such) and the cause of a conclusion (brain tumors, prejudices or whatever makes one think as one does). Lewis admitted in the course of debate that his use of the word *valid* was unfortunate.[18]

After the debate, Lewis was dejected. He told George Sayer that he felt his argument for the existence of God had been demolished.[19] However, Lewis did some further thinking on the whole issue of naturalism, which resulted in his rewriting chapter 3 of *Miracles* for the 1960 Fontana paperback version.[20]

Some Lewis scholars maintain that after the debate with Anscombe, Lewis made a deliberate decision to no longer write any strictly theological or apologetic works.[21] Sayer maintains that Lewis told him, with regard to *Miracles*, "I can never write another book of that sort."[22] Obviously, though, after Lewis thought the matter through, he did not give up on classical apologetics, as he did rewrite that chapter in *Miracles,* and that only a few years before his death. Though it seems Lewis was humbled by the encounter with Anscombe, he clearly continued to be a believer in Christ. Furthermore, he continued to stand by his early defenses of the Christian faith up to the time of his death. However, it would appear that after the debate with Anscombe, Lewis recognized the greater strength of intuitive and imaginative ways of leading people to faith in Christ, over and above his earlier and more strictly logical approach in his broadcast talks. Thus Lewis came to write *The Chronicles of Narnia* in order to "baptize the imaginations" of children.

At any rate, Lewis's argument from reason may be summed up as follows: If there is no reason, then the statement that there is no reason is unreasonable. If reason does exist, then it points to the reality of the supernatural realm. In *Mere Christianity* Lewis writes that atheism is too simple. If there is no meaning to the universe, we should never have found it out—just as, if there was no light in the universe and therefore no creatures with eyes, we would never know it was dark. The word *dark* would have no meaning.[23]

THE ARGUMENT FROM CHRIST

The fourth and most crucial prong of Lewis's defense of Christianity is his argument from Christ. In the second book of *Mere Christianity*, entitled "What Christians Believe," this line of argument follows Lewis's argument from morality. However, when Lewis begins to talk of Christ, he takes us a step further, a step higher, than we could possibly go in following his other arguments for the faith. The way of knowing truth through Christ is far more direct than the way of knowing truth through morality, reason or even through longing. At this point it might be said that we begin to move from "the logic of speculative thought" into "the logic of personal relations."[24]

Lewis spends the first two and one half chapters of "What Christians Believe" setting the stage for the argument from Christ. He briefly examines a few different "rival conceptions of God": atheistic materialism, pantheism, modernist Christianity (what Lewis calls Christianity-and-water), dualism and the Christian idea of God.

Lewis's final evaluation of atheistic materialism has already been mentioned above. Lewis rejects pantheism because it talks nonsense. The pantheist says that if you could only see cancer or a slum from the divine point of view, you would realize that it also is God.[25] Lewis calls this "damned nonsense." He rejects pantheism because it flies in the face of our deep-seated sense of right and wrong.

Lewis rejects Christianity-and-water because it is too simple. This conception of God asserts that there is a good God in Heaven; therefore all is right with the world. This leaves out the terrible doctrines of sin, hell, the devil and redemption. Lewis maintains it is no good asking for a simple religion because real things are not simple.[26]

Lewis claims that there are only two conceptions of God that face all the facts: the Christian one and dualism. What are the facts that must be faced? The facts are these: that the universe contains much that is obviously bad and apparently meaningless, and there are creatures like ourselves who know that it is bad and meaningless.[27] According to Lewis, only dualism and Christianity face these facts head on.

Dualism is the belief that there are two equal and independent powers behind the universe, one good and the other evil. However, the question that must be asked in regard to dualism is, Why do we call one power good and the other evil? When we call one power good and the other evil, we may be declaring our preference for good over evil. If this is the case, then we ought to give up talking about good and evil and make it clear that we are talking only about our preferences. The other alternative is to say that there really is good and evil. If there is good and evil, then by what standard are we judging? Whatever the standard, it is higher up than either good or evil, therefore the higher standard should be called God. Thus dualism falls apart.

The other problem with dualism is that a person cannot be bad for the mere sake of badness, but a person can be good for the mere sake of goodness. As Lewis notes, goodness is original; badness is only goodness corrupted.[28] Therefore dualism does not make full sense of the universe as we know it.

According to Lewis, the only conception of God that makes full sense of the universe is the Christian one, though the Christian view comes very close to dualism. Christianity maintains that God created everything good and then some of his creation chose to set up on its own, thus becoming evil. The difference between Christianity and dualism is that Christianity believes that God created the Dark Power, or the devil. However, Christianity agrees with dualism that this world is at war. This world is "enemy-occupied territory." Christianity is the story of how the rightful King of this world has landed here in disguise and is calling on us to take part in his plan of sabotage against the Dark Power.

In the chapter of *Mere Christianity* titled "The Shocking Alternative," Lewis answers the question, is this state of affairs (the battle of good against evil) in accord with God's will or not? He points out that God has not desired that evil should exist, but he has allowed it. Why? Because of free will. Why has God given free will to his creatures? Because without free will, human beings cannot love, for love is a choice.[29]

The second major question Lewis answers in this chapter is, What has God done in response to evil? Lewis tells us that God has done four things. First, he has left us with conscience. Second, he has left us what Lewis calls good dreams—the myths of various ancient societies that tell of a god who dies and comes to life again thereby giving new life to men. The third thing God has done in response to evil is hammer into one group of people, the Jews, that there is only one God and that he cares deeply about right conduct. The final thing God has done—and here is the real shock—is that he has become a man.

Thus Lewis leads into his christological argument for the probability of Christianity. The argument runs like this. (1) Among the Jews there turns up a man who goes about talking as if he was God. He claims to forgive sins. He says that he has always existed. He says that he is coming to judge the world at the end of time. (2) Such claims as Jesus made would not be unusual among pantheists, who believe that everyone is a part of God. But Jesus, being a Jew, would not have had this pantheistic concept of God in mind. What Jesus claimed is shocking because he was claiming to be the One outside the world who created it and was wholly different from any part of his creation.[30] (3) Therefore there are only three alternatives: either Jesus was a madman, something worse or the Son of God.

The "something worse" that Lewis suggests Jesus was, if he was not God or a madman, is that Jesus was a diabolical liar. Another apologist, Josh McDowell, writing many years later but building on Lewis's argument, presents us with a similar trilemma: either Jesus was a liar, a lunatic or Lord and God.[31] What Lewis does is to show us forcefully that a man like Jesus, who claimed to be God by his words and deeds, could not simply have been a great moral teacher. That is not an option left open to us.

Lewis contends that it is obvious to him that Jesus was neither a lunatic nor a fiend. These options are not consistent with Jesus being one of the greatest, if not the greatest of, moral teachers of all time. Therefore Lewis concludes that Jesus must be God.

However, those who have heard and seriously considered Lewis's argument from Christ raise some valid questions. How do we know that the presentation of Jesus' words and deeds in the New Testament is accurate? Couldn't it all be legends? Some people suppose that Lewis did not even consider such questions as these, but that is not the case. Lewis was well aware of various modern attacks on the historicity of the New Testament picture of Jesus. We will examine Lewis's response to those attacks in the next chapter.

SCRIPTURE

LEWIS'S FIRST PUBLISHED COMMENTS ON the nature of the Old Testament were written in *The Problem of Pain*. In chapter five of that book, on the Fall of Man, he avows that he has the deepest respect for pagan myths, still more for myths in Holy Scripture.[1] Then he goes on to tell us that the Genesis account of the Fall is not necessarily historical. For instance, we don't know how many men God originally created. We don't know the exact historical process of the Fall. Lewis asserts that the Fall may have concerned the literal eating of a fruit, but the question is of no consequence to him.[2]

In *Miracles*, published in 1947, Lewis tells us more about his views on the book of Genesis. He avers that the story in Genesis is told in the form of a folk tale, and he claims Jerome as his authority for this view.[3] Lewis states this same idea in an article written for *The Guardian* in 1943 entitled "Dogma and the Universe."[4]

Later in *Miracles*, Lewis describes exactly what he thinks is going on in the Old Testament. He suggests that the truth first appeared in mythical form and then by a long process of condensing or focusing finally became incarnate as history. In other words, myth became incarnate as history in Jesus Christ.[5]

It is vitally important to understand what Lewis means by myth. He does *not* use the word *myth* in the same sense as Reinhold Niebuhr, who defined myth as a symbolic representation of nonhistorical truth.[6] Lewis defines myth as "a real though unfocused gleam of divine truth falling on human imagination."[7]

According to Lewis, we can't say for certain where any one Old Testament story falls in this long process of myth becoming history. He feels confident that the memoirs of David's court are scarcely less historical than Mark or

Acts but that the book of Jonah is at the opposite end. In other words, Jonah is one of the fabulous stories of the Old Testament. Lewis conveys the same thought in a paper entitled "Is Theology Poetry?" which was originally read to the Socratic Club on November 6, 1944.[8] In that paper, he includes Noah's ark and the story of the sun standing still in the category of mythological stories from the Old Testament.

THE NEW TESTAMENT

The majority of Lewis's comments with regard to the historicity of the New Testament have to do with the Gospels. In *What Are We to Make of Jesus Christ?* originally published in 1950, he asserts that as a literary historian he is convinced that the Gospels are not legends. The Gospels are not artistic enough to be legends. They are clumsy; they don't work up to things properly. Most of the life of Jesus is unknown to us, as is the life of any other ancient person. But no person building up a legend would have allowed Jesus' biography to remain unknown. Apart from bits of the Platonic dialogues, Lewis asserts there are no conversations he knows of in ancient literature like those in the Fourth Gospel, and one must note that Lewis was quite familiar with ancient Greek and Roman literature. There is nothing like the Gospel of John, even in modern literature, until the realistic novel came into existence in the nineteenth century. In the story of the woman taken in adultery, it is said that Jesus bent down and wrote in the dust with his finger. Nothing comes of this incident. No one has ever based any doctrine on it. And the art of inventing little irrelevant details to make an imaginary scene more convincing is a purely modern art. Lewis suggests that the only explanation of this passage is that it really happened. The author of the Fourth Gospel put it in because he had seen it.[9]

Lewis makes a similar comment about the nature of the Gospels in *Surprised by Joy* when he is describing his response to the Gospels immediately prior to his conversion. He muses that the Gospels do not have the mythical taste. Yet the very content which they set down in their artless, historical fashion is precisely the content of the great myths.[10]

Lewis gets even more explicit in his comments on the historicity of the Gospels in a marvelous paper entitled "Modern Theology and Biblical Criticism." This paper was originally addressed to a group of young men studying for the ministry at Westcott House, Cambridge, on May 11, 1959. Writing about the incident of the woman caught in the act of adultery in the Gospel of John, Lewis maintains that there are only two possible views of such a text. Either it is reporting, perhaps with some errors but close to fact, almost as close as Boswell, or else some second-century writer anticipated the whole technique of the nineteenth-century novel.[11]

Other comments about the historicity of the New Testament are scattered throughout Lewis's writings. In "The World's Last Night," he posits that the fact that the evangelists mention things that at first might seem damaging to their case is the strongest argument for the historicity of the Gospels.[12] And in "Petitionary Prayer: A Problem Without an Answer," originally read to the Oxford Clerical Society on December 8, 1953, Lewis professes that he finds no difficulty in accepting the story of Jesus' and Peter's walking on the water as historical.[13]

REFLECTIONS ON THE PSALMS

Lewis's most lengthy treatment of the subject of Scripture comes in *Reflections on the Psalms*, published in 1958. At the beginning of the book he relates his belief concerning the nature of Scripture. He contends that the whole of Scripture is in some sense, though not all parts of it in the same sense, the Word of God.[14] He also maintains that the "contemptible" cursing Psalms are still of use to us as Christians.[15] He goes on to say what use he thinks we can make of these Psalms in his chapter on "The Cursings."

Lewis's most detailed treatment of the subject comes in the chapter simply titled "Scripture." In that chapter he affirms that the Old Testament writings are holy, inspired, the oracles of God. But this does not mean, for Lewis, that every sentence of the Old Testament carries historical or scientific truth. He claims that he is siding with Jerome and John Calvin on this point, neither of whom, he maintains, viewed the Old Testament in this way.

How does Lewis judge whether or not a particular story is historical? He makes it clear that the historicity of a story should not be rejected simply because it recounts miracles. We have no philosophical ground for supposing that miracles do not occur. In the case of Job, Lewis considers that book to be ahistorical simply because the text of *Job* itself does not connect the story to history.

In this chapter in *Reflections on the Psalms* Lewis again comments on the book of Genesis. He acknowledges that the account of Creation in Genesis may be derived from earlier Semitic stories. But this does not mar the value of the biblical creation story for him. For Lewis the Old Testament is literature taken into the service of God's Word. God's Word is not converted into literature, but literature is taken up to be the vehicle of God's communication.

Lewis believes that there was a Divine pressure on all the writers, editors and canonizers of Scripture. He admits that the human qualities of Scripture still show through. Those qualities include naivete, error, contradiction and even wickedness. The total result of this Divine pressure is not the Word of God in the sense that every passage in itself gives impeccable science or history. Rather, Scripture carries the Word of God. In order for us to receive the Word of God, we must steep ourselves in its tone or temper so as to learn the overall message.

Lewis holds to neither the fundamentalist view of Scripture nor to the Roman Catholic view of the church as being inerrant authorities. He argues that he cannot see where God has done in the Bible what the fundamentalist says he has done. In other words, Lewis has examined the phenomena of Scripture, and therefore he believes there is error in the Bible.

What kind of errors does Lewis suppose might be in the Bible? A letter that Lewis wrote to Professor Clyde S. Kilby of Wheaton College clarifies Lewis's position.[16] In that letter Lewis states that whatever view we hold of the divine authority of Scripture that view must allow for the following facts:

1. The distinction Paul makes in I Corinthians 7:10-12 between commands he gives from himself and those he gives from the Lord.

2. The apparent inconsistencies between the genealogies in Matthew and Luke as well as the apparent inconsistencies between the account of Judas' death in Matthew and in Acts.

3. Luke's account of how he got the content for his Gospel in Luke 1:1-4.

4. The ahistoricity, though not falsity, of at least some biblical narratives (i.e., the parables of Jesus, and possibly Jonah and Job).

In the same letter Lewis states that we cannot assume that any one passage of Scripture is inerrant in exactly the same sense as any other. For example, he says, we cannot assume that the numbers of Old Testament armies are statistically correct just because the story of the Resurrection of Jesus is historically correct. Lewis concludes by remarking that the kind of truth moderns sometimes demand of Scripture was probably not even envisaged by the ancient writers of Scripture.

By this account the only place where Lewis might definitely ascribe any kind of scientific or historical error to Scripture is in the case of the numbers of Old Testament armies reported in Scripture. In no case does Lewis purport that there is any doctrinal error in the Bible. Therefore we can at the very least say that Lewis held a high view of the inspiration and authority of Scripture even if not an inerrantist view.

As far as the apostle Paul goes, Lewis thinks his writing at times lacks lucidity and orderly exposition. However, the most important thing is that Paul's writings show us Christ operating in a man's life.

In regard to the teaching of Jesus, Lewis finds no imperfection there. However, Christ's teaching is not given to us in a systematic fashion, nor can the sayings of Jesus be reduced to a system. Perhaps Lewis's greatest line in the book comes at the end of his chapter on Scripture when he says of Jesus, "Systems cannot keep up with that darting illumination. No net less wide than a man's whole heart, nor less fine of mesh than love, will hold the sacred Fish."[17] God forces us to use our whole mind when we approach Scripture. God wants us to search the Scriptures in order to find in them the Word that he has for us. God wants us to use our whole heart in order to grasp Christ as he is witnessed in Scripture.

MODERN BIBLICAL CRITICISM

As I have mentioned already, Lewis delivered an excellent paper on the subject of modern biblical criticism at Westcott House, Cambridge, in 1959. Lewis's evaluation of modern biblical criticism is largely negative because, whatever such critics may know about the Bible, Lewis believes they have little ability as literary critics. Second, he does not highly value their modern "theology of the liberal type" because much of it is based upon the presupposition that Christ came very rapidly to be misunderstood and misrepresented by his followers. Lewis finds a priori improbability in that presupposition. Third, he disagrees with the modern theologian's constant use of the principle that the miraculous does not occur. Finally, he doubts the modern biblical critic's ability to reconstruct the genesis of the texts that he studies. For an elaboration of these points one should read "Modern Theology and Biblical Criticism" in full.

Again, Lewis has further comments on modern biblical criticism scattered throughout his writings. In "Why I Am Not a Pacifist," a paper delivered to the Oxford Pacifist Society sometime in 1940, he comments about the so-called historical Jesus. Any theory, he asserts, that bases itself on a supposed historical Jesus to be carved out of the Gospels and then set up in opposition to orthodox Christian teaching is suspect. There have been too many historical Jesuses—a liberal Jesus, a pneumatic Jesus, a Barthian Jesus and a Marxist Jesus. They are the cheap products of each publisher's list of new books, like the new Napoleons and new Queen Victorias. Lewis declares that it is not to such phantoms that he looks for his faith and salvation.[18]

In "Religion Without Dogma?" a paper that was originally read to the Socratic Club in 1946, Lewis similarly expresses his belief that a certain kind of literary criticism is a passing fad. He writes that the kind of criticism that discovers every old book was made by six anonymous authors well provided with scissors and paste and that every story of the slightest interest is unhistorical has already begun to die out in the studies he knows best. He notes that the period of arbitrary skepticism about the canon and text of Shakespeare is now over, and it is reasonable to expect that this method will soon be used only on Christian documents and survive only in the *Thinkers Library* and the theological colleges.[19] In "Modern Theology and Biblical Criticism" he expresses the hope that this approach to biblical criticism will soon blow over.[20]

This is not to say that Lewis derides all modern biblical criticism. He makes it clear that he is more disposed to accept textual criticism, that is, the science of trying to restore the original text of Scripture based upon the imperfect copies we have. Textual criticism seeks to sift through the variant readings of Scripture, where surviving ancient manuscripts disagree, and arrive at the most probable wording of the original author. Regarding source criticism Lewis is more skeptical, source criticism being, among other things, the attempt to reconstruct the whole *sitz em leben*, the situation in life, of each text of Scripture. Lewis is deeply skeptical of any New Testament

never give us grounds for criticizing the church. It is perfectly possible to accept B on the authority of A and yet regard B as a higher authority than A.
Lewis then gives the example of when he recommends a book to a student.
He first sends the student to the book, but having gone to it the student
knows (for Lewis has told him) that the author knows more about the subject than Lewis does.[29]

Perhaps Lewis's most complete treatment in a letter of the nature and authority of the Scriptures comes in his letter to Clyde Kilby on May 7, 1959,
a letter that we have already referred to. Lewis says that the curious thing is
that neither in his own Bible reading nor in his religious life as a whole does
the question of biblical authority in fact ever assume that importance that it
always gets in theological controversy. Lewis asserts that the difference between reading the story of Ruth and that of Antigone, which are both first-
class as literature, is to him unmistakable and even overwhelming. He claims
he has no reason to suppose that Ruth is unhistorical. But the question of
its historicity doesn't seem to arise until after reading the story. He affirms
that Ruth can still act on him as the Word of God even if it isn't historical.
All Scripture is written for our learning (2 Tim 3:16-17). "But learning of
what?" Lewis asks. He maintains that the value of some things (e.g., the Resurrection) depends on whether they really happened, but the value of others
(e.g., the fate of Lot's wife) do not depend upon their historicity. He believes
that where historicity matters it is plain. He affirms that the overall operation of Scripture is to convey God's Word to the reader, given that the reader
has the illumination of the Spirit and reads the Bible in the right spirit. But,
Lewis counters, this does not mean that the Bible also gives us true answers
to all the questions (often religiously irrelevant) that we might ask.[30]

COMMENT

Evangelical scholars might wish to point out that there are a few factors that
Lewis does not fully take into account in his view of the nature and authority
of Scripture. First, Lewis does not seem to take into account the statements
of Jesus about Scripture.[31] Second, he does not seem to consider the statements of the New Testament authors in regard to the nature and authority of
Scripture.[32] Third, Lewis does not appear to take account of the manner in
which the New Testament speaks of certain Old Testament characters

(Adam,[33] Noah, Job and Jonah) as historical.[34] In formulating his working view of Scripture, Lewis appears to consider the phenomena of Scripture more than he does Scripture's explicit claims of divine origin. While consideration of these explicit claims might not, to some scholars' minds, upend Lewis's view of the nature of Scripture, they do need to be considered.

In the end one must remember that the important thing to Lewis is that Christ is *the* Word of God, *the* revelation of God, and, for him, it is enough to say that Scripture testifies reliably to this Word. Formulating a systematic theology never seemed to be of the essence to Lewis's thought, much less formulating a consistent doctrine of Scripture, though he seems to be internally consistent in his views on Scripture over the course of his life. What is of the essence to Lewis is that we should open our hearts wide to receive "the sacred Fish," that is, Christ.

Perhaps Lewis's greatest contribution to our understanding of the nature and authority of Scripture is his ability to judge the nature of texts as a literary critic. Though some might disagree with Lewis's conclusions, his insights as a literary critic are still valuable. And when it comes to analyzing the literary genre of the Gospels there are few, laymen especially, who have been more perceptive than Lewis in the history of twentieth-century biblical criticism.[35]

THE
THREE-PERSONAL GOD

"THE THREE-PERSONAL GOD" IS THE TITLE OF Lewis's chapter on the doctrine of the Trinity in *Beyond Personality*, which was later reprinted as the fourth book of *Mere Christianity*. Lewis makes it clear that though he prefers such unique terms as "the three-personal God" and "beyond personality" to describe the Trinity, he does accept the orthodox doctrine of the Trinity.[1] Furthermore, it is apparent from Lewis's various writings and letters that he did not change his basic views on the Trinity over the course of more than thirty years as a practicing Christian.[2]

THE SOURCES OF LEWIS'S DOCTRINE OF THE TRINITY

Much of Lewis's recounting of the doctrine of the Trinity is based upon his first-hand reading of the church fathers as well as the New Testament.[3] Therefore the value of what Lewis gives us in his brief commentary on the doctrine is not originality but rather his ability to clearly illustrate the Trinity in simple language that modern readers can understand.

Lewis realizes that all three persons of the Trinity are incomprehensible,[4] that our knowledge of the Trinity is not exhaustive[5] and that there are no completely adequate illustrations in the created order of the uncreated, three-personal God. Yet Lewis makes some creative attempts to achieve the impossible. He says that the doctrine of the Trinity does not have the monolithic grandeur of unitarianism, nor does it have the richness of polytheism.[6] Nonetheless Lewis is able, by his compelling illustrations of the Trinity, to present the three-personal God in an extremely attractive fashion to the modern mind.

THE TRINITY IS LIKE A CUBE

The first thing that Lewis does, in *Beyond Personality*, to help us grasp the doctrine of the Trinity, is to suggest that the Trinity exists in another dimension beyond the three dimensions with which we are already familiar.

Lewis compares levels of being to various spatial dimensions. He notes how, on the human level, one person is one being, and any two persons are two separate beings. In the same way, in two dimensions (such as on a flat sheet of paper) one square is one figure, and any two squares are two separate figures. Lewis goes on to note how, on the divine level, there are still personalities; but at that level the personalities are combined in new ways that we, who don't live on that level, can't imagine. In the divine dimension there is a being who is three persons while remaining one being, just as a cube has six squares while remaining one cube.[7]

Apparently Lewis was criticized for drawing an analogy between the Trinity and a cube. This criticism came in the form of an article written by W. Norman Pittenger in *The Christian Century*, October 1, 1958 (pp. 1104-7). Lewis came up with a humorous reply in the November 26, 1958, issue of the same periodical. Lewis wryly remarked that he did not understand why it was vulgar or offensive, in speaking of the Holy Trinity, to illustrate from plane and solid geometry the concept that what is self-contradictory on one level may be consistent on another. He admitted he could have understood someone being shocked if he had compared God with an unjust judge or Christ with a thief in the night. But, Lewis maintained, mathematical objects seem to be as free from sordid associations as any the mind can entertain![8]

THE TRINITY IN THE PRAYER CLOSET

Lewis goes on to give us a second, very practical, illustration of the Trinity. He suggests that average Christians can see the Trinity at work when they say their prayers. When Christians pray, they are trying to get in touch with God the Father. The One prompting them to pray, from the inside, is God the Holy Spirit. And God the Son, from whom every Christian derives all real knowledge of God, is standing beside Christians, helping them to pray and praying for them. The whole threefold life of God is going on in every ordinary bedroom where every ordinary believer says his or her prayers.[9]

IN THE NEW TESTAMENT

Another thing Lewis does to show us the practicality of the doctrine of the Trinity is to recount how the doctrine developed in the New Testament church. The first Christians, before they became Christians, were mostly Jews who already knew Yahweh through the Old Testament Scriptures. Then Jesus came along, claiming to be God in the flesh. Through his life, death and resurrection, Jesus made his disciples believe that he really was God. Then, when the first disciples were formed into a community on the day of Pentecost, they discovered God, the Holy Spirit, working inside of them. Thus, through practical experience, Lewis postulates, the first disciples worked out a definition of the three-personal God.[10]

TWO BOOKS ETERNALLY RELATED

Lewis moves on, in the fourth chapter of *Beyond Personality*, to illustrate how the three persons of the Trinity relate to one another. He invites us to imagine two books lying on a table, one book on top of the other. Then imagine, he says, that the two books have been in that position forever and ever. Lewis uses this illustration to try and show that while the Son has always been dependent upon (resting on) the Father, none of the persons of the Trinity are prior to one another; they are all three co-eternal. The Father and the Son are like the books, the Father eternally supporting the Son, and the Son eternally resting on the Father.

ACT OF IMAGINING, MENTAL IMAGE AND WILL

Another illustration, borrowed from Augustine,[11] that Lewis uses, is that of the relation between the act of imagining, a mental picture and the will to imagine. The act of imagining causes the mental picture but is not really prior to, in any time sequence, the mental picture, and the will is involved at the same time, keeping the mental picture in one's mind. Lewis suggests that we must think of the Son in the same way—as always streaming forth from the Father, like light from a lamp, or heat from a fire, or thoughts from a mind. The Son is like the self-expression, or mental picture, of the Father who is like the act of imagination, and the Holy Spirit is like the will that constantly holds the picture of the Son in our minds.

Despite Lewis's great facility for coming up with or using other Christian theologians' illustrations of the Trinity, he still prefers the New Testament picture of a Father and a Son. He prefers this picture because God knows best how to describe himself.[12] And clearly the problem with some of the other images Lewis uses (i.e., a cube, or two books piled on top of each other) is that these images are impersonal.

GOD IS LOVE

Lewis borrows yet another illustration of the Trinity from Augustine.[13] Augustine likened the Trinity to a lover, his beloved and the love between them. Lewis asserts that the most important thing to know about the relations in the Trinity is that they are relations of love. The Father delights in his Son, and the Son looks up to his Father. If God were a single person before the world was made, then he could not be love, because love requires two or more persons. Lewis maintains that what Christians mean when they say "God is love" is that the living, dynamic activity of love has been going on in God forever and has created everything else. What grows out of this joint life of the Father and Son is a real person; he is in fact the third of the three persons who are God—the Holy Spirit. This Spirit of love is, from all eternity, a love going on between the Father and the Son.[14]

THE GREAT DANCE

Lewis develops Gregory of Nazianzus's idea of perichoresis. Lewis writes that God is not a static thing but a dynamic, pulsating activity—a life or a kind of drama. He is almost a kind of dance. The whole dance or drama or pattern of God's three-personal life is to be played out in each one of us. Or, to put it the other way around, each one of us has got to enter that pattern. We must take our place in the dance.[15]

Lewis's illustration of the relations of the Trinity being like a dance is a masterstroke. With this image we capture the joy of the relationships in the Trinity, a joy into which we are invited to enter. The image of the Great Dance is one that appears over and over again in Lewis's writings.

For example, in his chapter "Heaven" in *The Problem of Pain*, Lewis writes of this Great Dance with regard to the giving away of selfhood. To cling to self is death. But to give away self is life. For when self flies to and fro among human beings even the great master himself leads the revelry, giving himself eternally to his creatures and back to himself in the sacrifice of the Word. The eternal dance "makes Heaven drowsy with the harmony." All pains and pleasures we have known on Earth are but early intimations of the movements of that dance. In fact, as we draw nearer to the uncreated rhythm of the dance, pain and pleasure sink almost out of sight. For the dance is love himself. The Great Dance does not exist for us but we for it.[16]

One might wonder why Lewis has chosen the image of dance to represent the Trinity and the life of Heaven. He gives us an answer in chapter seventeen of *Letters to Malcolm: Chiefly on Prayer*. Lewis puts forward that in this "valley of tears" certain qualities of Heaven have no chance to get through, can project no image of themselves, except in activities that, for us here and now, are frivolous. How can one find any image of boundless freedom in the serious activities either of our natural or of our present spiritual life? It is only in our "hours-off," only in our moments of festivity, that we find an analogy. Dance and game are frivolous, unimportant on Earth, for Earth is not their natural place. Here they are a moment's rest from the life we were created to live. In this world everything is upside down. That which, if it could be prolonged here, would be a truancy is like that which, in a better country, is the goal of all goals. According to Lewis, joy is the serious business of Heaven![17]

Perhaps Lewis's most eloquent lines about the Great Dance come at the end of *Perelandra*, where he writes that in the plan of the Great Dance plans without number interweave, and each movement becomes in its season the fruition of the whole design to which all else has been directed. Thus each person is equally at the center of the dance by giving and receiving place. All are joined together by the union of a kneeling with a sceptered love.[18]

THE TRINITY IN LEWIS'S FICTION

Lewis is so deeply trinitarian in his thinking that there is a trinitarian cast to his fiction as well as his nonfiction. In *The Cosmic Trilogy* we hear of Maleldil the Young (God the Son), the Old One (God the Father) and the Third One (God the Holy Spirit).[19] In *The Chronicles of Narnia* we see Aslan (the Christ figure), and we hear of the Emperor-Beyond-the-Sea (God the Father), of whom Aslan is the son. Finally, there is the breath of Aslan, which brings back to life again the creatures turned to stone by the White Witch, similar to Jesus breathing on the disciples and saying,

"Receive the Holy Spirit" (Jn 20:22).

Walter Hooper says, "If the Chronicles of Narnia have a theological weakness, it is possibly that the Trinity (Father, Son and Holy Spirit) is not properly represented."[20] Perhaps the reason why Lewis does not represent or picture the Father and the Holy Spirit more than he does in *The Chronicles* is not due to lack of imagination on his part but rather to the fact that the Father and the Holy Spirit cannot, in the strictest sense, be pictured. God the Son is the only member of the Trinity who became incarnate. Thus he is the only member of the Trinity who can be properly pictured. Perhaps that is why Lewis focuses most of his attention in *The Chronicles* on developing the character of Aslan, the type of Christ. The fact that the Father and the Holy Spirit are not pictured is not a sign of weakness but rather a sign of Lewis's fidelity to Scripture and to the orthodox doctrine of the Trinity. However, this is pure speculation, and one must always keep in mind with regard to Narnia that Lewis was not writing an allegory.

Be that as it may, perhaps the most moving representation of all three members of the Trinity is found in chapter eleven of *The Horse and His Boy.* It is dark and the boy, Shasta, is alone and tired, traipsing across the countryside on his horse. Suddenly he realizes that there is some Thing beside him. "Who are you?" Shasta asks. By breathing on Shasta, the Thing reassures him that he is not a ghost. The Thing tells Shasta that he is a lion, the Lion who has been watching over Shasta and caring for him all through his young life. Again Shasta asks, "Who *are* you?" The Voice responds, "Myself," very deep and low so that the earth shakes. Then the Voice says again, "Myself," loud and clear and gay. And then a third time He says, "Myself," whispered so softly that Shasta can hardly hear it, and yet it seems to come from all round him as if the leaves rustled with the Voice. (Is there an echo here of the gentle whisper with which Yahweh spoke to Elijah in I Kings 19? And is there not a hint of the threefold name of God [Mt 28:19] who is thrice holy [Is 6:3]?) Finally, the night is turning to morning, and Shasta sees a golden light falling on them from the left. He thinks it is the sun, but he turns and sees a huge Lion from whom the light is coming. After one glance at the Lion's face Shasta dismounts and falls at the Lion's feet. The High King above all kings stoops toward him. Its mane, and some strange and solemn perfume that hangs about the mane, is all around Shasta. The Lion touches Shasta's forehead with its tongue. He lifts his face, and their eyes meet. Then instantly the pale brightness of the mist and the fiery brightness of the Lion roll themselves together into a swirling glory and gather themselves up and disappear.[21]

In this passage Lewis is surely at his best, presenting the Trinity of Christian theology in Narnian terms and doing it in a way that is powerfully attractive. It is the personal images of the triune God, like this one provided by Lewis, which make us as readers want to enter into the Great Dance with Aslan, Shasta and all the rest.

GOD'S SOVEREIGNTY
AND HUMAN RESPONSIBILITY

ONE OF THE AREAS OF POPULAR THEOLOGY where Lewis has unobtrusively made his mark is on the subject of God's sovereignty as it relates to the free will of humanity. Lewis, in his early apologetic writings, such as *The Problem of Pain* and *Mere Christianity*, clearly emphasizes a person's ability to come to Christ for salvation. This emphasis on human free will should come as no surprise to anyone who has read Lewis's writings. What many people do not realize is the emphasis that Lewis placed upon God's sovereignty in some of his later books. What follows is a chronological survey of Lewis's thoughts on this subject.

LEWIS'S EARLY CHRISTIAN WRITINGS

Lewis's first published words on this subject are in *The Problem of Pain*. Lewis writes that before all the relations of God to humanity there exists a Divine act of pure giving—the election of people to be loved by God. He theorizes that in the long run the soul's search for God can only be a mode or appearance of his search for the soul, since all comes from him, and since the very possibility of our loving is his gift to us. According to Lewis, our freedom is only a freedom of better or worse response to God's action, which is prior to all actions on our part.[1] In this statement Lewis echoes the Scripture which asks, " 'Who has ever given to God, that God should repay him?' For from him and through him and to him are all things. To him be the glory forever! Amen" (Rom 11:35-36).

Lewis's statement above seems to emphasize God's sovereignty more than human free will. However, in the same book, in Lewis's chapter on the Fall of Man, he raises objections to the doctrine of total depravity, thus emphasizing a person's ability to come to Christ for salvation. Lewis denounces the doctrine of total depravity, partly on the logical ground that if our depravity were total we should not know it, and partly because human experience shows that there is still much goodness in human nature.[2] It should be noted, however, that Lewis seems to misunderstand the doctrine of total depravity. Briefly stated, the doctrine of total depravity means not, as Lewis suggests, that people are as bad as they could be but rather that at no point are people as good as they should be. Total depravity states that every aspect of a person's being has been affected by sin, including the ability to choose. In fact, following Luther, the will is in bondage to sin.[3]

Another passage from *The Problem of Pain* that deserves comment is in the chapter on hell. Lewis says that the damned are successful rebels to the end and that the doors of hell are locked on the inside.[4] Here we see a clear emphasis on human free will. People go to hell because they choose to go there. The doors of hell are locked on the inside.

The book that probably made Lewis most famous during his lifetime was *The Screwtape Letters*, published in 1941. These are letters written, as it were, by a mature devil, Screwtape, to a younger tempter named Wormwood. Screwtape comments on what is, from his perspective, the problem of free will. Screwtape wonders why the Enemy (God) leaves room for human free will and supposes that it has something to do with the Enemy's nonsense about "Love." *How* God leaves room for free will is no problem at all, says Screwtape. For the Enemy does not foresee the humans making their free contributions in the future but sees them doing so in his unbounded Now. To watch a person doing something is not the same as making that person do it.[5] Here Lewis, through the pen of Screwtape, tries to answer for the first time in his own writings the whole problem of how human responsibility and God's sovereignty can be reconciled. Lewis also hints at the reason behind God's bestowal of free will; the reason behind it is love. Without the ability to choose, people will never truly love God.

Lewis comments further on the relation of love and free will in his *Broadcast Talks*, first published in 1943. Lewis queries, "Why did God give free will to human beings?" Because free will, though it makes evil possible, is also the only thing that makes love possible. A world of robots would hardly be worth creating. God has designed his higher creatures for the happiness of being voluntarily united to him and to each other in an ecstasy of love and delight, of which the most rapturous love between a man and a woman on this earth is but a dim reflection. To enjoy such a love, human beings must be free.[6]

Later in *Mere Christianity* Lewis talks about the possibility of losing one's salvation. He maintains that Christians can lose the Christ-life that has been put into them, and therefore they have to make efforts to keep it.[7] Lewis is so far consistent in his theology. If people can freely choose to come to Christ, they can also freely choose to leave the Christian fold.

FANTASY AND MORE APOLOGETICS

The first mention we have of the word *predestination* in Lewis's writings is in *Perelandra*, the second book of his space trilogy. The main character of Lewis's trilogy, Ransom, has been sent to Venus in order to prevent that planet's "Eve" from falling into sin. Ransom doesn't fully realize what his assignment is until he gets to Venus and sees the Un-man, the equivalent of the serpent, at work. All of a sudden it becomes clear that he was brought to Venus in order to destroy the Un-man. To Ransom, the deed seems impossible, but gradually an awareness breaks over him that by the same time tomorrow he will have done the impossible. He knows, almost as a historical proposition, that the deed is going to be done. The future act stands before him, fixed and unaltered as if he has already performed it. Lewis, the narrator, comments: "You might say, if you liked, that the power of choice had been simply set aside and an inflexible destiny substituted for it. On the other hand, you might say that he had been delivered from the rhetoric of his passions and had emerged into unassailable freedom. Ransom could not, for the life of him, see any difference between these two statements. Predestination and freedom were apparently identical. He could no longer see any meaning in the many arguments he had heard on the subject."[8]

Here we have, for the first time in the writings of Lewis, a concerted emphasis on God's sovereignty in salvation and in the general affairs of humanity. Lewis talks about there being no apparent movement of Ransom's will; the power of choice is simply set aside. Yet, at the same time, Lewis talks about Ransom emerging into unassailable freedom. Predestination and freedom are identical. How can this be? Lewis has more to say about this in later years.

For now, let us turn to what Lewis writes in *Beyond Personality*. In this book, Lewis tries more fully to reconcile the idea of God's foreknowledge and human free will. He writes about the difficulty created by believing that God is in time. Lewis asserts that everyone who believes in God believes that he knows the future. The question is, if he knows I am going to do such-and-such, how can I be free to do otherwise? The difficulty, Lewis says, comes from thinking that God is progressing along the timeline like us: the only difference being that he can see ahead and we cannot. If that were true, if God foresaw our acts in that sense, it would be very hard to understand how we could be free not to do them. But suppose, Lewis says, that God is outside and above the timeline. In that case, what we call "tomorrow" is visible to him in just the same way as what we call "today." All the days are present for him. We don't suppose that our actions in the present are any less free because God knows what we are doing. So why should we think differently about our actions in the future, if God is outside of time?[9]

Lewis borrows this idea from Boethius, a Christian philosopher born in Rome in A.D. 480. In book five of his *Consolation of Philosophy*, Boethius seeks to reconcile God's foreknowledge with human free will. God's knowledge is "not a kind of foreknowledge of the future but the knowledge of a never ending present." "God sees all things in his eternal present."[10] In response to *The Christian Century's* question, What books did most to shape your vocational attitude and your philosophy of life? Lewis listed *The Consolation of Philosophy* as one of the top ten most influential books in his life.[11] Lewis's line of thought suggests, in regard to human salvation, that God has predestined who will be saved based on his foreknowledge of who will choose him.

In any case, according to Lewis, God will not violate a person's free will. Again, in *Beyond Personality*, Lewis writes that our free will is trembling within us like the needle of a compass. However, ours is a needle that can choose. We can point to our true north, but we need not. Will our needle swing around and point to God? God can help it to do so, but he cannot force it, Lewis maintains. God cannot put out his hand and pull our needle into the right position, for then we would not have free will any more.[12]

Lewis returns to the relation of time, free will and predestination in *The Great Divorce.* In this work of fantasy Lewis places his master, George Mac-Donald, as one of the characters in the story. MacDonald says that every attempt to see the shape of eternity, except through the lens of time, destroys our knowledge of freedom. In other words, from within time we cannot fully understand how God's choices and our choices relate. MacDonald suggests that the doctrine of predestination destroys freedom by taking away human choice and giving all choice to God. But the doctrine of universalism also takes away freedom by saying that all will be saved in the end. The question is, Will they be saved with their consent or without it? MacDonald concludes that we *cannot* know eternal reality by a theological definition. Time itself, and all acts and events that fill time, are the definition of reality, and we must live out that reality.[13]

Around the same time as the publication of *The Great Divorce,* in 1946, Lewis also wrote an article for an Oxford periodical called *The Cherwell.* The article was entitled "The Decline of Religion," and in that article Lewis admits that conversion requires an alteration of the will, and that such an alteration is, in the last resort, not possible without the intervention of the supernatural.[14] Lewis again emphasizes God's sovereignty in salvation—the supernatural must intervene if conversion is to take place. But this does not rule out human free will. People still have a choice in the process and can presumably refuse the intervention of the supernatural.

In *Miracles,* published in 1947, Lewis again comments on God's sovereignty over all the events of life. He writes that where we have a God of purpose and of foresight who acts upon a totally interlocked nature, there are no accidents or loose ends. All results are intended from the beginning.[15] Later on in *Miracles,* Lewis draws the analogy of a play in order to explain the interrelationship of God's sovereignty and human free will. Just as every event in a play happens as a result of other events in the play but also as a result of the playwright's intention, so also in human life—every event happens as a result of human free will but also as a result of God's intention.[16]

Lewis uses this analogy of life as a play or a book in his *Broadcast Talks*[17] as well. What is fascinating about this analogy is that it emphasizes God's sovereignty more than human free will. If life is like a play and God is the playwright, then all events in life are planned from the beginning. Yet this analogy still allows for free will in a limited sense. The actors are free to play their parts in any way that they will, just so long as they don't change the script.

ASLAN'S SOVEREIGNTY IN NARNIA

We cannot fully examine Lewis's thought on any theological subject without paying some attention to the books for which Lewis will long be remembered, *The Chronicles of Narnia*. In *The Chronicles of Narnia* there are a number of incidents of relevance to this question of God's sovereignty and human responsibility. First, in *The Lion, the Witch and the Wardrobe* there is the event of Aslan offering his life for the traitor Edmund. Of course, this whole event represents Lewis's supposal of what redemption would look like in the world of Narnia. Aslan is the incarnate God in the world of Narnia, just as Jesus of Nazareth was the incarnate God in our world. Edmund, the traitor, is just like all sinners who have rebelled against God and sided with the enemy. What is most interesting about this incident is that Aslan initiates Edmund's salvation. Edmund doesn't seek out Aslan to free him from the clutches of the White Witch. Rather, Aslan rescues the prisoner Edmund and then lays down his life for Edmund on the Stone Table. Edmund is passive in the whole affair. In fact, we are not told much of anything about Edmund's response to Aslan, except that after Edmund was rescued, he and Aslan had a conversation that Edmund never forgot.[18]

Another dramatic incident from *The Lion, the Witch and the Wardrobe* takes place after Aslan's resurrection. Susan and Lucy accompany Aslan to the castle of the White Witch. At the castle, Aslan breathes on all of the creatures the White Witch has turned to stone, and they come to life again. This gives us a dramatic portrait of what the Bible calls regeneration or the new birth. In Ezekiel 36:26 (NIV) the Lord says, "I will give you a new heart and put a new spirit in you; I will remove from you your heart of stone and give you a heart of flesh." Aslan breathing on the stone figures is also reminiscent of the Lord breathing on the disciples in the upper room (Jn 20:22), though the former was for the purpose of regeneration, as it were, whereas the latter was for the purpose of mission.[19] Again, the startling thing about this is that the stone figures have no choice in the matter. They are totally passive. Bringing these stone figures to life is Aslan's work alone. One can hardly imagine a more striking portrait of monergistic regeneration, that is, a new birth that comes totally from the hand of God.

Another picture of regeneration that Lewis gives us in *The Chronicles of Narnia* comes in *The Voyage of the Dawn Treader.* Eustace Scrubb, who is a perfectly beastly little boy, turns into a dragon. After continuing in the state of dragonhood for some time, Eustace is suddenly approached by Aslan. Aslan invites Eustace to follow him, Eustace does, and Aslan leads him to a well at the top of a mountain. This well is wider than most, with great marble steps going down into the water, which is bubbling up out of the ground. At the well, Aslan tells Eustace that he must undress before entering. Eustace quickly figures out that Aslan must be talking about his dragon skin and that he must shed his skin before getting into the pool. Eustace scratches off one layer of skin after another, all to no avail. After each layer Eustace finds another layer underneath, as hard and wrinkled as the one before. Finally Aslan tells Eustace that he will have to let him undress him. Eustace submits to Aslan, and the first tear is so deep that it feels like it is going right into Eustace's heart. It hurts terribly, but Eustace is relieved, all the same, to have the ugly dragon skin removed. Then Aslan picks up Eustace and throws him into the water, and Eustace turns into a boy again. In this story of regeneration Eustace is active, in a sense. He submits to Aslan; he allows Aslan to tear his skin off. But the turning of Eustace from a dragon back into a boy is initiated and accomplished by Aslan.

Another intriguing statement is made by Aslan at the beginning of *The Silver Chair.* This time Eustace and a girl named Jill Pole call out to Aslan and ask him to let them come into his world. Once they get into Aslan's world through an open door, Eustace falls over a cliff and is blown far away by Aslan. Jill is left alone with the Lion, who tells her that he has called them there out of their own world to perform a certain task. This puzzles Jill a bit, and so she says to the Lion, "It was *we* who asked to come here." But then Aslan corrects her, saying, "You would not have called to me unless I had been calling to you."[20] Again we see Aslan taking the initiative. Aslan calls the children, and that enables them to call out to him.

Two Important Letters

Perhaps the one place where Lewis is most clear in communicating his thoughts on human free will and God's sovereignty is in two of his letters.

In a letter to "Mrs. Arnold" from Magdalen College dated October 20, 1952, Lewis contends that the question of free will and predestination is insoluble. He suspects that it is really a meaningless question. Lewis conjectures that the difference between freedom and necessity is clear on the physical level; we know the difference between making our teeth chatter and just finding them chattering with the cold. The difference begins to be less clear when we talk about human love. Do we like someone because we choose to or because we must? When we carry the discussion up to relations between God and human beings, the distinction has become, perhaps, nonsensical. When we are most free, it is only with a freedom God has given us. And when our will is most influenced by grace, it is still our will.[21]

In this letter Lewis shows his obvious distaste for discussing the whole subject. He does not like talking about issues that divide denominations. He prefers to stay in the realm of "mere Christianity." But the interesting thing in this letter is that he picks up the same idea that he voices in *Perelandra*, the idea that, at the highest level, freedom and predestination are the same thing. Lewis suggests that the whole problem of how human free will and God's sovereignty relate is impossible to solve. Again, Lewis stresses that it is best to leave discussion of the subject behind and get on with living and making choices.

Lewis apparently addresses a similar question from Mrs. Emily McLay when he writes to her from Magdalen College on August 3, 1953. Lewis relates predestination and free will in the following manner. First, he notes that every person looking back on his or her own conversion must feel that it was not of one's own doing. That, Lewis affirms, is the Pauline account, and he professes his certainty that it is the only true account of every conversion *from the inside*. However, Lewis counters, we must not turn this personal experience into a general rule and therefore say that all conversions depend on God's choice.[22] Generalizations are warranted only when we are dealing with matters to which our minds are adequate. But in this case, Lewis believes, our minds are not adequate to fully comprehend the truth. No one can fully reconcile God's sovereignty and human free will. Of course, Lewis admits, reality must be self-consistent, but until we can see the consistency, it is better to hold two inconsistent views than to ignore one side of the evidence. The real interrelation between God's omnipotence and human freedom is something we can't find out. Lewis ends the discussion with a practical quote from Martin Luther, who said, "Do you doubt if you are chosen? Then say your prayers and you may conclude that you are."[23]

LEWIS'S COMMENTS ON THE REFORMATION

Lewis may have discovered the quote from Luther when he was doing research for *English Literature in the Sixteenth Century*, published in 1954. In describing the Protestant experience of grace, Lewis notes that all the initiative for human salvation is from God. People's small and silly efforts cannot retain the joy of salvation any more than they can achieve that joy in the first place. Fortunately humanity need not achieve salvation by its own efforts. The happiness of salvation cannot be earned. Works merit nothing, though faith inevitably overflows into works of love. Faith alone saves, faith given as a sheer gift from God. Lewis notes that the Protestant doctrine of grace was at first not a doctrine of fear, as he thinks it later became when double predestination was emphasized by some Reformers. Rather, in its early stages, the Protestant doctrine of grace was all joy and hope. Lewis quotes William Tyndale, who says that the converted person is already tasting eternal life. Then Lewis mentions article seventeen of the Thirty-Nine Articles of the Anglican Church, which says the doctrine of predestination is "full of sweet, pleasant and unspeakable comfort to godly persons." But, one might ask, what about ungodly persons? Lewis maintains that inside the original Protestant experience no question regarding the ungodly arises. The early Protestants, according to Lewis, were not building a system. When they began to build a systematic theology, very troublesome problems and very dark solutions appeared. However, these horrors are astonishingly absent from the thought of the first Protestants, according to Lewis.[24]

What is interesting about Lewis's statement here is that the Thirty-Nine Articles do indeed address the issue of ungodly persons. The rest of article seventeen reads, "So, for curious and carnal persons, lacking the Spirit of Christ, to have continually before their eyes the sentence of God's Predestination, is a most dangerous downfall, whereby the Devil doth thrust them either into desperation, or into wretchlessness of most unclean living, no less perilous than desperation."[25]

A bit of Lewis's attitude toward Calvin and Calvinism is also suggested in *English Literature in the Sixteenth Century*. Lewis asserts that in the *Institutes* Calvin moves forward from the original Protestant experience to build a theological system, to extrapolate, to raise all the dark questions of predestination and give, without flinching, the dark answers. However, Lewis notes, the *Institutes* is a masterpiece of literary form. Lewis suspects that those who read the *Institutes* with most approval were troubled by the fate of predestined "vessels of wrath" about as much as young Marxists in the twentieth century were troubled by the approaching liquidation of the bourgeoisie![26]

SURPRISED BY JOY

In 1955 we have Lewis's account of his own conversion in *Surprised by Joy*. In it he once again emphasizes God's sovereignty in conversion. In his autobiography, Lewis draws an analogy from Shakespeare. If Shakespeare and Hamlet were ever to meet, it would have to be Shakespeare's doing. Hamlet could initiate nothing. Friendly agnostics talk cheerfully about "man's search for God." From Lewis's perspective, just prior to his conversion, he says you might as well have talked about the mouse's search for the cat! Lewis felt the unrelenting approach of a God whom he earnestly desired not to meet. He avows that when he became a theist, in 1929, he was the most dejected and reluctant convert in all England. He was dragged kicking and struggling into the kingdom with his eyes darting in every direction for a way of escape. "Compel them to come in" are Gospel words often abused by wicked people. But properly understood, those words plumb the depths of divine mercy. In fact, God's compulsion of us is really our liberation.[27]

Lewis goes on, in a later chapter, to consider freedom and necessity in the context of his conversion to Christianity. He describes his conversion as being like the experience of a man who, after a long sleep, still lying motionless in bed, suddenly becomes aware that he is awake. Is the act of waking an act of freedom or necessity? "Do freedom and necessity differ at their maximum point?" Lewis asks. He asserts that at that maximum point a man *is* what he *does*, there is nothing of the man left over or left outside of the act itself.[28]

LEWIS'S MATURE CHRISTIAN WRITINGS

It is another five years before we see anything from the pen of Lewis relevant to the question of free will and predestination. Then, in *The Four Loves*, Lewis comments directly on a Scripture that is relevant to the issue at hand. The

Scripture is Malachi 1:2-3, where God says, "I loved Jacob, and I hated Esau." Lewis notes how God's hatred of Esau is displayed in the story. The story pans out not as we would expect. Esau's earthly life is more blessed than Jacob's life. It is Jacob who experiences disappointments, humiliations, terrors and bereavements. But Jacob has something Esau does not have. Jacob is a patriarch. He passes on the calling and blessing of God; he even becomes an ancestor of Jesus Christ. God's love of Jacob seems to mean that Jacob is accepted for a high and painful vocation. God's hating of Esau involves his rejection for this vocation. Lewis maintains that there is no ground for assuming that Esau was a lost soul. The Old Testament says nothing about Esau's eternal destiny, according to Lewis.[29]

Lewis is still meditating on the darkness of some extreme forms of Calvinism when he writes *A Grief Observed* in 1961. He is not tempted, by the suffering and death of his wife, to question God's existence. However, he does question what kind of God exists. He asks whether one could seriously introduce the idea of a bad God through an extreme form of Calvinism. One could say that humanity is fallen and depraved. We are so filled with depravity that our idea of goodness itself is corrupted. Or worse than that—the very fact that we think something good is really evidence that it is bad. According to this theology, God has all the characteristics we regard as bad: unreasonableness, vanity, vindictiveness, injustice and cruelty. But all these blacks (as they seem to us) are really whites. It's only total depravity that makes them look black to us. However, Lewis avers, this, for all practical (and speculative) purposes, cleans God off the slate. The word *good*, when applied to God in this way, becomes meaningless: like abracadabra.[30]

Lewis's final written comments on this subject are delivered to us in *Letters to Malcolm: Chiefly on Prayer*. Lewis has attempted to write a book on prayer for at least the last ten years of his life. Finally, in his last year, 1963, the book comes together on paper and is sent off to the publisher. In the book Lewis contends that Scripture sails over the problem of grace and free will. He quotes Philippians 2:12-13: "Work out your own salvation in fear and trembling, for it is God who worketh in you." Lewis asserts that it is only our presuppositions that make the first and second halves of this verse appear contradictory. We assume that divine and human action exclude one another like the actions of two fellow creatures. The reality, Lewis conjectures, is that before all worlds, God, in his creation and providence, takes into account all the situations produced by the acts of his creatures.[31]

An interesting thing to note about Lewis's comments on this subject in *Letters to Malcolm* is his debt to Austin Farrer. Farrer was warden of Keble College, Oxford, from 1960 until his death in 1968. He was a renowned Anglican theologian and preacher. Lewis became a friend of Austin Farrer and his wife, Katherine, during his own marriage to Joy Davidman Gresham. A couple of Farrer's books from Lewis's library still exist at the Wade Center of Wheaton College in Wheaton, Illinois. In Farrer's *The Glass of Vision*, Lewis underlined the following paragraph: "Now it is by no means clear that the finite excludes the infinite in the sense in which one finite excludes another. . . . The creature and the Creator are both enacting the creature's life. . . . Upon this double personal agency in one activity turns the verbally insoluble riddle of grace and freewill."[32]

THE LAST INTERVIEW

Before we come to any final conclusions about Lewis's thought on human responsibility and God's sovereignty we must consider one more thing that Lewis has to say on the subject. The following comments are not in any of Lewis's books. Rather, these comments come out of the last official interview that Lewis gave before his death. The interviewer is Sherwood Eliot Wirt, then editor of Billy Graham's *Decision* magazine. In the course of the interview, Wirt asks Lewis, "Do you feel that you made a decision at the time of your conversion?" Lewis says he would prefer to put it the other way around—that he was decided upon. He maintains that his decision was not so important. He was the object rather than the subject in conversion. Then Wirt presses Lewis further, "That sounds to me as if you came to a very definite point of decision." And Lewis responds by asserting that the most deeply compelled action is also the freest action. He chose, but it really did not seem possible to do the opposite.[33]

Again we see the influence of Farrer upon Lewis. Another one of Farrer's books contained in Lewis's library, now at Wheaton, is *Lord, I Believe*. In that book Lewis underlined and marked the following sentence: "the assistance of God does not remove the reality of our decisions; when we are most in God, then we are most freely ourselves."[34]

What is so startling about Lewis's final comments on this subject are the words "I was decided upon." This hardly sounds like the Lewis who wrote *The Problem of Pain* and *Mere Christianity*. How can he say that his decision was not important, that he was decided upon? And how can Lewis say, "I chose, yet it really did not seem possible to do the opposite"? One thing is for certain. There is a decided emphasis, in Lewis's last interview, on God's sovereignty in Lewis's own salvation.

CONCLUSION

We have heard the early, strident Lewis, the apologist insisting upon the vital importance of human free will in *The Problem of Pain* and *Mere Christianity*. We have heard the more mature, imaginative and gentle Lewis emphasizing God's sovereignty in *Perelandra*, *The Chronicles of Narnia* and in his autobiography, *Surprised by Joy*. We have seen the influence on Lewis's thought by the theologian Austin Farrer. But will the real Mr. Lewis please stand up?

I think, in the end, the real C. S. Lewis does stand up. He is the C. S. Lewis who is not, in the end, interested in reconciling human free will and God's sovereignty along logical-causal lines. He is the C. S. Lewis who is sure in his own case that his decision for Christ was not all that important. What is important is that he was "decided upon." God's decision made all the difference in C. S. Lewis's life, as it has in many other lives before and since.

CREATION

C. S. LEWIS BELIEVED IN A GOD WHO created all that exists. He believed that the Creation account in Genesis was the best one on the market. Yet, believing that the opening chapters of Genesis were told "in the form of folk tale"[1] left open the possibility for Lewis of accepting certain aspects of evolution into his theology, thus making Lewis a theistic evolutionist.

THE BIBLICAL DOCTRINE OF CREATION

In order to grasp Lewis's theology of Creation let us first note several things about Lewis's understanding of the biblical doctrine of Creation.

First, Lewis makes clear that he believes the Genesis account to be inspired, though it is derived from extrabiblical sources. He claims he has no difficulty in accepting the view of scholars who say that the account of Creation in Genesis is derived from earlier Semitic stories that were pagan and mythical. However, Lewis believes that the retelling of these Semitic stories in Genesis achieves the idea of true Creation and of a transcendent Creator. According to Lewis, God guided this process.[2]

Second, Lewis clearly believes in creation "out of nothing," that God did not make the universe out of any preexisting raw material. Lewis suggests that the Christian idea of Creation is that God made up space and time, heat and cold, and all the colors and tastes, all the animals and vegetables, "out of his head" as a person makes up a story.[3]

Lewis illustrates this concept of divine creation in *The Magician's Nephew*. Aslan, the great Lion, creates Narnia by singing, just as in the Bible the Lord created the heavens and the earth by his Word.[4] In Lewis's story, when a line of dark firs spring up on a ridge, they are connected with a series of deep,

prolonged notes from the mouth of Aslan, and when the Lion bursts into a
rapid series of lighter notes, primroses suddenly appear in every direction.[5]

One important implication for Lewis, which flows out of God being the
Creator of all that exists, is the fact that therefore everything human beings
do is derivative. Lewis believed strongly that originality was the prerogative
of God alone and that, even within the Trinity, originality seemed to be con-
fined to God the Father. Therefore the duty and happiness of the creature is
found in being derivative, in reflecting God's sole originality like a mirror.[6]

This has profound implications for Lewis's understanding of what we
normally call artistic creation. Lewis avouches that creation as applied to human authorship is a misleading term. Human authors only rearrange elements God has provided. There is not a vestige of real creativity in human
beings. Lewis invites us to try and imagine a new primary color, a third sex,
a fourth dimension, or even a monster that does not consist of bits of existing animals stuck together. What happens when we try to imagine thus?
Nothing happens because, strictly speaking, human beings create nothing.
An author's work never means to others quite what he intended, because the
author is only recombining elements made by God and already containing
his meanings. Because of those divine meanings in the author's materials it
is impossible that the author should ever know the whole meaning of any of
his own works. In fact, the meaning he never intended may be the best and
truest meaning. Writing a book, Lewis insists, is much less like creation than
it is like planting a garden or begetting a child. In all three cases human beings are only entering as one cause into a causal stream that works in its own
way.[7] The reality of God's creation and originality was so woven into the
warp and woof of Lewis's everyday thinking that he consistently denied any
originality for his own books.

A third thing that Lewis sees in the biblical concept of Creation is that
there is a certain amount of "crucifixion" involved in the act of creation.
Lewis writes in Letters to Malcolm that when God creates, he makes something
to be not himself. To be created is, in a sense, to be ejected or separated from
God. Lewis surmises that there is anguish, alienation, a crucifixion involved
in the creative act, yet God judges the end goal to be worth it.[8]

A fourth point that Lewis makes is that God was not under any necessity
to create. In The Four Loves, Lewis states that there is no hunger that needs to

be filled in God; there is only plenteousness that desires to give. The doctrine that God was under no necessity to create is essential. Without it, Lewis maintains, we can hardly avoid the conception of what he calls a "managerial" God, a being whose function is simply to "run" the universe. Why would God need to create when in himself, in the Trinity, he is already Sovereign of a far greater realm? Lewis asserts that we must keep before our eyes the vision of Lady Julian of Norwich wherein God carried in his hand a little object like a nut, and that nut was "all that is made." The God who needs nothing loves us into existence only so that he may love and perfect us.[9]

In other words, we are created for God's pleasure. Lewis elaborates on this in *The Problem of Pain*. He writes that human beings are not the center of Creation. God doesn't exist for the sake of humanity. Human beings do not even exist for their own sake. Lewis quotes Revelation 4:11: "Thou hast created all things, and for thy pleasure they are and were created." We were made so as to become objects in which the Divine love might rest well pleased.[10]

However, Lewis also notes a second reason for creation. People were created to enjoy God and all his creation. Lewis writes that if it were not for our body one whole realm of God's glory—all that we receive through the senses—would go without praise. Mere animals cannot appreciate creation, and angels are pure minds who understand colors and tastes better than the greatest scientists. But do the angels receive God's creation through senses as we do? Lewis thinks not. He fancies that the beauties of nature are a secret God has shared with human beings alone. That is one of the reasons why we were made—and why the resurrection of the body is so important.[11] Lewis echoes the first question and answer of the Westminster Shorter Catechism: "What is the chief end of man? Man's chief end is to glorify God, and to enjoy him forever."[12] For Lewis, the enjoyment of God is one of the main reasons for human existence.

One reason why Adam and Eve could fully enjoy God and his creation in the Garden was because God's original creation was completely good,[13] and according to Lewis, the goodness of God's creation was not completely lost after the Fall. Lewis exults in the beauty of God's creation throughout his writings. His fictional works overflow with descriptions of the glories of God's creation, whether those glories are on Earth or on other planets, as in *The Cosmic Trilogy*, or in other worlds such as Narnia. And we can gather from the various biographies written about Lewis that he got tremendous joy out of nature in his everyday life.[14] The ability to describe the beauty of God's creation, with some attention to detail, is a gift that the Lewis brothers shared.[15]

Lewis believed that this biblical doctrine of Creation is rare in that it seldom appears outside of the Bible in other religions or mythologies. The only place outside of the Bible where Lewis sees something akin to the biblical doctrine of Creation is in Plato. And that is an amazing leap, Lewis posits, not made without him who is the Father of lights. In other words, Plato could not have arrived at the true understanding of Creation without the inspiration of God. But, Lewis argues, this biblical understanding is not normally found in pagan religion.[16]

Lewis held that belief in the biblical doctrine of Creation unites evangelicals and Anglo-Catholics against liberals and modernists. Furthermore, not only does this belief unite evangelicals and Anglo-Catholics with each other but also with the Christian religion as understood "everywhere and by all," to quote St. Vincent of Lerins. Lewis lamented the lack of a label to describe all supernaturalist Christians, though he put forward "Deep Church" and Richard Baxter's "mere Christians" as possible labels.[17] Lewis did not believe, however, that holding to the biblical doctrine of Creation committed one to believing in a specific manner of creation or a specific way of picturing that creative process by which God created human beings.[18]

THE CREATION OF HUMANITY

Lewis makes it clear in *The Problem of Pain* that he believes that animals existed long before people.[19] This is one of the tenets he accepts from the evolutionists. For Lewis, this does not conflict with the biblical teaching about the creation of the first human beings or the creation days of Genesis I. Remember that for Lewis, the early chapters of Genesis are told in the form of a folk tale. Therefore it could be argued that Lewis viewed the creation days of Genesis I as a literary framework rather than viewing them as six twenty-four-hour days.[20] According to Lewis, the Bible does not limit us to belief in any definite period of time in which the creation of humanity followed the creation of animals.

Lewis indicates that he believes it possible, and in no conflict with the Bible, that God raised one of the primates eventually to become human. Genesis 2:7 (NIV) says, "The LORD God formed the man from the dust of the ground and breathed into his nostrils the breath of life, and the man became a living being." Commenting on this verse, Lewis writes that humanity is clearly made out of something else. Man is an animal, but he is an animal called to be or raised to be something more than an animal. Lewis asserts that the difficulties he has with evolution are not religious. Therefore, on the ordinary biological level, one of the primates is changed so that it becomes a human being, but human beings remain in some sense primates and animals. Human beings are taken up into a new life without relinquishing the old.[21] In another place, Lewis theorizes that for long centuries God perfected the animal form that was to become human and the image of himself. God gave to this animal hands whose thumb could be applied to each of the fingers, jaws, teeth and throat capable of articulation, and a brain sufficiently complex to execute all the material motions of rational thought. Lewis muses that this creature may have existed for ages in this state before it became human.[22]

A third tenet that Lewis accepts from the evolutionists is the possibility that the human race started from multiple numbers of human beings rather than a single pair. At times Lewis indicates his belief in a historical Adam and Eve.[23] However, he is open to the possibility that God may have created many human beings in this original, paradisal state.[24]

A fourth tenet of evolution that Lewis accepts is the idea that prehuman forms of life are recapitulated in the human womb. This point, which evolutionists use to try and prove that humanity evolved from lower life forms, Lewis accepts as a matter of course.[25]

THE BIBLE AND MODERN SCIENCE

So far we have seen that Lewis sees no final conflict between the Bible and true science. In fact, Lewis believes that modern science in some cases supports the biblical view of nature. For instance, Lewis notes how the physics of his time demonstrated that nature is not everlasting. The universe had a beginning and will have an end. Lewis quotes Professor Whittaker, who said in the Riddell Lectures of 1942, "It was never possible to oppose seriously the dogma of the Creation except by maintaining that the world existed from all eternity in more or less its present state." And, Lewis concludes: this fundamental ground for materialism has now been withdrawn.[26] In the same article, Lewis goes on to note how the process of entropy supports the Christian view of things rather than the creative evolutionary view.[27] Elsewhere Lewis writes that creative evolution, as imagined by Shaw and Bergson, is too convenient a theory.[28]

However, Lewis contends, we must be cautious of building our case for Creation on any current scientific theory, for those theories change as quickly as the shifting sands.[29] The mystery of origins ultimately lies outside the discovery of science.[30]

SCIENCE OR SCIENTISM?

Lewis has been criticized as being anti-science, but this is unfounded. Lewis has no quarrel with true science, though he does have a number of reservations regarding what he calls scientism. Walter Hooper gives a good summary of Lewis's thoughts on science and scientism in *C. S. Lewis: A Companion and Guide.* By scientism Lewis meant "a certain outlook on the world which is casually connected with the popularization of the sciences, though it is much less common among real scientists than among their readers."[31]

That Hideous Strength has been especially accused of maligning science and scientists. However, as Lewis pointed out, the only true scientist in the story is William Hengist, and he leaves the N.I.C.E. after finding out what its true purpose is. Lewis wrote in his preface to *That Hideous Strength* that the story was a tall one about devilry, the serious point of which was given in his *Abolition of Man.* That serious point is that getting rid of the moral law can lead to the abolition of man by nature. Thus at the end of *That Hideous Strength,* the animals, upon whom the N.I.C.E. have conducted experiments, turn on their experimenters and eat them.

Lewis understood that some would perceive *The Abolition of Man* as an attack on science. However, Lewis maintained that by defending objective value he was also defending the value of knowledge upon which true science is based. In the same book Lewis notes a similarity between magic and applied science, both of which are interested in subduing reality to the wishes of human beings rather than conforming the soul to reality. In this pursuit magic and science are prepared to do "disgusting and impious" things such as digging up and mutilating the dead.[32] Lewis held out some hope, however, for a "regenerate science" that would explain reality without explaining away, a science that would study the It without losing sight of what Martin Buber called the I-Thou relation.[33]

EVOLUTION, EVOLUTIONISM AND THE NEXT STEP

As we have already seen, Lewis believed that certain parts of evolutionary theory might be correct, and in the strictly scientific theory of evolution he saw no conflict with the Bible. However, Lewis strongly held that evolutionism, the belief that life on Earth is getting better and better, is a myth. And by myth, in this instance, he means a picture of reality that results from imagination.[34] Lewis considers this myth to be a wonderful story, but not one that is true to reality. He points out that an illegitimate transition is often made from the Darwinian theory in biology to the modern myth of evolutionism, developmentalism or progress in general. Lewis documents how the myth arose earlier than Darwin's theory, in advance of all evidence. He notes two great works that embody an idea of a universe where the "higher" always supersedes the "lower." One is Keats's poem *Hyperion*, and the other is Wagner's Ring cycle. Both works of art, Lewis emphasizes, are earlier than the *Origin of Species.* The idea that the myth is a result of Darwin's biology is unhistorical. On the contrary, Lewis contends, the attraction of Darwin's theory of evolution was that it gave to a preexisting myth of evolutionism the scientific reassurances it required.[35]

Perhaps one reason why Lewis does not have any religious difficulty with accepting the biological concept of evolution is because he believes that creation is taking place at every moment, not just at one point millions of years ago. The reason Lewis views creation in this way is because of his understanding of God being outside of time. He explains that there is no question of God, at one point in time, adapting the material history of the universe to free acts that human beings perform at a later point. To God, all the physical events and all the human acts of time are present in an eternal Now. The liberation of finite wills and the creation of the whole material history of the universe is, to God, a single act. God did not create the universe long ago; rather, he creates the universe every minute.[36]

Along with this idea, Lewis has no problem accepting the idea that humanity is in the process of evolution, though he would prefer to say that humanity is in the process of being created, since the latter terminology implies a personal God who is involved in the whole process.[37]

Lewis takes this idea of humanity being in the process of evolution and uses it in a unique way: to suggest that the next step in human evolution has already happened, and the next step is that of people, who are merely creatures of God, becoming the children of God.[38]

THE VALUE OF LEWIS'S APPROACH

Whether the biological theory of evolution is right or wrong was irrelevant to Lewis. If it were found to be wrong or right, either way, it would have had no effect on Lewis's Christianity. What Lewis wanted to do as an apologist was to show that there was no final conflict between true science and the Bible. The value of Lewis's theistic evolutionary stance, whether one agrees with it or not, was that it allowed Lewis to focus on what he considered to be more important issues and to lead his readers to consider what he thought to be more vital religious questions.

THE FALL

LEWIS'S MOST DETAILED TREATMENT OF the Fall is contained in *The Problem of Pain*. In fact, Lewis has a chapter titled "The Fall of Man." At the beginning of that chapter, Lewis states that human beings, after the Fall, are a horror to God and to themselves, and are now ill-adapted to the universe—not because God made people that way originally but because people have made themselves so by abusing free will.[1]

Lewis asserts that the sole function of the doctrine of the Fall is to guard against two sub-Christian theories: monism and dualism. Monism states that God is above good and evil. Dualism states that while God produces good, some equal and independent power produces evil. Christianity asserts that God is good and made all things good, but that one of the good things he made was free will in his rational creatures so that, by their very nature, these rational creatures contained the possibility of evil.[2]

After positively stating the doctrine of the Fall, Lewis goes on to mention two things this doctrine does not do. It does not answer the question, Was it better for God to create than not to create? and it cannot be used to show that it is just to punish individuals for the faults of their remote ancestors.[3]

Next Lewis comments on the statement of the church fathers that we sinned in Adam. This concept is somewhat impenetrable to Lewis's mind. He thinks it important, but he doesn't understand it.[4] At the end of the chapter on the Fall, Lewis declares that the theory that we were physically present in Adam's loins does him no good,[5] yet he wrestles for a few pages in this chapter with the idea, stated in I Corinthians 15:22, that in Adam all die. Lewis claims that this statement implies that man as he really is differs from the way we usually think of him. To Lewis, the Scripture implies some sort of interanimation between individuals. In effect, he asks: How can we be in Adam or in Christ? His answer is a guess: just as the Holy Spirit can be really present in each of us, so perhaps, in some sense, each human spirit can be present in other people. He notes how the Old Testament ignores our modern concept of the individual. He supposes that we participated in Adam's Fall in some way deeper than that suggested by mere legal fiction, metaphor or causality. Lewis may be right in this regard.

One interpretation that Lewis does not seem to fully consider is the interpretation that Adam acted as our federal head. In other words, Adam represented all of humanity when he made the choice to eat the forbidden fruit in the Garden of Eden, just as the president of the United States represents American citizens in decisions made as president. Lewis, it would appear, dismisses this idea as a mere legal fiction.

Perhaps what Lewis wrestles with the most is the seeming lack of fairness in God, that God condemns all of humanity for one man's sinful choice. He answers this problem by saying that God could remove the results of the Fall, but this wouldn't be any good unless he removed the results of every sin. And if he did this we would not be living in a stable world, and God's action would effectively remove human choice.[6]

The next thing Lewis does in this chapter is to contrast the myth, or story of the Fall, in Genesis 3 with the doctrine, or systematic theological statements about the Fall, that developed from it. Here again we must remember that when Lewis is talking about the myth in Genesis 3 he does not mean something necessarily or completely unhistorical. Rather by myth he means "a real though unfocused gleam of divine truth falling on human imagination."[7] In the doctrine, the magic of the forbidden fruit has dropped out and the story is simply one of disobedience. Though the myth, Lewis believes, contains deeper truths than the doctrine, he does not believe he can penetrate the profundity of the myth, so he focuses on the doctrine of the Fall.[8] Lewis does explore the mythic dimensions of the Fall in *Perelandra* and *The Magician's Nephew*.

Lewis goes on to answer two more arguments against the biblical doctrine of the Fall. First, he shows that the doctrine of the Fall has not been proven false by modern science.[9] Second, he answers the argument that the first man could not sin because there couldn't have been a law to sin against because law takes centuries to develop. Lewis contends that the problem with this argument is that it assumes that the first sin was a social one, whereas the traditional doctrine points to a sin against God. Such a sin does not take long centuries of human development before it can be committed. Lewis agrees with Augustine that the first sin was a result of pride. This sin, the sin of choosing self over God, can be committed without complex social conditions. Lewis cites several examples to support his case.[10]

What exactly happened when human beings fell? Lewis offers his account of what he thinks may have been the historical fact. First, Lewis relates his theory of theistic evolution. Then he asserts that all bodily functions were under the full control of the human spirit prior to the Fall.[11] Human beings also commanded all the animals, and humanity rested totally in God. God came first in humanity's love and thought, without painful effort. The best among us would bow down before Paradisal Man if he were to appear before us today.[12]

According to Lewis, Paradisal Men fell from their original perfection when someone or something whispered that they could become as gods. So human beings chose to be on their own.[13] According to Lewis, we have no idea in what particular act or acts the Fall found expression because what we have in Genesis 3 is written in the genre of myth, not the genre of historical narrative. He believes that the Fall may have happened, in a historical sense, exactly the way Genesis relates it, but that is of no consequence to him.[14]

Lewis's view of Genesis 3 raises the question: Did the Fall happen at a particular point in time, or is Genesis 3 merely a description of what happens in the individual history of each human life? The historicity of the Fall is not denied by Lewis's view of Genesis 3 as myth. It is possible to tell of a historical event using the literary genre of myth.

One major result of the Fall was that the human spirit lost control of the human organism.[15] Lewis draws this idea from Augustine.[16] God began to rule the human organism not by the laws of the human spirit but by the laws of nature. Lewis develops this idea from Richard Hooker, the Anglican theologian.[17]

According to Lewis, the human spirit could still, after the Fall, turn back to God, but only by painful effort.[18] Lewis denies that he is making a contribution, at this point, to the Augustinian-Pelagian debate.[19]

Lewis affirms the doctrine of original sin. The sinful condition of Adam, after the Fall, was transmitted by heredity to all later generations, but Lewis phrases this doctrine in his unique way. He posits that a new species sinned itself into existence.[20]

Lewis again introduces the image of the Great Dance, saying that the world is like a dance in which good comes down from God and then is disturbed by evil rising up from the creatures. The ensuing conflict is resolved by God's assumption of the suffering nature that evil produces.[21]

OTHER THEOLOGICAL WORKS

Lewis's comments on the Fall in his other theological books and essays are in line with his comments in *The Problem of Pain*. In *Miracles*, Lewis shows how death is a result of the Fall. He affirms the orthodox doctrine—that human death is a result of human sin and human beings, as originally created, were immune to death.[22] He notes that physical death may be regarded as a punishment ("In the day ye eat of that fruit ye shall die"), as a mercy or even as a safety device. How is death a mercy? It can be viewed as such because by willing and humble surrender to death Man undoes his act of rebellion and makes even physical death an instance of that higher and mystical death. Bodily death, so welcomed, becomes blessed spiritual death to self, if the human spirit so wills—or rather if the human spirit allows the Spirit of the willingly dying God so to will in it. Death is also a safety device because, once humanity has fallen, immortality in its present state would be a horror.[23]

In his address titled "Membership," Lewis shows how political equality is a necessary result of the Fall. Fallen humanity is so wicked that it cannot be trusted with any irresponsible power over its fellows. That, says Lewis, is the true ground of democracy. God did not create an egalitarian world. Lewis believes that the authority of parent over child, husband over wife, learned over simple, was as much a part of God's original plan as the authority of man over beast. He believes that, if human beings had not fallen, patriarchal monarchy would be the sole lawful government, but since humanity has learned sin, the result is, as Lord Acton says, that "power tends to corrupt, and absolute power corrupts absolutely." Equality, says Lewis, is as necessary as clothes. Equality both results from the Fall and is the remedy for it. To Lewis's mind, any attempt to reintroduce paradisal lines of authority on the political level would be as foolish as taking off one's clothes in public.[24]

In *Mere Christianity,* Lewis uses the metaphors of the hole and the rebel to describe the Fall. What sort of hole has humanity gotten into? Human beings have tried to set up on their own, to behave as though they belong to themselves. Fallen people are not just imperfect creatures who need improvement; they are also rebels who need to lay down their weapons. Laying down their weapons, surrendering, saying they are sorry, realizing that they have been on the wrong road and getting ready to start life over again from square one—that is the only way for human beings to get out of the hole they have gotten themselves into.[25]

In his essay "Religion and Rocketry," Lewis speculates on what it would be like if fallen people were to meet unfallen creatures in outer space. He supposes that at first, fallen people would have a grand time jeering at, duping and exploiting the innocence of an unfallen race. However, he doubts whether the half-animal cunning of fallen humanity would long be a match for the godlike wisdom, selfless valor and perfect unanimity of unfallen creatures.[26] In *Perelandra,* Lewis takes this one thought and develops it into a book.

References to the Fall appear several times in *God in the Dock.* In "Some Thoughts," Lewis suggests that some hazy ideas of the Fall can be found even in paganism.[27] In "The Sermon and the Lunch," he notes that after the Fall no organization or way of life has a natural tendency to go in the right direction.[28] Monasticism and family life are both affected negatively by the Fall. And in a letter to *The Church Times* he asserts that belief in the Fall, among other doctrines, unites the evangelical and the Anglo-Catholic against the liberal and the modernist. This doctrine is part of the Christian religion as understood "everywhere and by all."[29]

In "The Poison of Subjectivism" Lewis again argues against what he understands to be the doctrine of total depravity. He maintains that our knowledge of the Law has not been ruined to the same extent as our power to fulfill it. He notes how Paul, in Romans 7, asserts our inability to keep the moral law and, at the same time, our ability to perceive the law's goodness. Our righteousness may be filthy rags, but, Lewis contends, Christianity gives us no quarter for believing that our perceptions of righteousness are in the same condition. Our perception of the law may be impaired, but we are not blind. Lewis holds that a theology that represents people's practical reason as radically unsound is heading for disaster. If what God means by "goodness" is utterly different from what we judge to be good, there is no difference left between pure religion and devil worship.[30]

LETTERS

Lewis also comments on the Fall throughout his letters. In a letter to Mary Willis Shelburne he notes that all human beings are fallen creatures and therefore very hard to live with![31]

In one of his letters to his friend Dom Bede Griffiths, Lewis notes the effect of the Fall on our work. He points out that Adam was a gardener before he was a sinner. Therefore, there can be two degrees or kinds of work— one that is wholly good and necessary to the animal side of our nature, the other a punishment due to the Fall.[32]

In another letter Lewis answers a question about the relation between the Fall and evolution. He comments that there is no relation of any importance between the Fall and evolution. Evolution states that organisms have changed, sometimes for the better, sometimes for the worse. The doctrine of the Fall states that at one particular point in time humanity tumbled down a moral precipice. Lewis maintains that there is neither opposition nor support between the two doctrines. Evolution, he asserts, is not a doctrine of moral improvements but of biological changes—some improvements and some deterioration.[33]

Lewis mentions in a letter to Wayne Schumaker that Milton's great success in *Paradise Lost* lies in affirming the doctrine of the Fall without losing the quality of myth, though Milton does lose this quality, to Lewis's mind, in books 11 and 12.[34] It would appear that Lewis's goal in all of his works was to practice creedal affirmation of the doctrine of the Fall while continuing to explore the mythic elements of it.

LITERARY CRITICISM

Lewis comments on the Fall even in his books of literary criticism. Whereas some Christian writers would find pleasure itself to be sinful, Lewis does not. To think that pleasure is sinful, for Lewis, is a sub-Christian idea. In *The Allegory of Love* he summarizes the thought of Albertus Magnus. Magnus maintains that the real problem for fallen human beings is not the strength of their pleasures but the weakness of their reason. If human beings had not fallen, they could have enjoyed any degree of pleasure without losing sight, for a moment, of God.[35]

In *A Preface to Paradise Lost* Lewis summarizes Milton's understanding of the Fall. What is the Fall all about? It is about disobedience—doing what you have been told not to do. The Fall is the result of pride—of being too big for your boots, forgetting your place, thinking that you are God. This, Lewis says, is what Augustine thought and what the church has always taught. This is what Milton states in the first line of *Paradise Lost,* and this is what all Milton's characters reiterate from every possible point of view throughout the poem as if it were the subject of a fugue.[36]

POEMS

A reference to the Fall also appears in Lewis's poetry. In "Eden's Courtesy," he talks about the wall of fear erected between man and beast. He attributes this wall to the Fall. The only way to take down the wall, he surmises, is to first tame sly fox, timorous hare and lording lion in oneself, for the brutes within are archetypal of the brutes without.[37]

FICTION

As mentioned earlier, it is in *Perelandra* and in *The Magician's Nephew* that Lewis explores the mythic elements of the Fall. In *Perelandra* he makes an interesting comment on the relation between truth, myth and fact after the Fall. He contends that these three were divided only by the Fall and that on Earth the sacraments exist as a reminder that this division is neither wholesome nor final. The Incarnation is the beginning of the disappearance of this distinction. On Perelandra the triple distinction of truth, myth and fact has no meaning. Whatever happens on Perelandra is of such a nature that earthlings would call it mythological.[38] Therefore, when we talk about Lewis exploring the mythical dimensions of the Fall, it by no means implies that we are talking about a departure into purely nonhistorical fancy.

What Lewis does in *Perelandra* and in *The Magician's Nephew* is to give us his supposal of what the Fall averted would look like on Venus and in Narnia. In both stories temptation consists of an appeal to desire and a blurring of the lines of truth. In *Perelandra*, Tinidril overcomes the temptation of the Un-man, and in *The Magician's Nephew*, Digory overcomes the temptation of Jadis, the Queen of Charn. Thus in both stories a fall is averted by obedience to the law. Digory obeys the writing on the garden gate by not eating one of the silver apples. Tinidril obeys Maleldil by leaving the Fixed Land before nightfall. These laws correspond to the law that God gave Adam and Eve—not to eat of the tree of the knowledge of good and evil (Gen 2:17).

Another similarity is that in both stories evil comes from the outside. In *Perelandra*, evil comes to the planet Venus from Earth in the form of Weston. In *The Magician's Nephew*, evil comes to Narnia from Charn in the form of Jadis. Lewis is drawing on Milton's *Paradise Lost*, where evil is introduced to the world from the outside through Satan being expelled from Heaven, taking up residence on Earth and assuming the form of a serpent.[39] Milton draws this concept from his interpretation of certain biblical passages.[40] There can be no doubt that Lewis believed in a fall of Satan that took place prior to humanity's Fall.[41]

In *The Magician's Nephew*, Lewis combines the biblical elements of the tree of life and the tree of knowledge of good and evil.[42] Aslan tells Digory that it is his desire to plant in Narnia a tree that Queen Jadis will not dare to approach so that Narnia will be protected from her evil for years to come. Aslan asks Digory to go and pluck an apple from a tree in the center of a garden, atop a green hill far outside of Narnia in the Western Wild. Digory is to bring that apple back to Aslan so that, from its seed, a similar tree may grow in Narnia. When Digory arrives at the garden he finds in its center a tree with gleaming silver apples. He plucks one and is on his way out when he encounters Jadis, who has already eaten one of the apples. Jadis tempts Digory to eat one of the apples by telling him that if he does not stop and listen to her, he will miss out on some knowledge that will make him happy for his whole life.[43] Jadis goes on to tell Digory that the apple he has in his pocket is the apple of life and that if he eats of it, he will live forever. Thus the tree in the garden in the Western Wild is both a tree of knowledge and a tree of life. The real temptation to Digory lies in the thought that this apple might heal his mother of her terminal disease. However, Digory resists the temptation and takes the apple back to Aslan uneaten. Aslan has Digory plant the apple in Narnia, and it quickly grows into an immense tree. Aslan confirms that eating the apple will give eternal life, though for Jadis it will be a life of eternal misery. Then Aslan permits Digory to pluck an apple from the newly planted tree to take back to his mother. Aslan says that the apple will not, on Earth, give endless life, but it *will* heal.[44] Thus Lewis restores the myth of the magic apple while at the same time preserving the central doctrinal lesson of the apple—the importance of obedience to revealed truth.

The result of the Fall averted, in Narnia and on Perelandra, is a good that we have not seen in our world since our first parents gave into the temptation presented to them. So, at the end of *Perelandra*, two creatures of the low worlds, two images of God that breathe and breed like the beasts, step up the step at which Adam and Eve fell, and they sit on the throne of what they were meant to be. Because this enthronement did not happen in our world, a greater thing has happened here, Lewis believes.[45] To that greater thing that happened in our world we now must turn.

THE PERSON AND
WORK OF CHRIST

LEWIS CAME TO BELIEVE IN JESUS OF NAZARETH as the God-man when he was almost thirty-three years of age. Years later Lewis asserted that he found nothing else in all literature quite like the Gospels. The pagan myths that he so loved were like the Gospels in one way. Histories were like it in another. But nothing was simply like it, and no person was like the Person depicted in the Gospels. That Person was as real and recognizable as Plato's Socrates or Boswell's Johnson. Yet that same Person was lit by a light from beyond the world. Lewis came to believe that here, and here only, myth became fact; the Word became flesh; God became man in Christ.[1] Thus Jesus Christ became central to Lewis's life and writing as the puzzle pieces of existence fell into place for him on a motorcycle journey to Whipsnade Zoo.[2]

Lewis's theological writings elucidate his views of the Person of Christ, the grand miracle of the Incarnation, the related miracle of the Virgin Birth, and the Atonement. Along the way he also makes clear his belief in the orthodox doctrines of the Resurrection and Ascension of Christ. (We will examine Lewis's view of the Second Coming in the last chapter of this book.) However, no commentary on Lewis's theology of Christ would be complete without a brief look at the greatest character of his fiction—Aslan, for it is the great lion who gives us Lewis's perspective on the very character of Jesus Christ.

THE PERSON OF CHRIST

In *Mere Christianity* Lewis states the doctrine of the Person of Christ most forthrightly. He is the second Person of the Trinity. He is the Son of God, but not in the sense that he had a beginning. Lewis notes the importance of the language of begetting. We say that the Father begets or produces the Son; we say begetting, not making, because what the Father produces is of the same kind as himself. Unfortunately, even the use of the word *begotten* suggests that the Father existed before the Son, just as a human father exists before his son. But this is not true when it comes to the Trinity. There never was a time before the Father produced the Son. The Son is the self-expression of the Father, what the Father has to say, and there never was a time when he was not saying it.[3] In traditional theological language, the Father and the Son are co-eternal.

At the same time, Lewis makes clear in other places that he believes in the headship of the Father in relation to the Son, and therefore that the Son is subject to the Father.[4] Once again, the Son is the self-expression of the Father. Or, as Lewis says elsewhere, Christ is the true Word of God[5] who imitates what he sees the Father doing.[6]

In a letter to Mrs. Frank L. Jones written on February 23, 1947, Lewis states his beliefs about the two natures in the one Person of Christ. He points out that the doctrine of two natures in the one Person of Christ does not mean that Christ had a human body with the divine nature taking the part of the normal human soul. It means that a real man with human body and human soul was so united with the second Person of the Trinity as to make one Person. Lewis draws the analogy to our human nature wherein our animal body and animal "soul" (i.e., instincts, sensations, etc.) are so united with an immortal rational soul as to be one Person. He asserts that Christ's human soul was so unswervingly united to the God in him that he had one will. But Jesus had the feelings of any normal man. Hence he could be tempted and he could fear. Because of these human feelings he prayed, "If it be possible, let this cup pass from me." Yet, because of the perfect union with his divine nature he also unwaveringly prayed, "Nevertheless, not as I will but as thou wilt."[7]

When it comes to understanding the relation of these two natures in the one Person of Christ, Lewis admits that the doctrine is beyond comprehension, though not completely out of sync with what we see in the rest of God's creation. We cannot imagine how the divine Spirit lived within the created and human spirit of Jesus. Then again, we can't conceive how his human spirit, or that of any person, lives within a body.[8]

Lewis also makes clear that this union of two natures in one Person in Christ is irreversible. This union admits no divorce. Once the second Person of the Trinity takes on humanity, he will not lay it down again.[9] Lewis believed that this truth needed to be especially emphasized in his day. In *Reflections on the Psalms*, he expressed his feeling that we stress the humanity of Christ too exclusively at Christmas, and the deity too exclusively after the Resurrection. It's almost as if we think Christ once became a man and then presently reverted to being simply God. We think of the Resurrection and Ascension rightly, says Lewis, as great acts of God. But we recognize less often how these acts are also his triumph as man.[10]

Also in *Reflections on the Psalms*, Lewis comments on the roles of Christ as priest and king. He notes the peculiar correspondence between Christ and Melchizedek. Christ, like Melchizedek, claims to be a priest, though not of the priestly tribe, and also king. For Jewish converts to Christianity, this removed a difficulty. They might be brought to see how Christ was the successor of David, but it would be impossible to say that Christ was the successor of Aaron. He was not of the right Israelite tribe for that role. However, by comparing Christ with Melchizedek one could see how Christ was a priest independent of and superior to Aaron. For Gentile Christians, Lewis says, the shoe is on the other foot. They are more likely to emphasize the priestly, sacrificial and intercessory character of Christ and understress his role as king and conqueror. The Scriptures present him as both our great priest and king.[11]

In addition to mentioning Christ's roles as priest and king, Lewis also comments on Christ's role as our example in a few places. For instance, how should we behave in the presence of evil people? Jesus speaking to the woman at the well, dealing with the situation of the woman caught in the act of adultery or eating with the "tax collectors and sinners" is our example.[12] In *The Four Loves*, Lewis says that our imitation of God in this life must be an imitation of God in the flesh. Jesus is our model. Not just the Jesus of Calvary, but the Jesus also of the workshop, the roads, the crowds and the clamorous demands; the Jesus who faced surly opposition, the Jesus who lacked all peace and privacy, who constantly experienced interruptions, this Jesus is our example. The earthly life of Jesus, which is so strangely unlike anything we can attribute to the life of God in itself, is apparently not only like, but is, the divine life operating under human conditions.[13]

Most important, Lewis asserts that it is through Christ alone that we can best find God. "Look for Christ and you will find Him, and with Him everything else thrown in."[14]

THE GRAND MIRACLE

Lewis maintains that the Incarnation is the central, the grand miracle of Christianity. Every other miracle prepares for, exhibits or results from the miracle of God becoming man.[15] For Lewis, the Incarnation is the missing piece that makes sense of the whole jigsaw puzzle of our existence.[16]

Lewis's favorite language for describing the Incarnation is that of descent and re-ascent. He writes:

> In the Christian story God descends to re-ascend. He comes down; down from the heights of absolute being into time and space, down into humanity; down further still, if embryologists are right, to recapitulate in the womb ancient and pre-human phases of life; down to the very roots and sea-bed of the Nature He has created. But He goes down to come up again and bring the whole ruined world up with Him. One has the picture of a strong man stooping lower and lower to get himself underneath some great complicated burden. He must stoop in order to lift, he must almost disappear under the load before he incredibly straightens his back and marches off with the whole mass swaying on his shoulders. Or one may think of a diver, first reducing himself to nakedness, then glancing in mid-air, then gone with a splash, vanished, rushing down through green and warm water into black and cold water, down through increasing pressure into the death-like region of ooze and slime and old decay; then up again, back to colour and light, his lungs almost bursting, till suddenly he breaks surface again, holding in his hand the dripping, precious thing that he went down to recover. He and it are both coloured now that they have come up into the light: down below, where it lay colourless in the dark, he lost his colour too.[17]

Why did the Son of God become man? Lewis, echoing Irenaeus and Athanasius, avers that the Son of God became a human being so that people might become children of God.[18] Christ came down to Earth in order to lift us up.

Lewis describes the Incarnation even more plainly, and humorously, in *Mere Christianity*. He says that the Eternal Being, who knows everything and created everything, became not only a man but, before that, a baby, and before that a fetus. If we want to get the real idea of it, then we need to think how we would like to become slugs or crabs![19]

While it is amazing that God should become man so that we might become gods, Lewis denies that the Incarnation implies any merit on our part. Rather, the Incarnation implies the reverse; it implies a demerit and depravity on our part. No creature that deserved salvation would need to be saved. Healthy people don't need a doctor.[20]

Lewis has a couple of unique ways of describing the Incarnation. In *Letters to Malcolm*, he suggests that the Incarnation can be described as Heaven drawing Earth up into it. He asserts that when God the Son took on the human body and soul of Jesus, he took on with it the whole environment of nature—locality, limitation, sleep, sweat, aching feet, frustration, pain, doubt and death. The pure light walked in the darkness and the darkness, thus received into the heart of Deity, was swallowed up. In his uncreated light the darkness was drowned.[21]

In *Christian Reflections* Lewis describes the Incarnation as God putting himself as a character into his own novel. He notes how there is a real example of this in Dante's *Divine Comedy*. Dante is the poet outside the poem who is inventing the whole and a character inside the poem. Other characters meet him and hold conversations with him. Lewis contends that God is like Dante in that he has written the poem of life, but in Christ he has also entered as a character into the poem. However, Lewis admits the analogy breaks down in that everything the poem contains is merely imaginary; the characters have no free will. They can say to Dante only the words that Dante (the poet) has decided to put into their mouths. Lewis believes that God can do better. He can make characters who not only appear to have an independent life but who really have it. Still, Lewis's analogy furnishes a crude model of the Incarnation in two ways. First, Dante the poet and Dante the character are in a sense one, but in another sense two, just as God the Father and God the Son are one God in two persons. Second, the other people in the poem meet and see and hear Dante, but they don't have a clue that Dante is also the one making the whole world in which they exist, nor do they realize that he has a life of his own, outside the poem and independent of it. In the same way, people in first-century Palestine met and saw and

heard Christ, but many of them had no idea that he was the God who created them.[22]

Lewis's analogy answers a question posed by the doctrine of the Incarnation. How did the whole universe keep going while God in Christ was a baby
or while he was asleep? Lewis answers these questions in *Mere Christianity* by
pointing out that we cannot fit Christ's earthly life in Palestine into any time
relation with his life as God, beyond all space and time.[23] The reason we can't
do this is because his life as God is outside of time. He is outside of the novel
he has written. However, he has also put himself as a character into that novel.
The timeline in the novel has no relation to the timeline of the Author's life.

Another question Lewis asks is how could Christ simultaneously be the
God who knows everything and also a man asking his disciples "Who
touched me?"[24] His answer is that Christ, in the flesh, was not omniscient.[25]
He admits it is hard to understand how Christ, as God, could be ignorant.
But if he was God and he said he could be ignorant, then ignorant he could
really be! Lewis calls attention to the answer of the theologians, that the God-
man was omniscient as God and ignorant as man. Such a state of affairs cannot be imagined. However, Lewis reminds us, the physical sciences, no less
than theology, propose for our belief much that cannot be imagined.[26]

Another aspect of the character of the incarnate Lord, which Lewis
comments on in a few places, is his sinless character. Lewis talks about the
sinless man suffering for sinful people.[27] He notes how we have been taught
by the apostle Paul that he who was without sin became sin for our sake.
In other words, Lewis posits, Christ plumbed the depth of the worst suffering that comes to evil people who at last know their own evil.[28] He also
points out that some of the Psalms anticipate a Sufferer to come who will
be holy and innocent.[29]

One thing Lewis rejects is any attempt to reconstruct a historical Jesus
apart from the one presented to us in the Gospels. The senior devil,
Screwtape, writes to his junior tempter, Wormwood, that they must once
again encourage the conception of a historical Jesus. Screwtape notes how in
a previous generation the devils promoted the construction of a historical
Jesus along liberal and humanitarian lines. And, says Screwtape, the demons
are now putting forward a new historical Jesus along Marxian and revolu-
tionary lines. The advantages of these ever-changing constructions are many,

says Screwtape. All these historical Jesuses direct people's devotion to something that does not exist, for each historical Jesus is unhistorical! The Gospels say what they say and cannot be added to. Therefore each new historical Jesus has to be dug out of the Gospels by suppression at one point and exaggeration at another.[30]

THE VIRGIN BIRTH

A smaller miracle related to the grand miracle of the Incarnation is that of the Virgin Birth. The doctrine of the Virgin Birth tells us something of how God accomplished the Incarnation, though the doctrine does not give us the details we might like to know. Lewis states the doctrine of the Virgin Birth most clearly in a letter to Mrs. Sonia Graham dated June 13, 1951. The doctrine is simply that Jesus had no physical father and was not conceived as a result of sexual intercourse. The exact details of such a miracle are not part of the doctrine. Lewis affirms that our starting point for understanding this doctrine should be to read Matthew 1 and Luke 2.[31]

Most of Lewis's comments on the Virgin Birth are designed to show that this miracle, while being an intervention of the supernatural into the natural, does not, strictly speaking, violate the laws of nature. In *Miracles*, he answers those who say that the Virgin Birth is scientifically impossible. He points out that Joseph knew, as well as any modern gynecologist, that in the ordinary course of nature, women do not have babies unless they have lain with men. Before the Virgin Birth took place, Joseph would have agreed that such a thing was scientifically impossible. When Joseph finally realized that Mary's pregnancy was not due to unchastity, he accepted the conception and later birth as a miracle. Lewis notes that belief in miracles is possible only in so far as the laws of nature are understood.[32] Later on he points out that it is inaccurate to define a miracle as something that breaks the laws of nature. Miracles do not break the laws of nature. If God creates a miraculous sperm in the body of a virgin, that sperm does not proceed to break any laws. The laws of nature take over, pregnancy follows, and nine months later a child is born![33]

THE ATONEMENT

When it comes to discussing the Atonement Lewis seeks to answer several questions. Why did Christ die? For whom did he die? How does his death cover sin, make us one with God, in short, accomplish people's salvation? It should be noted that *Atonement* is not a term often used by Lewis. He believed that this term, along with many theological terms, needed translation in order to be understood by the modern mind.[34] So you will not see the word *Atonement* very often in the discussion that follows.

Why did Christ die? Lewis makes it clear in his address titled "Membership" that Christ did not die for human beings because of some value or merit in them. He died for humanity not because each human soul is lovable but because he is love.[35]

A couple of pages later, Lewis answers the question, For whom did Christ die? It was not for societies or states that Christ died, but for individuals.[36] In *Mere Christianity*, he asserts that Christ would have died for you if you had been the only person in the world who needed a Savior.[37] Lewis can make this assertion indiscriminately, to all of his readers, because he believes that all humanity is saved by Christ's death, in principle. All that is left for individual people to do is to appropriate that salvation for themselves.[38]

The question Lewis spends the most time trying to answer is How did Christ's death accomplish people's salvation? He gives his answer to this question in a chapter titled "The Perfect Penitent" in *Mere Christianity*.

Lewis begins by saying that before he became a Christian he was under the impression that a Christian had to believe one particular theory as to what the point of Christ's dying was. What he came to see later was that no theory about the point of Christ's death was really at the core of Christianity. He maintains the core Christian belief is that Jesus' death has somehow put us right with God and given us a fresh start. Theories as to how his death did this are separate from the reality itself.[39] He makes it clear in a number of places that he believes the Christian is not under any obligation to accept any one theory of the Atonement.[40]

However, in *Mere Christianity*, Lewis relates his theory of how Christ's death has accomplished salvation. He begins with the Anselmic or satisfaction theory of the Atonement[41] and works out his view from there.[42] He says that this is the theory most people have heard of, that we have been "let off" because Christ volunteered to bear a punishment in our stead. He admits that on the surface this is a very silly theory. He asks, "If God was prepared to let us off, why on earth did He not do so? And what possible point could there be in punishing an innocent person instead?" Then Lewis answers his own question by saying that in the case of a debt, there is plenty of point in a person who has some assets paying a debt on behalf of someone who has no assets.[43]

Lewis goes on to point out that the kind of hole that human beings got themselves into is that they tried to set up on their own, to behave as if they belonged to themselves, and the only way out of this hole is for people to surrender to God, lay down arms and apologize. The problem is that only a bad person needs to surrender in this way but only a good person can surrender perfectly. We cannot accomplish this surrender in our own power, so God must help us. When we speak of God helping us we mean that God must put a bit of himself into us. We need God's help to do something that it is not in God's nature to do—to surrender, to submit, to suffer, to die. Thus God helped us by becoming a man so that he could do these things in our stead. Christ could surrender his will, suffer and die because he was man; he could do it perfectly because he was God. That is the sense in which he pays our debt and suffers for us what he need not suffer.[44] However, Lewis reminds us that if his expression of the doctrine of the Atonement doesn't help, we are free to drop it. It is not his theory of the Atonement that counts but rather the reality of the Atonement.

THE RESURRECTION OF CHRIST

Lewis clearly believes in the bodily resurrection of Christ from the dead.[45] He likens the Resurrection of Christ to a tin soldier coming alive[46] and to a diver bringing up some precious object from the deep.[47] He is clear about the centrality of the Resurrection of Christ to the early Christian proclamation, contending that the preaching of Christianity and the preaching of the Resurrection were synonymous in the early church. The Resurrection and its consequences *were* the good news that the early Christians took throughout the Roman Empire.[48]

Lewis points out that the apostles did not regard Jesus' Resurrection as evidence for the immortality of the soul.[49] They already believed in that before the Resurrection of Christ. We expect the Gospels to tell of a risen life that is purely spiritual. However, if that is what the Gospels are about, then what more misleading way of communicating the reality of the Resurrection could possibly be found than telling of a risen Christ who eats broiled fish (see Lk 24:36-43)?[50]

Lewis answers the objection that the disciples were merely hallucinating and only imagined that they saw Jesus risen bodily from the grave. He points out that any theory of hallucination breaks down on the fact that on three separate occasions this hallucination was not immediately recognized as Jesus (see Lk 24:13-31; Jn 20:15; 21:4)! Why didn't God get the face of the hallucination right? Is the One who created all faces such a bungler that he cannot even work up a recognizable likeness of the man who was himself?[51]

THE ASCENSION OF CHRIST

Lewis believed that we ought not to isolate the doctrine of the Resurrection of Christ from that of his Ascension.[52] He points out that all the biblical accounts suggest that the appearances of the risen body of Christ came to an end. He admits that the way this end is described presents greater difficulties to the modern mind than any other part of Scripture. All sorts of primitive crudities are implied: the vertical ascent of Christ like a balloon, the local Heaven, the decorated chair to the right of the Father's throne. Certainly, Lewis allows, we may get rid of the report of the Ascension by admitting that it is recorded in only two places, Mark and Acts. However, we can get rid of the Ascension only if we are willing to regard the resurrection appearances as those of a ghost or hallucination, and Lewis has already shown us why this is unacceptable. If Christ rose bodily from the grave, then that body had to go somewhere. You cannot take away the Ascension, Lewis argues, without putting something else in its place.[53]

So how does Lewis handle the apparent crudities of the Ascension story? He points out that the statement that Christ "sat down at the right hand of God" is a metaphor, a poetical quotation from Psalm 110.[54] He maintains there is no question of a human body existing in interstellar space. The Ascension belongs to a new nature. We are discussing only what the connection between the old nature and the new, the precise moment of transition, would look like.

In order to explain the Ascension to modern minds Lewis tries to disentangle the various senses of the word Heaven.

1. The life of God beyond all worlds.

2. Blessed participation in that life by one of God's creatures.

3. The whole nature wherein rescued human spirits, still remaining human, can enjoy such participation fully and forever. This is the Heaven Christ went to prepare for us.

4. The physical Heaven, the sky, the space in which Earth moves.

He elucidates that what enables us to disentangle these senses is not any special spiritual purity but the fact that we are the heirs to centuries of logical analysis. He cautions us against the supposal that the writers of the New Testament mistook Heaven in sense four or three for Heaven in sense two or one. He points out that you cannot mistake a half sovereign for a sixpence until you know the English system of coinage. In the apostles' idea of Heaven all these meanings were latent, ready to be brought out by later analysis.[55] Thus, Lewis concludes, if God were to represent his Son's transition from Earth to Heaven, in sense one, how would he do it, for first-century minds to conceive, other than by having his Son appear to go up into Heaven, in sense four?

ASLAN AS A PICTURE OF CHRIST

Finally, the character of Aslan in *The Chronicles of Narnia* gives us a picture of the Person and Work of Christ in several ways.

First, Aslan gives us a picture of the character of Christ. In the character of Aslan, Lewis combines the tenderness and strength that he believed were so perfectly combined in Christ. Mr. Beaver probably gives the best description of Aslan in all of *The Chronicles* when he says that Aslan is the King, the Lord of the whole wood, the One who alone can save Mr. Tumnus. Aslan is the son of the great Emperor-Beyond-the-Sea, the great Lion who isn't safe but is good.[56]

Second, Aslan gives us a picture of the *Work* of Christ. Aslan is the Creator of Narnia in *The Magician's Nephew* just as Christ is referred to as the Creator of the universe in John 1:3. Since we have examined this in depth in the chapter on Creation we will not go into it further here.

Aslan is the Redeemer. He gives us a picture of the Work of Christ in redemption in that he gives his life for Edmund as a substitute. Aslan describes his sacrifice as that of a willing victim who had committed no treachery but who was killed in a traitor's stead. When such a victim offers himself as a substitute, death itself starts working backward.[57]

Aslan gives us a picture of Christ as the Sustainer in *The Horse and His Boy*. Aslan is the lion who forces Shasta to join with Aravis. He is the cat who comforts Shasta among the tombs. He is the lion who drives the jackals away from Shasta while he sleeps. He is the lion who gives the horses the new strength of fear for the last mile so that Shasta reaches King Lune in time. And Aslan is the lion Shasta does not even remember who pushed the boat in which he lay, a child near death, so that it came to shore where a man sat, wakeful at midnight, to receive him.[58] In fact, it could be argued that Sustainer is the predominant role of Aslan throughout *The Chronicles of Narnia*, even when he is not a visible part of much of the action. Even in those times, Aslan is still playing the most significant role, behind the scenes, guiding each character who is one of his followers and providing for their needs.

Aslan gives us a picture of Christ as the coming one in *The Last Battle*. He is the one who brings the history of Narnia to an end as he stands at the stable door and wakes Father Time from his sleep.[59] As a result, all the stars begin falling from the Narnian sky. Lewis here is echoing the prophecy of Isaiah:

> All the stars of the heavens will be dissolved
>   and the sky rolled up like a scroll;
> all the starry host will fall
>   like withered leaves from the vine,
>   like shriveled figs from the fig tree. (Is 34:4)

The final chapters of *The Last Battle* echo many biblical prophecies about the end times, especially the book of Revelation, which shows us Christ bringing our world to an end. We will examine this more closely in the final chapter of this book when we talk about *The World's Last Night*.

THE HOLY SPIRIT

LEWIS HAS VERY LITTLE TO SAY, explicitly, about the Person and Work of the Holy Spirit. Certainly, he has a good bit to say about the Trinity, as we have seen in an earlier chapter. However, about the Holy Spirit in particular he is comparatively silent.

Leanne Payne in *Real Presence: The Holy Spirit in the Works of C. S. Lewis* maintains that Lewis's terminology of the Spirit is implicit, like that of the early church fathers.[1] It is not clear that Payne proves her point. It is kind of like saying that there must be an invisible cat in the chair precisely because you don't see him. Payne attributes much teaching on the Holy Spirit to Lewis, but she may be reading into his writing what isn't there. Payne's case is a hard one to prove because Lewis's language in talking about the Spirit is not more explicit.

In *Mere Christianity* Lewis more often speaks of the "Christ-life" than of the Spirit. He says that Christians can lose the Christ-life that has been put into them, but at the same time this Christ-life inside them repairs them all the time, enabling them to repeat in some degree the kind of voluntary death that Christ died. Any good in Christians comes from the Christ-life inside them. Lewis makes clear that when Christians say the Christ-life is in them, they do not mean simply something mental or moral. They mean that Christ is operating through them.[2] To the Christian who has carefully read the New Testament, these are all veiled references to the Work of the Holy Spirit. Lewis is more explicit in *The Problem of Pain* when he says that the Holy Spirit can be present and operative in the human spirit.[3] It is this actual presence of the Spirit, not the sensation of his presence, that begets Christ in us.[4]

One reason why Lewis may have been reluctant to write more directly about the Holy Spirit is because he felt he was a novice when it came to understanding the nature of the Spirit and his operations. At the beginning of his sermon entitled "Transposition" he says that for him to speak about the nature of the Holy Ghost or the modes of his operation would be an attempt to teach when he himself has nearly all to learn.[5]

Perhaps Lewis does not speak more explicitly about the Spirit because his Christian reading focused more on the early church fathers, who lived in a time when the Holy Spirit and his operations were not more broadly spoken of. After all, even such great theological confessions as those coming out of the Reformation did not speak explicitly about the Holy Spirit, except in connection to the other members of the Trinity. We must also remember that Lewis was writing before the charismatic movement in the church became more widespread. In "Transposition" Lewis speaks of the glossolalia phenomenon breaking out only here and there in revival meetings. The charismatic movement has affected not only Pentecostal and charismatic churches. All churches are talking and writing more about the Holy Spirit today than they were during Lewis's lifetime.

Maybe another reason why Lewis does not speak more often and more explicitly about the Holy Spirit is because the role of the Holy Spirit was less clear to him than that of the Father or the Son. Toward the end of *Mere Christianity*, in the section entitled "Beyond Personality," Lewis begins to talk more specifically about the Holy Spirit because he is talking about the Trinity. In this section of the book he is not as reticent to talk directly about the Holy Spirit because, in these chapters, he is addressing himself more to Christians than to non-Christians. Yet even here he notes how vague the Holy Spirit may seem to some people. He contends this is the case because in the Christian life we are not usually looking *at* the Holy Spirit; rather, he is always acting through us. If the Father is out there in front of us, and the Son is standing at our side, helping us to pray, trying to turn us into fellow children, then we must think of the Holy Spirit as someone inside of us or behind us. Lewis declares that the Holy Spirit is really the love of God working through us, through the whole community of Christians. The Holy Spirit is the love that has been going on between the Father and Son for all eternity.[6] As we saw in the chapter on the Trinity, Lewis is fond of Augustine's image of the Trinity, where the Father is the lover, the Son is the beloved and the Holy Spirit is the love between them. This emphasis comes out in *The Problem of Pain* as well.[7]

As we have seen, Lewis emphasizes that the presence of the Holy Spirit in the life of the Christian is more important than the feeling of the Holy Spirit. His actual presence is what begets Christ in us. Lewis writes that the presence of God is not the same as the sense of the presence of God. Our supposed sense of his presence may be due to imagination whereas his actual presence may be attended with no "sensible consolation." Lewis draws an analogy to sex. He points out that the act of conceiving a child ought to be, and usually is, attended by pleasure. But the pleasure itself doesn't produce the child. We may experience sexual pleasure without producing a child, or we may produce children without pleasure. He argues that the spiritual marriage of God and the soul works in the same way. The sense of the presence of the Holy Spirit is an added gift for which we should give thanks when it comes.[8] In another place he urges that we should accept the sensations of the Holy Spirit with thankfulness, like birthday cards from God, but we should remember that these sensations are only greetings, not the real gift. The real thing is the gift of the Holy Spirit. The sensations are merely the response of our nervous system. We ought not to depend upon the sensations. The Holy Spirit may be most operative when we feel him the least. Sensations, to use another image, are merely the push to start us off on our first bicycle. We will have much pedaling to do later on. Such pedaling will be good for our spiritual leg muscles. We should enjoy the push while it lasts but enjoy it as a treat, not as something usual.[9]

Lewis talks briefly about the descent of the Spirit at Pentecost in *Reflections on the Psalms*. He confesses that there is a mystery here that he will not even attempt to sound.[10] He obviously believed in the historical descent of the Holy Spirit at Pentecost, and perhaps the role of the Holy Spirit as the giver of gifts was important to him as well. Douglas Gresham, Lewis's stepson, suggests that this was the reason why Lewis retained the character of Father Christmas in *The Lion, the Witch and the Wardrobe*, even after friends like J. R. R. Tolkien told him that they felt Father Christmas was out of place in the story. According to Gresham, Father Christmas, in his giving of gifts to the children and to the beavers, is symbolic of the Holy Spirit as the giver of spiritual gifts, and Lewis felt it was important to maintain that aspect of the story.[11]

Lewis makes clear that he believes the Holy Spirit gave the gift of tongues or glossolalia to Christ's followers at his descent on the day of Pentecost. However, Lewis is doubtful of the spiritual validity of the modern-day experience of tongues. He admits that glossolalia has often been a stumbling block to him, an embarrassing phenomenon. He finds it hard to believe that in all instances of glossolalia the Holy Spirit is operating. He suspects that it is usually an affair of the nerves. However, Lewis asserts, we cannot as Christians shelve the story of Pentecost or deny that on that day the speaking with tongues was miraculous. For the people spoke not gibberish but languages unknown to them, though known to other people present. He contends that it looks, therefore, as if the same speaking in tongues that is sometimes only natural is at other times (or at least at one other time) supernatural.[12]

Lewis goes on to show how glossolalia is an instance of what he calls transposition. What is clear is that while Lewis accepts the New Testament story of the gift of tongues and therefore the validity of speaking in tongues, he questions whether the modern experience of speaking in tongues has the same spiritual validity as the experience recorded in the New Testament.

This is not to say that for Lewis the Holy Spirit is not active in our day. On the contrary, the Holy Spirit is the One who actively begets Christ in us. And once he begets Christ in us, he helps us to grow in Christ. One of the ways the Holy Spirit does this is through prayer.

Apparently, for Lewis, Romans 8:26 (NIV) was a very important verse. That is where Paul says, "In the same way, the Spirit helps us in our weakness. We do not know what we ought to pray for, but the Spirit himself intercedes for us with groans that words cannot express." Lewis echoes this verse more than once in his writings. In a letter to Mary Willis Shelburne, he mentions that he has been praying for a letter to come from her, and then he receives the letter that day. He professes it is as if, in tenderness for his small faith, God moved him to pray for the very thing that he was about to give. Lewis then comments on how true it is that our prayers are really God's prayers: he speaks to himself through us.[13]

Again, echoing Romans 8:26 in *Letters to Malcolm,* Lewis asks if prayer, in its most perfect state, is not a soliloquy, God speaking to God. He includes a poem in this chapter to illustrate the point. The poem is presented as though written by an anonymous author but undoubtedly it is Lewis's own poem.

They tell me, Lord, that when I seem
To be in speech with you,
Since but one voice is heard, it's all a dream,
One talker aping two.

Sometimes it is, yet not as they
Conceive it. Rather, I
Seek in myself the things I hoped to say,
But lo!, my wells are dry.

Then, seeing me empty, you forsake
The listener's role and through
My dumb lips breathe and into utterance wake
The thoughts I never knew.

And thus you neither need reply
Nor can; thus, while we seem
Two talkers, thou art One forever and I
No dreamer, but thy dream.[14]

Immediately after relating this poem Lewis cautions that the word *dream* makes the poem perhaps too pantheistic. In other words, we need to be careful of saying that we as humans are just a mode, or attribute, or appearance of God's one being. That is not the case. We, as human beings, are distinct from God as his creation, but we can have relationship with God the Father through the Son and by the Spirit. In fact, we can never be completely separate from him without experiencing annihilation, for "in him we live and move and have our being" (Acts 17:28 NIV). At any rate, the Work of the Holy Spirit in the prayer life of Christians was important to Lewis, for he even uses this doctrine as a defense against non-Christians' charge that Christians speak only to themselves in prayer.

According to Lewis, another way in which the Holy Spirit is active is in guiding the Christian. He guides our decisions from within when we make them with the intention of pleasing God. However, he affirms, the Holy Spirit also speaks to us through Scripture, the church, Christian friends and other books.[15]

As we saw in an earlier chapter, Lewis does not limit the inspiration or illumination of the Holy Spirit to Scripture. According to Lewis, the Holy

A third thing that we need to recognize is the amazing claim made by Jesus of Nazareth. He claimed to be God not only directly but also indirectly by claiming to forgive sins. Lewis points out how Jesus told people that their sins were forgiven, but he never consulted the other people whom their sins had undoubtedly injured. Jesus behaved as though he was the one chiefly offended in all offenses. This makes sense only if Jesus was God, only if he was the one whose laws are broken and whose love is wounded in every sin.[6]

If we come to terms with these facts—that we have broken the moral law of the universe and are in need of forgiveness, that only a personal God can grant cosmic forgiveness and that Jesus made the amazing claim to forgive sins and thus claimed to be God—then we are ready to hear what Christianity has to say about forgiveness of sins.

A DEFINITION OF FORGIVENESS

In his essay *On Forgiveness*, Lewis gives a definition of what forgiveness is. It comes in a context where he is talking about the difference between forgiving and excusing. He maintains that what we often are asking God to do is not to forgive us but to excuse us. There is a huge difference between the two. Forgiveness agrees that we were in the wrong and promises never to hold it against us ever again. Excusing says that we weren't really at fault. However, if we were not really to blame, then there is nothing to forgive.[7]

Jeremiah 31:34 (NIV) conveys the essential promise of forgiveness. God says, "For I will forgive their wickedness and will remember their sins no more." "Not remembering" is not the same as forgetting. God, being omniscient, does not forget anything. When he says that he will not remember our sins any more, it means that he will not bring them up against us ever again.

THE BASIS OF FORGIVENESS

Lewis points out the ultimate and immediate bases for forgiveness in *The Problem of Pain*. He says that mere time does not cancel sin. Guilt is cleansed only by repentance and the blood of Christ.[8]

Lewis has captured the essence here of biblical forgiveness. There can be no forgiveness without the shedding of blood.[9] Without the shedding of Christ's blood, we cannot be forgiven by God for our sin. Lewis also notes, in *The Problem of Pain*, that a person who does not admit guilt cannot accept forgiveness. Forgiveness must be accepted as well as offered if it is to be complete.[10]

REALLY BELIEVING IN GOD'S FORGIVENESS

In 1947 Lewis was invited by Father Patrick Kevin Irwin to write an essay on the topic of forgiveness for the parish magazine of the Church of St. Mary, Sawston, Cambridgeshire. In that essay Lewis writes that believing in the forgiveness of sins is not as easy as he once thought. Real belief in forgiveness very easily slips away if we don't keep working at it.[11]

Lewis was truly speaking from personal experience in the above mentioned essay because just a few years later, in 1951, he wrote to his friend Sister Penelope that he didn't really believe in God's forgiveness of his own sins until a month before writing to her. He thought he believed but then realized it was a sham. He cautions that therefore we must never *say* we believe or understand anything because at any moment a doctrine we thought we believed may blossom into a new reality.[12]

Lewis went into more detail about this new reality in a letter to Father Don Giovanni Calabria, written later that same year. He tells Father Calabria that for some time he believed that he believed in the forgiveness of sins. But suddenly on St. Mark's day the truth of forgiveness appeared in his mind with a new, blazing clarity. Then he realized that never before had he believed in forgiveness with his whole heart. There is a great difference, Lewis asserts, between the affirmation of the intellect and that faith which is fixed in the very marrow of our bones, the faith that Hebrews calls substance.[13]

This new realization of God's forgiveness of his sins was confirmed again in a letter to Mary Willis Shelburne, written several years later. Lewis reaffirms that he had been a Christian for many years before he really believed in the forgiveness of sins, before his theoretical belief became reality.[14]

It is doubtful, in referring to this 1951 experience, that Lewis was talking about the feeling of being forgiven. In another letter to Mary Willis Shelburne, he denies any great importance to the feeling of being, or not being, forgiven.[15]

The experience of 1951 was for Lewis something much deeper. What led him to say, twenty years after his conversion to Christianity, that he had just that year come to really believe that God had forgiven his sins? Biographer A. N. Wilson calls this Lewis's "second conversion" and relates it to the death in January 1951 of Mrs. Moore, who had lived with Lewis for thirty years.[16] Lewis attributed this new understanding to the prayers of Father Calabria.[17] Whatever the reason behind Lewis's fresh experience of forgiveness it is clear from his letters that he felt a new lease on life after this point.

FORGIVING OTHERS

Much of Lewis's writing on forgiveness does not focus so much on our personal experience of God's forgiveness but on the forgiveness that the Christian is obligated to give to others. In his essay on forgiveness written for Father Irwin, he notes that God will not forgive us unless we forgive other people for their sins against us. He declares there is no doubt about this because it is in the Lord's Prayer and was emphatically stated by Jesus.[18]

In a chapter on forgiveness in *Mere Christianity*, Lewis gives some practical advice regarding our forgiveness of others. He suggests that we need to start by forgiving those closest to us. He also declares, as many other Christians have said before and since Lewis's time, that we need to hate the sin but love the sinner. Lewis relates how this didn't make much sense to him when other Christians first told him to do it. Then he noticed how he had been doing this with himself for years without realizing it; he hated the bad things that he did, but he still loved himself, cared for himself. Lewis notes that loving your enemy does not mean withholding punishment for wrongdoing. We may in some situations have to kill our enemies (Lewis was not a pacifist), but we must not hate and enjoy hating.[19]

Lewis suggests to Mary Willis Shelburne that forgiving others should be one of our main tasks as Christians. Once we have experienced God's forgiveness, we should spend most of our remaining strength in forgiving. We need to lay all our old resentments down at the wounded feet of Christ.[20]

FORGIVING OTHERS IS HARD

Lewis makes it clear that this job of forgiving others is difficult. Being a Christian means forgiving the inexcusable, just as God has forgiven the inexcusable in us. This is hard. Maybe it isn't so hard to forgive a single great offense, but what about the seemingly unending provocations of daily life? How can one forgive those who don't seem to change very quickly—bossy mothers-in-law, bullying husbands, nagging wives, selfish daughters, deceitful sons? The only way, Lewis says, is to remember where we stand. We must mean our words when we say to God, "Forgive us our trespasses as we forgive those that trespass against us."[21]

The reason why forgiveness is so difficult is because we human beings have a hard time keeping the promise of forgiveness. Lewis notes how the work of forgiveness has to be done over and over again. We may forgive someone and try to kill our resentment, but then a week later we may start thinking again about the original offense, and we discover that old resentment blazing away as if nothing had been done about it. Lewis says we need to forgive others seventy times seven not only for 490 different offenses but sometimes for only one offense.[22] He remarks that this forgiving of the same offense every time it recurs to the memory is a real tussle. What he finds helpful is to look for some action of his own that is open to the same charge as the one he's resenting. If he still hurts to remember how A let him down, he tries to remember how he let B down. If he finds it difficult to forgive those who bullied him at school, he remembers and prays for those he bullied.[23]

Lewis was not speaking as an armchair theologian about forgiveness. According to his letters, he struggled with forgiving others through his whole Christian life. This very real, personal struggle also appeared in his fictitious *Letters to Malcolm*. He remarks to Malcolm how, on one particular day, while at prayer, he was suddenly able to forgive someone he had been trying to forgive for over thirty years.[24] However, while Malcolm was fictional, the incident Lewis refers to was not. Lewis reveals the identity of the person he had been trying to forgive in one of his real letters to Mary Willis Shelburne on July 6, 1963. There he comments that only a few weeks prior, he realized that he at last had forgiven the cruel schoolmaster who so darkened his childhood.[25] The person Lewis struggled to forgive through his whole life was Oldie, the sadistic schoolmaster of Belsen, as he called this horrid school of his boyhood in *Surprised by Joy*.[26] This teacher, who regularly caned the children under his care, was certified insane shortly after the school closed, and he died a few years later.

Perhaps this is the type of situation Jesus was addressing when he said, "And when you stand praying, if you hold anything against anyone, forgive him, so that your Father in Heaven may forgive you your sins" (Mk 11:25 NIV). When we stand praying, we need to tell God of our willingness to forgive the person in question, whether that person is living or dead. If we are inwardly unwilling to forgive others, then we cannot expect forgiveness from God. So what we need to do is to tell God that we are ready to forgive and ask him to remove all bitterness and resentment from our hearts. Surely something like this is what we all need to do in regard to the Oldies in our lives.

THE PRACTICE OF FORGIVENESS

This sums up the core of what Lewis has to say about forgiveness. However, he does make just a few other points about the practice of forgiveness.

In one of his letters, he says that a sin repented and forgiven is gone, annihilated, burned up in the fire of divine love, but there is no harm in continuing to "bewail it." It is all right to express sorrow over sin once forgiven but not to ask for pardon, for we have that from God already.[27]

In this letter, Lewis once again shows himself to be an astute observer of the soul. Most Christians have experienced exactly what he is talking about. We often remember a sin from our past, and, if we are walking in a relationship with God, we are mortified by the thought of that past sin. But what are we to do about it? If we have already confessed the sin to God and to anyone else whom we may have hurt, if we have already received forgiveness from God and others, we don't need to confess and receive forgiveness all over again. However, we may still, as Lewis suggests, bewail the sin and express our sorrow for having been the kind of people who could commit such sins. We may also do one thing more. We may thank God that he has already forgiven us through Christ's shed blood. Thanking him for what he has already done keeps us from setting up ourselves as a higher tribunal, and it keeps us from rejecting the forgiveness he has already given us.

A practical aid to feeling forgiveness, which Lewis mentions in his letters, is the aid of confessing one's sins to a priest. He writes of the contrast between the Roman Catholic Church and the Anglican Church in regard to confession. Rome makes confession compulsory for all, whereas the Anglican Church makes it permissible for any. Lewis does not doubt that there can be forgiveness without confession to a priest. However, experience shows that many people do not feel forgiveness, do not effectively believe in the forgiveness of sins, without the rite of confession. He asserts that the enormous advantage of coming *really* to believe in forgiveness is well worth the horrors of a first confession.[28]

In October 1940, Lewis decided to begin seeing an Anglican priest for weekly confession. He chose as his spiritual director Father Walter Adams, one of the priests of the Anglican Society of Saint John the Evangelist in Cowley, a town neighboring Oxford. This society was locally known as the Cowley Fathers or the Cowley Dads. Lewis wrote to Sister Penelope on October 24, 1940, about his decision to make his first confession the following week. He says that it was one of the hardest decisions he ever had to make, and so he posted a letter to the Cowley Fathers before he had time to change his mind![29]

Biographer George Sayer suggests that worries about the writing of *The Screwtape Letters* drove Lewis to seek out a spiritual director.[30] Whatever initially drove him to do this, it is clear that he continued the practice for many years. On April 14, 1952, he wrote to Don Giovanni Calabria that he felt like an orphan because his aged confessor and most loving father in Christ had just died.[31] Lewis continued for the rest of his life to go to confession, but he never again took up with another spiritual director as he had with Father Adams.[32] It is clear, however from his letters, that he experienced the truth of James 5:16 (NIV): "Therefore confess your sins to each other and pray for each other so that you may be healed. The prayer of a righteous man is powerful and effective." Lewis says that the effect of a righteous confessor in his life was indeed powerful and effective.

One final note regarding the practice of forgiveness where Lewis gives advice is in *The Four Loves*. He comments on how a game, a joke, a drink together, idle chat, a walk or the sexual act can all be modes in which we forgive or accept forgiveness. He asks, who would not rather live with ordinary people who get over relational disturbances quietly, letting a meal, a night's sleep or a joke mend everything?[33]

Upon learning about the importance of forgiving other human beings, it is a great temptation for some Christians to become fussy in their practice of forgiving others. One can become so over scrupulous about confessing sins and asking forgiveness that it becomes an irritation to others. The constant guidance of the Holy Spirit is needed to know just when to confess a particular sin or to know when it is best to let a game, a joke or a walk mend all. Also needed is the power of the Holy Spirit to enable the confession and granting of forgiveness, whether that is done verbally or enacted as Lewis describes.

FAITH AND WORKS

IT IS HARD TO SORT OUT THE EXACT relationship that C. S. Lewis saw between faith and works because he resisted coming down on either the Protestant or the Roman Catholic side of the question. This was obviously due to his desire to be a proponent of mere Christianity, not the defender of the doctrine of any particular denomination or wing of the church. However, we can divide what Lewis had to say on this topic into three segments: works before faith, faith, and works after faith.

WORKS BEFORE FAITH

Lewis's experience shortly before his conversion was such that he made an attempt at moral behavior. In *Surprised by Joy* he insisted that an attempt at complete virtue must be made. When he first seriously examined his life in this regard, he said he found within himself a zoo of lusts, a bedlam of ambitions, a nursery of fears, a harem of fondled hatreds. He found that he could not last one hour without continual conscious recourse to what he at that time called Spirit.[1]

In looking back upon his experience, Lewis believed that this was a necessary step toward adult conversion. One must first attempt to obey the moral law. Then when one sees that it is impossible to fully obey it in one's own strength, the turn to God can take place. He described this dilemma in *The Problem of Pain* by saying that the moral law may be transcended, but not until we have first admitted its claims upon us. We must first try with all our strength to meet those claims and then face head-on the fact of our failure.[2]

In *Mere Christianity* Lewis says that this is the main thing we learn from a serious attempt to practice virtue—that we fail. If we have any idea of

God setting us a sort of exam on which we might get good marks, such an idea has to be wiped out. If we have any sort of bargain in mind, any idea that we could somehow put God in our debt, this idea must be expunged from our minds.[3]

It is clear from this passage that Lewis believed our works merit us nothing. It is essential to true conversion that we come to the point of recognizing this. Lewis goes on a few pages later in *Mere Christianity* to say that the road back to God is a road of moral effort, of trying harder and harder. In another way, though, it is only giving up that is ever going to bring us home. All our trying must lead up to the essential moment at which we turn to God and say, "You must do this, because I can't."[4]

What Lewis has described to this point is what Paul calls the role of the Law, leading us as a tutor to Christ. "So the law was put in charge to lead us to Christ that we might be justified by faith" (Gal 3:24 NIV).

FAITH

In what sense does the Christian leave it to God and give up the attempt to be justified by works? Lewis clearly distinguished between faith as intellectual assent and faith as trust.[5] Intellectual assent, the belief that certain things about God and Christ are true, is absolutely necessary. Lewis maintained, however, that such a faith has no religious dimension. One must go on from faith as intellectual assent to faith as trust in a Person. In *Mere Christianity* he says we must trust that Christ will somehow share with us his perfect human obedience that he carried out from his birth to his crucifixion. The amazing truth is that Christ offers us something for nothing; he even offers everything for nothing. The whole Christian life consists of accepting this extraordinary offer.[6]

In three of his letters to Mary Willis Shelburne, Lewis emphasized the importance of trusting God to change us and not turning Christianity into a system of law. In his letter of November 6, 1953, he writes about God that he always has to do all things in us—all the prayers, all the virtues.[7] Then, in his letter of February 20, 1955, he states that we mustn't make the Christian life into a system of mere law, because it raises scruples when we don't keep the routine or it raises presumption when we do. Nothing, he says, gives us a more spuriously good conscience than keeping petty rules, even if there has been a total lack of real charity and faith on our part.[8] Finally, in his letter of November 9, 1955, he writes that we can't even change ourselves; we can only ask God to do so, meanwhile keeping on with the ordinary practices of religious devotion.[9]

It would seem that the overwhelming emphasis in Lewis's writing is on the importance of faith, trusting God to do in us and for us what we cannot do for ourselves. In his essay on "Membership," he paraphrases the apostle Paul when he says that we are saved by grace; in our flesh dwells no good thing; we are, through and through, creatures not creators, derived beings, living not of ourselves but from Christ.[10]

In his sermon "A Slip of the Tongue," Lewis confesses that any efforts of his will cannot end once and for all his craving for "limited liabilities," in other words, his desire for a safe life. Only God can end this desire. However, what God does for us, he does in us. The process of doing it will appear to us to be the daily or hourly repeated exercises of our wills, renouncing certain attitudes. This must especially be accomplished each morning, for it seems that the wrong attitude grows all over us like a new shell each night![11] In Reflections on the Psalms he maintains that we must hope in the mercy of God and the Work of Christ alone, not in our own goodness.[12]

One of Lewis's most extended comments on the relation of faith and works, though he doesn't use that terminology in the context, is toward the end of The Four Loves, in the chapter on charity. He asserts there is always the temptation to believe that God loves us because we are intrinsically lovable, not simply because he is love. He quotes John Bunyan, who said of his first and illusory conversion, "I thought there was no man in England that pleased God better than I." Lewis contends that depth beneath depth, like the layers of Eustace's dragon skin, and subtlety within subtlety, there remains some lingering idea of our attractiveness. What we must truly recognize is that we are mirrors whose brightness comes, if it is there at all, from the sun that shines upon us. We must become "jolly beggars" who recognize our total need for God and his grace. Trying to hold on to what we think is our innate goodness, we have been like ocean swimmers who want to keep a toehold in the sand, when to lose that hold will mean surrendering ourselves to a glorious tumble in the waves. The consequence of parting with our last claim to intrinsic goodness is real freedom.[13]

WORKS AFTER FAITH

Lewis does talk about good works that follow from faith. It would not be true to his thought to neglect the role that works play after conversion. If we return to *Mere Christianity*, we will see just what trusting Christ involves. Trusting him means trying to do all that he says. Lewis declares there is no sense in saying we trust a person if we do not take his advice. When we have truly handed ourselves over to Christ, we will be trying to obey him in a new way, a less worried way. We will be obeying him not in order to be saved but because he has begun to save us already. We will no longer be hoping to get to Heaven as a reward for our actions, but we will want to act in certain ways because we have already had a glimpse of Heaven inside our hearts.[14]

Lewis goes on to comment more specifically on the relation between faith and good works. He claims that he has no right to speak on such a difficult question, but it seems to him like asking which blade in a pair of scissors is most necessary. A serious moral effort is the only thing that will bring you to the point where you throw up your hands in despair. Faith in Christ is the only thing to save you from that despair, and out of that faith in him good works will inevitably come.[15]

Some readers of Lewis may think that he saw works as meriting salvation in some way. In fact, some of his writing gives this suggestion. The parable of the sheep and the goats is one of the stories taught by Jesus about which Lewis thought long and hard. He points out that in this parable there is nothing about predestination or even about faith; all depends on works.[16] Then in a letter written on November 8, 1952, he says something that has seemed curious to many. He suggests that every prayer sincerely made, even to a false god or to a very imperfectly conceived true God, is accepted by the true God. He thinks that Christ saves many who do not think they know him, because Christ is, however dimly, present in the good side of the inferior teachers that some people follow. Again he refers to the parable of the sheep and the goats in Matthew 25. He remarks on how those who are saved, according to this passage, do not seem to know that they have served Christ.[17] He elaborates on this in *The Four Loves*, saying that he takes the whole parable to be about the judgment of the heathen, because the parable begins by saying, in the Greek, that the Lord will summon all "the nations" before him. However, he concludes this passage in *The Four Loves* by saying that such a Gift-love, as exhibited in the sheep, comes from God's grace.[18]

Those who have heard of Christ must come to him through faith, but Lewis holds out hope, fostered by the parable of the sheep and the goats, that even those who haven't heard of Christ may be saved by grace. As he writes in *Mere Christianity*, God has not told us what his arrangements will be for those who have not heard of Christ. Lewis asserts strongly that Christ is the only way of salvation. However, he maintains, we don't know that only those who have heard of Christ will be saved through him.[19]

Emeth, one of the characters in *The Last Battle*, is the working out of this idea in story form. Emeth serves the false god Tash but is nonetheless saved by Aslan. And Emeth displays a combination of faith and works. Emeth's mistaken faith in Tash and works mistakenly done in the name of Tash are accepted by Aslan. Aslan explains that Tash and he are so different that no evil service can be done to him and no good service can be done to Tash. If anyone swears by Tash and keeps his oath for the oath's sake, it is by Aslan that he has truly sworn, even though he doesn't know it, and it is Aslan who will reward such a man. Furthermore, if any person commits cruelty in Aslan's name, it is really Tash whom he serves, and by Tash his deed is accepted.[20]

In the end the reader needs to see that there is no contradiction here with Lewis's basic teaching, that we are saved by the grace of Christ. Some are saved by his grace when they are enabled to put their faith in him in this life. Others, Lewis holds out hope, will be saved by Christ's grace even though they have not heard of him in this life. The bottom line for Lewis is that people are not saved because they do works of love but that they do works of love because they are saved. Or, as he puts it in *Mere Christianity*, man does not think God will love him because he is good but that God will make him good because God loves him.[21] God's work, God's love, God's grace come first. We receive that grace and that love through faith, and out of that faith we do good because we love him who first loved us.

SATAN AND TEMPTATION

WHEN C. S. LEWIS WROTE *THE SCREWTAPE LETTERS* he was not simply indulging his love of fantasy. He believed in the existence of the devils. He points out that there are two errors we can fall into in regard to the devils. One is to disbelieve in their existence. The other is to believe and have an unhealthy interest in them. Satan welcomes equally the materialist and the magician.[1] Screwtape contemplates the victories that can be won by tempting human beings to one or the other of these extremes or a delightful (from his perspective) combination of both.[2]

In the preface to *Screwtape*, Lewis claimed that his belief in the devils was not a part of his creed,[3] for belief in Satan did not appear in any of the early creeds of the church. Rather, he held his belief in the devils as a personal opinion.

Lewis had some experience with the occult. He was first introduced to it through his matron at Cherbourg School in Great Malvern, England. This is one factor that led to him becoming an atheist at the age of thirteen.[4] The occult held great fascination for him for a time, but when he reached Oxford and met real Spiritualists, such as W. B. Yeats,[5] the lust for it had passed.[6] Lewis also saw firsthand the effects of involvement in the occult on Dr. John Askins, brother of his adopted mother, Mrs. Moore. Lewis cared for Askins through fits of madness, right up to the time of Askins's death. This made Lewis determine never to have anything more to do with Spiritualism.[7]

After his conversion, Lewis believed, along with the Scriptures and most of Christendom, that certain angels, by the abuse of their free will, became enemies of God and therefore enemies of humanity as well. He held that the devils were supernatural beings.[8] However, he was not a dualist; he did not believe that Satan was the opposite of God but rather the opposite of the archangel Michael.[9] Satan was created by God, and he continues to exist only by feeding off of the good that God originally put into him, feeding off of that good and corrupting it, twisting it, into evil.[10] Satan cannot create anything. He can only spoil what God has created.[11]

SATAN'S FALL

How did Satan go wrong? Lewis points out that the moment you have a self, there is the possibility of putting yourself first. This was the sin of Satan. He wanted to be God, and he taught this same sin to the human race.[12] It was through the great sin of pride that the devil became the devil.[13] Satan has no sense of humor, for humor involves seeing yourself with a sense of proper proportion. Lewis, quoting G. K. Chesterton, says that Satan fell through force of gravity![14]

Lewis believed that Satan's fall took place prior to humanity's.[15] This seems to agree with Scripture, for how else are we to explain the presence of the serpent in the Garden tempting Eve?[16] Lewis held that Satan may, after his fall, have corrupted the animal kingdom before humanity came on the scene, bringing about animal suffering.[17] Lewis also points out that our Lord on one occasion attributed disease to Satan.[18]

Lewis deftly paints a picture of Satan's fall from a different perspective in his novel *Out of the Silent Planet*. The chief character, Ransom, when he is on the planet Malacandra (Mars), sees a picture of our solar system on a stone. In the picture, each one of the planets is shown with its corresponding Oyarsa (archangel). However, rather than seeing a flame-like figure pictured next to the earth, Ransom sees a deep depression cut out to erase it.[19] The Oyarsa of Malacandra later explains this to Ransom. He tells Ransom that the Oyarsa of the earth was once greater and brighter than he was, but he became "bent" before any life appeared on the earth. The Oyarsa of Malacandra explains that the Oyarsa of earth also wanted to spoil other worlds beside his own, and so there was war in Heaven and the bent Oyarsa was driven back and bound in the air of the earth.[20] Lewis was both grieved and amused when, out of sixty reviews of *Out of the Silent Planet*, only two reviewers showed any knowledge that his idea of the fall of the Bent One was anything but his own creation.[21]

Of course, Screwtape has his own version of Satan's fall. He claims that

Satan (Our Father Below) had a conversation with God (the Enemy) before humanity was created. God told him that he could foresee a certain episode about a cross taking place. When Satan questioned him about it, God told him of his love for human beings. Satan, not being able to accept this, suddenly removed himself an infinite distance away from God, thus giving rise to the story that he was forcibly thrown out of Heaven.[22] However, as Lewis insists, we must be careful about believing anything that Screwtape says.[23]

Lewis points out that in God's version of the story, the Fall did not take him by surprise, nor did it frustrate his plans. Once again Lewis proposes that the world is like a dance in which good, coming down from God, is disturbed by evil coming up from his creatures, and the resulting war is resolved by God assuming the suffering that evil produces.[24]

A Universe at War

Since the Fall there is no neutral ground in the universe. We live in the midst of a war-torn battlefield. Every inch is claimed by God and counterclaimed by Satan.[25] As this war rages on, Satan causes nature's depravity[26] as well as causing disease.[27] However, in the war between God and Satan, God uses Satan's weapons against him. God in Christ faces the temptations that Satan poses and resists them completely.[28] Satan produces death in us as a consequence of the Fall. But then God-become-Man willingly takes that death upon himself. He dies our death that we might live his life. This is how God uses Satan's main weapon against him,[29] and in the end, if we are to believe the story, God defeats Satan.[30]

Satan's War Strategy: Temptation

Central to Satan's war strategy is temptation, a general pull toward self-centeredness. Lewis declares that God designed the human machine to run on himself. Satan tempts us to run the human machine on the wrong juice.[31] Satan wants us to think of evil as liberating[32] when in reality it is enslaving (see Rom 6:16-23). Also central to Satan's strategy is his constant attempt to darken our intellect.[33] Satan tries to take advantage of the peaks and troughs of daily human life along with their attendant emotions.[34]

Lewis believed that after our early youth, the devil seldom tries to deceive us with direct lies.[35] Rather, the enemy exploits the truth in order to deceive people.[36] Satan always sends errors into the world in pairs, pairs of opposites, like totalitarianism and individualism, solitary living and collectivism. Satan encourages us to spend a lot of time thinking about which error is worse so that we will be drawn to the opposite one. However, we must not be drawn into either. We must walk straight through the middle of both on the narrow path that God marks out.[37] The devil tempts us to avoid the ditch on one side of the road by swerving into the ditch on the other side. To Screwtape's mind, all extremes, except extreme devotion to the Enemy, are to be encouraged.[38]

The tempter tells us to be careful of how much our acceptance of grace is going to cost us in the end. He tempts us to be wary of getting in over our heads. Most professing Christians have felt this wariness in the form of the desire to perform the bare minimum that God requires. Of course God also encourages us to count the cost, but he does it with a different motive. He wants us to see that we cannot pay the price of obedience ourselves but that we must rely on him to help us every step of the way. To God's way of thinking, being in over our heads is the best place for us, because only then will we learn to rely on him more fully.[39]

Satan believes in the existence of God, but not in such a way as to trust him.[40] He teaches human beings to doubt God as well. The devil tempts us to doubt God at precisely those moments when God wishes to give us more of his grace. The devil is most active around the altar or on the eve of conversion.[41] One gets more grace, however, if one plods steadily through the distractions of Satan.[42]

A number of Satan's fiery darts are aimed at our human sexuality. Lewis had personal experience of this, to which he refers, sparingly, in his autobiography.[43] According to Lewis, the rule of chastity requires either marriage, with complete faithfulness to one's partner, or else total abstinence from sexual activity.[44] Screwtape says that the second alternative has been made very difficult for humans to achieve since the Fall. The devils have been trying, for the past hundred years or so, to close up the first alternative as a way of escape by making humans think that the only proper basis for marriage is the precondition of falling in love. This keeps humans who cannot remain chaste from pursuing marriage because, they reason, "I am not in love with anyone. Therefore it would be wrong for me to marry." The whole business about falling in love also destroys many marriages when couples fall out of love with each other and then into love with other people. This is one form of sexual temptation that involves much more than the basic animal drive for copulation.[45]

In regard to the purely animal element of sexuality, Screwtape recommends to Wormwood that he attack his patient's chastity through failure on the patient's part to attend to the proper diet, while making his patient think that his lapse is due to lack of spirituality.[46] Furthermore, Wormwood should make his patient think that there is no hope of getting rid of him except by yielding to temptation, when in reality only those who continue resisting temptation know how strong that temptation is.[47] Wormwood should also try to convince his patient that chastity is unhealthy.[48] Screwtape counsels that the trough periods of human undulation are better than the peak periods for attempting attacks on chastity. The sexual drive is stronger during the peaks, but the same energy can be used in other ways during those peak periods. Better to attack the patient's chastity when his whole inner world is drab and dull.[49]

While temptations to unchastity can be great and frequent in some people, the devil is content to see human beings become more chaste or honest if he can replace those sins with the great sin of pride, making them think that all other sins are beneath their dignity. The devil loves curing one fault by giving us a greater one.[50] According to Screwtape, the devils also use the great sinners, dictators and demagogues, film stars and crooners, to draw a multitude of others into hell with them.[51]

TEMPTATION IN LEWIS'S FICTION

Temptation in Lewis's fiction, beside *Screwtape*, takes place in a few different ways. In *The Lion, the Witch and the Wardrobe*, the White Witch tempts Edmund through physical desire for Turkish Delight and enslaves him through addiction. The more Edmund focuses on feeding his addiction, the more he lets down his guard. The White Witch also appeals to Edmund's vanity. She tells him that she will make him a prince because he is so handsome and clever.

In *The Silver Chair*, the Lady of the Green Kirtle tempts Prince Rillian, Puddleglum and the children by using physical means. She enchants them using a green powder that works like incense when it is thrown on the fire.

She also seduces them through strumming on a mandolin. The Green Witch tempts them to doubt the existence of Narnia and the Overworld in general. She convinces them that Narnia and our world and Aslan are but dreams made up out of things they have seen in Underworld.

Finally, Puddleglum breaks the spell by sticking his webbed foot on the hearth, thus partially putting out the fire and reducing the enchantment of the green powder. Puddleglum also breaks the witch's spell by an argument that runs thus: So what if there is no Narnia and no Aslan? Our play world licks your real world any day. And how, after all, could we dream up a play world that is better than the real one? After Puddleglum's statement, the mental battle against the witch's enchantment turns purely physical as the witch is transformed into a giant serpent. Prince Rillian then does battle with her and kills her with his sword.

In *The Magician's Nephew*, the Queen of Charn tempts Digory to break his promise to Aslan and steal an apple of youth to take to his dying mother. The queen questions Aslan's good intentions. Digory is hard pressed to know what to do for a few moments, but then the queen presses her case too far, too quickly. She tells Digory that no one need know of his broken promise or of his theft, for he needn't take Polly home with him. Suddenly Digory realizes once again how mean the queen really is, and her temptation loses its power. Digory quickly departs with Polly, on Fledge, the first flying horse.

Another one of Lewis's stories where the mental battle with evil turns physical is *Perelandra*. On the planet of the floating islands, Perelandra (Venus), the evil Weston tempts the first lady of that planet, Tinidril, to dwell on the Fixed Land, something that Maleldil (God) has forbidden. Weston entices her first to *think* about dwelling on the Fixed Land. Then he tries to separate her mentally from the authority of her husband, the king.

In Weston's second attempt to seduce the Green Lady, he tries to convince her that drawing back from his new idea of dwelling on the Fixed Land is beneath her dignity. He tells her that these new ideas will make her wiser, older. Ransom, who is sent by Maleldil to Perelandra to help avert the Fall on that planet, lamely interrupts Weston's conversation with the Green Lady and tells her not to listen. Weston then appeals to the Green Lady's courage, telling her that wanting to learn of death is like her desire to tackle waves that seem too big at first. Weston tries to convince Tinidril that Maleldil wants her to learn these new things so that she will stand on her own two feet and be, as we would say, grown up. Then Weston tells her that to wait for Maleldil's voice, when he wants her to make a decision on her own, is a kind of disobedience. Conversely, Weston casts doubt on the idea that Maleldil always wants to be obeyed. He suggests that perhaps there is a certain type of disobedience that Maleldil wants his creatures to commit so that they will grow "older." To this Tinidril responds with one of the best lines in *Perelandra:* "To walk out of His will is to walk into nowhere."[52]

Weston then tries to talk Tinidril into believing that Maleldil's prohibition against living on the Fixed Land is an arbitrary commandment, meant to be broken. To this, Ransom counters that this command may have been given to teach Tinidril sheer obedience in a situation in which she can see no other reason to obey than her love for Maleldil.

Ransom goes on to tell Tinidril what came of the first disobedience in our world. Weston counters by noting that the first disobedience in our world also brought about good and brought Maleldil to Earth in the form of a man. Ransom is forced to admit this truth, but he also notes that the first good, which would have been, was lost forever. He asks Weston if Maleldil coming to Earth brought him any good. This elicits a wolf-like howl from Weston, who is thereafter transformed, semi-permanently, into the Un-Man.

The tempting process in *Perelandra* is the most complex in all of Lewis's fiction and lasts for days on end. The Un-Man goes on to tell Tinidril stories of supposedly brave women on Earth who committed heroic disobedience. Then he tries to teach her vanity through clothing her in bird feathers and giving her a mirror to look at herself. The latter brings more fear than vanity to Tinidril's heart. From here the situation devolves into what amounts to a catfight between the Un-Man and Ransom, finally ending in the Un-Man's death at the hands of Ransom.

Thus we see temptation taking place in several ways in Lewis's fiction. There are the purely physical sources of seduction displayed in *The Lion, the Witch and the Wardrobe* and *The Silver Chair.* Then there is the temptation to vanity in *The Lion, the Witch and the Wardrobe* and *Perelandra.* There is the temptation to doubt the existence of the real world and the existence of Aslan in *The Silver Chair.* We see the evil queen in *The Magician's Nephew* trying to get Digory to break his promise to Aslan by using Digory's good desire to help his

mother. Finally, we see the most subtle temptations of all posed tediously by
Weston to Tinidril in *Perelandra*, the temptation to an unfallen creature to put
self before God.[53]

How to Combat Satan

In addition to the physical ways of combating evil, another way of resisting
the devil is by prayer. Lewis comments, however, that when one prays for
certain virtues one must really want to have them.[54] Only reason and faith
working together can win the battle against Satan when he tries to assail us
with doubts.[55] Lewis quotes Martin Luther, who said, "The best way to
drive out the devil, if he will not yield to texts of Scripture, is to jeer and
flout him, for he cannot bear scorn."[56] The fact that Lewis includes this
quote at the beginning of *Screwtape* suggests that perhaps the book was written in order to "drive out the devil." We, Lewis's readers, have the pleasure
of testing this method by continual rereading of *Screwtape*!

Lewis repeatedly emphasizes the importance of pressing on in our battle
against Satan and temptation.[57] One example he gives is that of the pervert
who is a man of good will, saddled with an abnormal desire that he never
chose, fighting hard, yet time after time defeated. Lewis believes the continued avoidance either of triumph or despair and the ever-renewed struggle
against temptation is a great triumph of grace.[58] We must act mercilessly toward little indulgences and not allow even these to trip us up.[59]

In another sense, Lewis tells us that no temptation is overcome until one
stops trying to overcome it. That is, temptation is not overcome until a person tries his hardest, realizes he can't do it on his own, and hands himself
over to Christ. Then one begins to resist temptation in a much less fussy and
worried manner.[60]

Lewis's Achievement

Lewis's great achievement in regard to his teaching on the devils is in his depiction of them. By his depiction of the devils, his theological art, he makes
us more ready to accept his doctrine. And Lewis points out the importance
of using the right symbolism. He prefers Dante's depiction of angels and
devils to Milton's. Dante's devils are full of rage, spite and obscenity, whereas
Milton's devils are attractive in their grandeur and high poetry. Lewis

chooses to depict Screwtape as a bureaucrat because he likes bats better than bureaucrats! Since we still live in a "managerial age," as Lewis did, we can still despise Screwtape as we are meant to.[61]

Second, Lewis's creative depiction of the devils—desiring to eat one another—presents a desire we are familiar with in everyday life.[62] Haven't we all known a boss who viewed all of his hirelings as merely an extension of his enterprise or a lover who wanted to merely possess his beloved?[63] That desire to suck in, rather than to push people out to stand on their own and become more themselves, is familiar to us all. Thus Screwtape in a sense becomes more real to us as his motivations are more identifiable.

A third thing that makes Lewis's devils more believable is that they are subtle; Screwtape is less interested in the Second World War than he is in the accomplishments he can achieve by leading one human patient down the soft slope of gradual sin and degradation.[64] Screwtape is most interested in effecting small choices rather than large changes that might awake us to the peril of our spiritual condition.[65] The less dramatic the temptation, the better it is.[66]

Fourth, Lewis is counterintuitive in the way that he represents the demons and temptation. This, I think, makes Lewis's theology all the more intriguing to his readers. For instance, Lewis claims that his appetites would give him no trouble if his imagination would just be obedient.[67] We expect a moralist to harp on the problem of our appetites, but Lewis does not. He points out over and over again how the greatest sins are all spiritual, not physical.

Another point about which Lewis is counterintuitive is with regard to the temptation to connivance—the temptation to laugh at, admire, approve or justify the wickedness of others. Lewis says we need to avoid the company of wicked people, not because we are too good for them but because we are too weak. To handle such situations successfully may require not simply good intention, humility and courage but also social and intellectual talents that God has not given us. Therefore it is not self-righteous but merely prudent to avoid the "company of the wicked."[68]

In *Screwtape* there are temptations not only to the gluttony of Excess, which we expect, but also the temptation to the gluttony of Delicacy, which we do not expect.[69] These and many more are the subtleties with which Screwtape intrigues the readers of his letters. Is it any wonder that *The Screwtape Letters* has remained one of the best-selling of all of Lewis's books?

THE TAO

C. S. LEWIS USES THE CHINESE WORD *TAO* to describe the Way of ultimate right that human beings were originally designed to follow. He equates it with the Jewish understanding of the Law.[1] The second chapter of *The Abolition of Man* summarizes Lewis's argument for the existence of God based upon the existence of the Tao. Lewis shows us[2] from history, experience and conscience that the Tao exists and that we have all failed to follow it. In *Christian Behavior,* the third book of *Mere Christianity,* he further tells us that there are three parts to morality, or the Tao. Morality is concerned with three things: harmony and fair play between individuals, tidying up or harmonizing things within each individual and the purpose of human life as a whole.

Lewis uses the illustration of ships sailing in formation. The Tao tells the ships how to keep from running into each other or drifting apart, how to keep their engines in good running order and what direction they need to head in. Lewis tells us that we can all—Christian and non-Christian—cooperate on the first point.[3] He believes that while all people are corrupt and incapable of keeping the Law by their own power, most people are still able to perceive what the Tao is.[4] He maintains that it is on the second point that disagreements begin and on the third point those disagreements become serious.

Lewis then moves on, in *Christian Behavior,* to describe the cardinal virtues of prudence, temperance, justice and fortitude. The cardinal virtues, he argues, are the ones that all civilized people recognize. Here again we are talking about an area of morality where Christians and non-Christians can cooperate.

However, one wonders if as many people today recognize the universal Tao as they did in Lewis's day.[5] If the apostle Paul was correct, then all people do recognize this deep down in their hearts.[6] The problem seems to be that our society is taking steps toward the abolition of man that Lewis described in his book by the same name.[7] Whether this abolition of man is truly possible is a topic worthy of discussion.[8] Perhaps a major part of the problem is that Christians have forgotten the Ten Commandments and failed to practice them. As Lewis asserts, moral collapse follows spiritual collapse.[9] If society around us is collapsing morally, perhaps it is because the church has already collapsed spiritually. In response, Lewis would urge that Christians need to begin to value again the clean air and sweet reasonableness of the Christian ethics that in a more Christian age they learned to take for granted.[10]

In the chapter on "Social Morality" in *Christian Behavior*, Lewis makes several points. First, Christian morality is no new morality. Second, Christianity does not have a detailed political program. Third, the New Testament does give us some hints as to what a Christian society would look like. Lewis surmises that we should feel the economic life in a Christian society to be very socialistic but the family life and code of manners to be rather old-fashioned. Fourth, a Christian society would probably not have an interest-based economy. Finally, giving to the poor would be an essential part of a Christian society.

Lewis is careful to point out that a Christian society is not going to be realized until we want it, and we are not going to want it until we become fully Christian. He contends that we cannot make people good by the law.[11] Thus we are driven on from the first concern of morality, fair play between individuals, to the second concern of morality, harmonizing things inside the individual. He maintains that both steps must be attempted at once, even though we cannot fully achieve the first step until we achieve the second.[12]

In this regard, Lewis agreed with the sixteenth-century Reformers when they said that one use of the law is to restrain corruption in society. Lewis believed that the laws of the state should be formed upon the basis of natural law.[13]

In the next chapter in *Mere Christianity*, "Morality and Psychoanalysis," Lewis deals with the second concern of morality. He tells us that psychoanalysis, apart from the philosophical additions of Freud and others, does not contradict Christianity. Christianity deals with our moral choices whereas psychoanalysis deals with the raw material of choice, the various feelings and impulses of our psychological outfit and tries to make that outfit more normal. God does not judge us for our psychological outfit but for our moral choices.[14] For instance, we may have a psychological predisposition to alcoholism. God does not judge us for that, but he does want us to make the proper moral choices in spite of our psychological makeup. He wants us to abstain from alcohol if we have a tendency to alcoholism. Furthermore, God promises help to accomplish the end he appoints.[15]

In the chapters that follow in *Mere Christianity*, Lewis deals with distinctly Christian behavior: Christian sexual morality, Christian marriage, forgiveness, humility, charity, hope and faith. In these chapters, Lewis moves between the second and third concerns of morality. He posits that if I truly loved my neighbor as myself, then most of the things that the Law tells me are my duty would flow out of me naturally. The problem is that appropriate Christian behavior is impeded by my sin. Not to follow the Law is to abandon humanity. To act spontaneously as a Christian is not yet possible. Therefore acting in accordance with the Law as a matter of duty is essential. The Law exists to be transcended, but it cannot be transcended until I admit its claims upon me.[16] Until I reach perfection, the Law is there as a tutor to lead me to Christ.[17] I must try to act as a Christian today whether I feel like it or not. One day, I will always feel like acting as a Christian should.[18]

Christ is the one who helps us to transcend the Law. We must, in a sense, pretend to love God and our neighbor. While we are pretending, Christ comes alongside of us and turns our pretense into reality. We catch his good infection. Growing in the Christian life is more like painting his portrait in our lives than like obeying a set of rules.[19] Lewis suggests that after the first few steps in the Christian life we begin to realize that God must do everything for us, and we need to let him work in us.[20] We need to ask our Lord to change us, while at the same time we keep on with our sacraments, prayers and ordinary rule of life.[21]

In conclusion, Lewis agreed with what the sixteenth-century Reformers saw as the three uses of the Law: to restrain corruption in society, to lead us as a tutor to Christ and to be a guide to Christian living. However, Lewis went beyond the Reformers by reminding us that the Law exists to be transcended and that transcending the Law begins to occur when we move from following a set of rules to painting Christ's portrait in our lives by God's power. The use of the Law in the life of the Christian is a dynamic activity, not a static one, because Christ has fleshed out the Law for us in his life. Instead of merely obeying a rulebook, we must put on Christ if we are to transcend the Tao.

VENUS

IN *THE FOUR LOVES*, LEWIS CALLED SEXUALITY by the name Venus. He pointed out that sexuality may operate with or without Eros, that is, with or without the experience of falling in love. Lewis did not subscribe to the modern idea that the presence of Eros is what makes a sexual act pure. He argued that if this were the case, then we all come of tainted stock because most of our ancestors were married off to partners chosen by their parents. They obviously experienced Venus without Eros, and Lewis contends they did right. Conversely, the sexual act committed under the inspiration of Eros may still be plain adultery.[1]

AGAINST THE MODERN GRAIN

Lewis thought that many modern people were in his time being encouraged to take Venus too seriously. The psychologists have us so convinced that we must pursue complete sexual adjustment that it would seem some couples go to bed with sex manuals in hand. Lewis thought this ridiculous. He agreed that sex is serious. It is serious theologically because it is the body's part in marriage, which is an image of the union between God and humanity.[2] Lewis believed that one of the purposes of sex was to symbolize the hidden things of God.[3] Second, sex is serious because it is the human expression of a natural sacrament, the marriage of Sky-Father and Earth-Mother. In the sexual act we are not merely ourselves, but we act as representatives. In the sex act all masculinity and femininity are momentarily focused in one man and one woman.[4] Third, sex is serious because of the moral obligations involved and the seriousness of becoming a parent and ancestor. Fourth, sex often has an emotional seriousness to the people involved. However, Lewis points out that eating is also serious for several reasons, but we don't bring eating guides to the dinner table. We can't be completely serious about Venus without doing violence to our humanity. If we banish play and laughter from the marriage bed, then we will let in a false goddess. Besides, Lewis asserts, Venus is a mocking spirit who makes sport of us. The times when we feel most desirous of sex are just those times when we are most indisposed, and when we have leisure to engage in the act, we often find the desire has flown. This, says Lewis, is all part of the game, and sensible lovers laugh even when they are caught out in the game.[5]

Another problem that Lewis observed about sex in the modern world is that there is a tendency to rush human beings on to the mating season and keep them there as long as possible, thus losing the real value of the other parts of life. Lewis thought this a senseless attempt to prolong the one stage of life that is neither the wisest, happiest nor the most innocent period. He thought commercial motives might be behind it since people in the mating season have the least sales resistance. Lewis, when he wrote this observation, commented that he was happy to be beyond the age when one expects and desires to attract the opposite sex. The mating season is natural enough in and of itself but is distorted and unnecessarily prolonged in our modern culture.[6] Lewis believed that sexual rapture is given to lead us to offspring and family life. To ask that those raptures return is to try to prolong the honeymoon when a man ought to be thinking, for instance, about the careers of his growing sons.[7] In *Out of the Silent Planet*, Ransom is amazed to learn that one of the reasoning species of that planet, the hrossa, is naturally continent and monogamous. At last it dawns on Ransom that it is not the hrossa but his species that are strange in this regard, always wanting to have the springtime of love over again. Hyoi, one of the hrossa, tells Ransom, "Undoubtedly, Maleldil made us so. How could there ever be enough to eat if everyone had twenty young? And how could we endure to live and let time pass if we were always crying for one day or one year to come back—if we did not know that every day in a life fills the whole life with expectation and memory and that these *are* that day?"[8] To ask for the springtime of love over again is to pray the fatal prayer that God will not answer in the affirmative, that one-word prayer, "Encore!"[9]

Nonetheless Lewis had a very positive view of human sexuality as it was originally created to operate by God. He believed that sexuality is the transposition into a minor key of that creative joy that in God is unceasing and irresistible.[10] If Freud had ever met Lewis, he might have thought that Lewis's experience of joy, or *sehnsucht*, was a substitute for sex. Lewis would not have agreed. On the contrary, Lewis said that while joy is not a substitute for sex; sex is often used as a substitute for joy.[11]

Lewis believed that since the Fall, we need legal equality just as we need to wear clothes, but underneath we want the naked body to remain alive. Under the covering of legal equality we want the whole hierarchical dance and harmony to continue, and we want the naked body to appear, among other places, in the marriage bed. Lewis says we need as much equality as possible in our marriage laws, but consent, even delight, in inequality at some level is an erotic necessity. Some women, fostered on a defiant idea of equality, recoil at the mere sensation of male embrace, thus shipwrecking marriage. Modern women, taught by Freud to consider the act of love the most important thing in the world, are inhibited by feminism from the surrender that will alone make that act successful.[12]

Sexual Morality

Lewis pointed out in *Letters to Malcolm* that sex in and of itself cannot be moral or immoral, any more than gravitation or nutrition can be moral or immoral. However, the sexual *behavior* of human beings does fall into the realm of morality.[13]

Christianity, through its moral outlook—insisting on compassion and the sanctity of the human body—softened the brutalities of the ancient world in all departments of life, including the sexual arena.[14] One of the problems with sexual infidelity is that the society that tolerates it is a society adverse to women.[15] We see this so much in our society, which is so indulgent of sexual promiscuity. Women are most often the ones left having to rear the children on their own because of the male's flight from one sexual conquest to another. This is an economical as well as an emotional hardship for women. Biblical Christianity, if followed, runs directly counter to this modern scheme of things and is much more supportive of women in this regard than other modern philosophies.

Lewis corrects a mistaken account of the biblical view of sexuality. He declares that the Fall did not have to do with sex but with putting the self first. Genesis suggests that corruption in our sexual nature followed the Fall as result; it did not precede it as cause.[16]

Lewis joyfully recounted, in a letter to his brother in 1940, the successful lecture by Charles Williams to the undergraduates of Oxford on the subject of Milton's *Comus*, which was really on the subject of chastity. He declared it was a beautiful sight to see a whole room full of modern young men and women sitting spellbound as they listened to such a subject. He considered that no lecture so important had taken place in the Divinity School at Oxford since the great medieval or Reformation lectures. He relished the opportunity, for once, to see a university doing what he thought it was originally formed to do—teach wisdom. He thought there was great power in this direct approach by Williams as it disregarded the contemporary climate of opinion and preached squarely the value of chastity.[17] Obviously Lewis thought Williams's approach was the right one, since he adopted a similar approach to the subject in his own broadcast talks a couple of years later.

In his broadcast talk on "Sexual Morality," reprinted in *Mere Christianity*,[18] Lewis makes several points about the morality of sex. First, he says we should not confuse the Christian rule of chastity with the social rule of modesty. The latter changes from culture to culture, whereas the Christian rule of chastity remains the same. We must be careful of assuming that just because a person violates our rule of modesty that this means he or she has also broken the Christian rule of chastity.

Second, he comments that chastity is the most unpopular of Christian virtues. The rule, Lewis contends, is either marriage with total fidelity to one's partner, or else total abstinence from sex. This is such a difficult rule for us to accept that we can conclude only one of two things. Either Christianity is wrong or the sexual instinct has gone wrong, and Lewis cites some reasons for thinking the sexual instinct has gone awry. One reason for thinking this is that the sexual instinct goes way beyond the biological purpose for sex, which is to beget children. The appetite for food oftentimes goes beyond our physical need for food; we often eat too much as human beings and get fat. Lewis says we may eat for two but not for ten. However, if some people indulged their sexual appetite completely they could populate a small village. Lewis goes on to ask: Wouldn't we think that something had gone wrong with a society where people gathered in darkened theaters and began salivating as the curtain was raised on a mutton chop? And yet we try to think nothing is wrong in our society when people gather in darkened theaters to see the curtain raised on nude bodies. One possible conclusion in the first case is to assume that the people who salivate over mutton chops in theaters are being starved to death. However, if you find that those same people are receiving adequate food, then you will have to change your conclusion. Lewis argues there is no evidence of sexual starvation in our society. Therefore we may conclude that something has gone wrong with the sexual instinct. Furthermore, perversions in our appetites for food are rare. You rarely see people wanting to do something with food other than eat it. But perversions of the sexual instinct are numerous in our culture. Lewis concludes that the problem with sex is not that talk of it was hushed up by the Victorians. Talking endlessly about sex has not cured our problems with it. From the Christian perspective, we have nothing to be ashamed of in sex itself, but we should be ashamed of how the sexual instinct has gone awry.

Lewis maintains that before we can be cured we have to want a cure. He notes that it is easy to fool ourselves in this matter, as the unconverted Augustine did, and think we want a cure when we don't really want it yet. Lewis notes that it is hard to want a cure for our sexual problems because the devil tempts us and the media tries to make us feel that the desires we are trying to resist are so natural and healthy. Sex, apart from excess and obsession, is normal. However, the media takes this truth and twists it into a lie. Surrendering to all of our sexual desires can lead to disease, jealousy, lies and everything that is the opposite of health. Most of our desires have to be controlled in some way unless we want to ruin our lives. Christian principles regarding sex are certainly stricter than the prohibitions that other philosophies suggest. However, we also can expect the blessing of God's help if we try to follow his rules.

Lewis is a practical moralist when it comes to sexuality. He recognizes that sometimes virginity is lost less in obedience to Venus than in pursuit of being inside the Inner Ring.[19] Sometimes we give up on chastity not because we want sexual intercourse but because we want to be part of the in crowd and we can't resist peer pressure. Other times, Lewis suggests, human beings don't attempt chastity because they think it is impossible. However, if God tells us that the thing must be attempted, then we must do so, just as we must attempt an answer at a compulsory question in an exam or else be flunked. Lewis declares it is wonderful to find out what you can do when you are forced to do it.

Nonetheless perfect chastity will not be attained merely by human effort. We have to ask for God's help, and if we continue to fail we must keep picking ourselves up. Sometimes this is the first thing God helps us to do. He helps us to keep getting back on the horse, and then eventually we will be able to ride the horse of our human sexuality without falling off.[20]

Lewis demystifies another Freudian bogey when he points out that repressed sexuality is not the same as suppressing or resisting our sexual desires. The latter does not lead to the former, so we need not be worried about it, as some psychologists want us to be.

Finally, Lewis makes clear that sexual sin is bad, but it is the least bad of all sins. He suggests that a cold, self-righteous snob who goes to church regularly may be nearer to hell than a prostitute. But it is better to be neither!

CONTRACEPTION

In regard to contraception, the few statements that Lewis does make are in the negative. In *The Abolition of Man*, he contends that by contraception future generations are denied existence. When contraception is used as a means of selective breeding, future generations are made to be what the present generation wants them to be and without the consent of the former.[21] We see this being attempted in our day. How prophetic Lewis was on this point. In *That Hideous Strength*, which is Lewis's illustration in fiction of *The Abolition of Man*, Mark and Jane Studdock decide not to have children, at least not for a long time, so that Jane can continue her career as a scholar.[22] Merlin later refers to Jane as the falsest lady alive. He says this is due to the fact that by her will, and her husband's will, she is barren, and thus the child that would have been born, by whom the enemies of Logres should have been exiled for a thousand years, has not been born. A great opportunity has been missed, irretrievably.[23] Finally, in a letter to Sheldon Vanauken, Lewis tells Van that his and his wife's choice not to have children was wrong.[24] Clearly Lewis had a decidedly negative view of the use of contraceptives.

HOMOSEXUALITY

In *Surprised by Joy,* Lewis claimed that homosexuality was a vice to which he was never tempted and that he found it opaque to the imagination.[25] For this reason he refused to say anything too strongly against the pederasty that he encountered at Malvern College, where he attended school from the age of fifteen to sixteen.[26] Lewis did not rate pederasty as the greatest evil of the school because he felt the cruelty displayed at Malvern to be a far greater sin. Lewis thought that pederasty was most attacked because it was the most disreputable and unmentionable sin, by adult standards, and because it was a crime in English law. He thought this attack was hypocritical.[27]

Lewis also abhorred the modern notion that friendship between two men is unconsciously homosexual. He maintained that those who cannot conceive of friendship as a love, in and of itself, but only see friendship as a guise for Eros, show that they have never experienced true friendship. Lewis says that even kisses, tears and embraces are not necessarily signs of homosexuality. If they were, then the results would be too comic, for Johnson and Boswell embraced each other, and they were obviously both heterosexual. One might add the example of David and Jonathan from the Old Testament, another pair of male friends who embraced, kissed and cried together but who were both heterosexuals. Lewis suggests that if we do not have such demonstrations between male friends in our culture today, it is we, not our ancestors, who are out of step.[28]

In regard to homosexuality Lewis believed that the physical satisfaction of homosexual desires is sin. This leaves the homosexual no worse off than the heterosexual who is prevented from marrying for whatever reason. According to Lewis, our speculation about the cause of homosexuality is not what matters. We have to rest content with ignorance. Lewis cites the case where the disciples ask Jesus why a certain man was born blind.[29] The disciples were told that it was not because of the man's sin or his parents' sin that he was born blind. Rather, the man was born blind so that the work of God might be displayed in his life. Lewis applies this to the condition of homosexuality and makes the point that every disability, homosexuality included, conceals a vocation. To discover this vocation the homosexual must accept sexual abstinence. Lewis speculates that the Christian homo-

sexual might be able to provide a certain kind of sympathy and understanding to others that mere men and women cannot give. The Christian homosexual should not seek to evade this vocation through mock marriage to his
own sex, even if carnal acts are not involved, nor should he wear the clothes
of the other sex in private. Rather, the Christian homosexual must try to
cultivate the duties, burdens and virtues of the other sex. In short, the tribulation of homosexuality, like all other tribulations, must be offered to
God, and then he will guide.[30]

Lewis did not think that homosexual acts should be considered criminal.
He thought that of all sins in the world, homosexuality should be of least
concern to the state.[31] Lewis argued with regard to the homosexual issue
that one is fighting on two fronts: for the persecuted homosexual against
busybodies who have no right to know about this aspect of people's private
lives, and for ordinary people against the highbrow homosexuals who dom-
inate the world of criticism and who won't be very nice to you as an author
unless you are on their side.[32]

It is quite possible that Lewis's views on homosexuality were influenced
by his lifelong friendship with Arthur Greeves, a man who struggled with
homosexual desires. Lewis's relationship with Greeves developed in him a
deep compassion for the homosexual, especially the Christian homosexual.
However, Lewis did not allow this relationship to alter his biblical understanding of homosexual practice as a sin.[33]

RESURRECTED SEXUALITY

Lewis believed the biblical dictum—that life in the new creation will not be
a sexual life.[34] He conjectured that we are like the boy, who when told about
sex, asks if you eat chocolate while you are doing it. To the boy, eating chocolate is the supreme pleasure of his life, and he can't imagine anything better,
so he can't imagine how sex without chocolate will be any good. In the same
way, we cannot imagine how the resurrected life without sex will be any good
because we can't imagine a more excellent ecstasy than sex. However, that
more excellent ecstasy will be a reality nonetheless. The fact that life in the
new creation will not be a sexual life does not mean, however, that the distinction between the sexes will disappear. Lewis suggests that what is no
longer needed for biological purposes may still be retained for splendor.[35]

The resurrected life will be trans-sensuous and trans-sexual. The appetites of the body will disappear not because they are atrophied but because they are engulfed.[36] As Lewis said in his great sermon, *The Weight of Glory*, we are half-hearted creatures, playing around with sex when so much more is offered to us. We are far too easily pleased.[37] We have something even better than sex awaiting us in Heaven, if only we will be willing to move on to that more excellent ecstasy.

MARRIAGE AND DIVORCE

BEFORE HIS CONVERSION, LEWIS REFERRED to a friend's engagement as "that fatal tomb of all lively and interesting men."[1] Lewis later came to value a common life more than a solitary one.[2] After his conversion, he noted that Christianity had exalted marriage as a state of life more than any other religion,[3] and Lewis found many reasons to exalt marriage. He notes that many Christian mystics have regarded marriage and sexual union as an image that expresses the desired union between God and humanity.[4] However, he also notes the effects of the Fall on marriage and the family, commenting that after the Fall, no way of life has a natural tendency to go right. Monogamous family life will not instantly make a person holy and happy. Marriage and the family, just like all other institutions, must be offered to God. Only then will they become the channels of particular blessings and graces.[5]

REASONS FOR MARRIAGE

In a letter to a former pupil Lewis affirms that the three reasons for marrying are (1) to have children, (2) because you are unlikely to be able to live a life of total sexual abstinence and marriage is the only innocent outlet, and (3) to be in a partnership. He asserts that being in love, while all well and good, is an inadequate basis for marriage. This is the case because many ages, cultures and individuals have not experienced Eros, and Christianity is for all ages. Second, Eros often unites people who are unsuitable for each other. Third, Eros is transitory. That, suggests Lewis, is why the Prayer Book begins with something biological and solid, the begetting of children, as a proper basis for marriage.[6]

ONE FLESH

Lewis begins his chapter on "Christian Marriage" in *Mere Christianity* by talking about the "one flesh" nature of marriage.[7] This means that the husband and wife are to be regarded as a single organism, just as a key and lock are one mechanism, or a violin and bow are one instrument. Lewis believed, as did Paul (see 1 Cor 6:16), that whenever a man lies with a woman, a transcendental relation is set up between them that must be eternally enjoyed or else eternally endured.[8] Regarding the relation of spouses in eternity, Lewis thinks that the union between the risen spouses will be as close as that between the soul and its risen body because of the one-flesh nature of marriage. However, the risen body is the one that has died.[9] This one-flesh relationship must not, and in the long run cannot, live to itself, any more than an individual can live to oneself. The one-flesh marriage relationship was made for God and, in him, for its neighbors.[10] Lewis believed there should be a clear understanding between a man and a woman before they marry that God must come first in their lives, even before their relationship with each other.[11]

Lewis also notes the limitations of the one-flesh nature of marriage. He comments that one can't really share someone else's weakness, fear or pain.[12] In speaking of his wife's death he reiterates that they were one flesh, or one ship, and now that the starboard engine has gone, he, the port engine, must chug along somehow until they make harbor.[13] Yet another way Lewis has of looking at bereavement and the one-flesh nature of marriage is to say that bereavement is not the interruption of the dance but the next figure.[14] However, the bereaved person, now cut off from his spouse, shouldn't pretend that he is whole and complete.[15]

"One flesh" refers not just to a sexual combination but a total combination. Lewis avers that the monstrosity of sexual intercourse outside of marriage is that it tries to separate the sexual union from all the other kinds of union that were designed by God to go along with it.[16]

DIVORCE

As a consequence, Christianity says that marriage is for life. Lewis notes that there are differences between denominations in regard to their attitudes about divorce. Some do not allow it. Some allow it only in special cases. Lewis contends it is a great pity that the churches should disagree about something so important. However, the great thing, Lewis says, is to notice that the various denominations agree with one another more than they agree with the outside world. He notes that all the churches, at least in his day, agree that divorce is more like having your legs cut off than it is like dissolving a business partnership. He says that none of the churches agree with the modern view that divorce is simply a matter of rearranging partners, something that can be done whenever two people fall out of love with each other and in love with other people.[17]

Lewis counseled a woman by letter whose husband was committing adultery. In that letter, he passes on the counsel of his advisor that she should refuse to have intercourse with her husband and, furthermore, her husband should not mention the mistress in his house. Lewis comments that he cannot see the point of the latter. He asserts that he can't help the woman on the practical arrangements but that he can guide her in terms of her spiritual response to the situation. He notes in a subsequent letter that his advisor was passing on this advice in order to help her endure the situation with her husband, not to sanction it.[18] In a letter to the same woman a few years later he maintains that the only question is whether she can divorce her husband in such a way as to be free to remarry. He notes the differing positions on this matter in the Orthodox, Roman and Anglican communions. He believes she is free to divorce her husband but not to remarry, thus following the position of the Anglican bishops at Lambeth in 1888. However, he cautions the woman by reminding her that he is not an authority on the subject and that she should speak to one or two sensible clergymen in "our own Church." Lewis notes that some Anglican theologians would say she should not divorce her husband.[19]

Lewis reminds those who are married, or considering divorce, that they have made a promise to stick to their partner until death. He is very strong on this point and the importance of keeping one's promises, saying that if a couple doesn't believe in permanent marriage, then it would be better for them to live together rather than take vows they don't mean. This, in the eyes of the church, means fornication, but, as Lewis points out, two wrongs don't make a right. It would be better not to commit fornication, but if you are going to do it, then it would be good not to add to fornication the sin of lying.[20]

Lewis does not think that Christians should make divorce difficult for everyone else. He thinks there should be two distinct kinds of marriage: one governed by the state with rules enforced on all citizens, and the other governed by the church with rules enforced only on its members.[21]

Eros and Marriage

Lewis notes how some Christian writers are afraid that the intensity of Eros in marriage might distract one from devotion to God. On the contrary, Lewis asserts, the gnat-like cloud of petty anxieties and decisions about what to do in the next hour can interfere with our prayers much more than the passion of Eros within marriage.[22]

He points out that the idea of being in love as the only basis for marriage leaves no room for marriage as a contract or promise at all. If love really is all, then a promise adds nothing to it and should not be made. But lovers know better. All lovers have a natural inclination to bind themselves by oaths. The love songs of the world are full of it. Christianity does not force upon Eros something that is foreign to it. It only asks us to take our promises seriously and follow them through to the end. Of course this promise, "until death do us part," commits the lovers to staying together even if they fall out of love. A promise must be made about actions, not about feelings, because one can't do much about one's feelings.[23]

Lewis asks the question that many people ask today: "What is the point of staying married when you are no longer in love?" He answers the question by pointing out that marriage provides a home for the children, and it protects the woman from being dropped whenever the man is tired of her. After all, she may have given up her career to get married, and she may be in a real fix financially if a divorce takes place.[24]

Lewis takes a bit longer to explain the third reason for staying together even when you are no longer in love. He maintains that we need to think in terms of good, better and best, not just good and bad. People tend to think, too simply, that it is good to be married if you are in love and bad to be married if you aren't. Being in love is a good thing but not the best thing. Being in love does not last. But ceasing to be in love doesn't mean that a couple needs to stop loving. Agape or charity means doing what is best for the other person. Lewis urges that it is on the fuel of this love that marriage must run;

falling in love is simply the explosion that gets marriage started. Those who are willing to submit to the loss of the thrill of being in love but stay married are those who will find new thrills later on.[25] Lewis's theology on Eros in marriage reminds one of the line from Browning's poem, "Grow old along with me, the best is yet to be."

In a letter to Sheldon Vanauken, Lewis mentions that he wonders whether bereavement is not the easiest and least perilous of ways to lose youthful love, for it must always be lost in some way. Every natural love must be crucified before it can be resurrected, and the happy old couples enjoy the rebirth.[26] There is always a disappointment when lovers get married and have to settle down to the laborious work of living together.[27] When a couple falls out of love they can do one of four things: (1) look for other persons to be in love with, (2) settle for marriage without any feeling, (3) try to recover the feelings they had when they first fell in love, or (4) move through the time of death in their marriage to a new resurrection. Lewis recommends the fourth as the best option.[28]

Another mistake people make regarding Eros is that they think it is irresistible. That is why some people give up so easily on their marriage when they find themselves in love with another person. However, it is in our hands to choose what we will do with that momentary feeling we may have toward another person who is not our spouse. We can nurture that feeling or cut it off at the root. Lewis avers that if our minds are full of novels and plays and sentimental songs and our bodies full of alcohol then we will seek to inflame what might have been a mere passing feeling for someone else. If we do that, it is our own fault, not the fault of Eros.[29]

On the subject of Eros and its effect upon marriage and divorce, Lewis pointed out, in the last article he wrote for publication, that we have no right to sexual happiness. This so-called right, which is claimed whenever someone wants to divorce a spouse to live with someone else, is based on a mistaken understanding of the right to pursue happiness. Lewis reminds us that what the American founding fathers meant by the "right to pursue happiness" was the right to pursue happiness by all lawful means. The sexual motive is taken to condone behavior that for any other end would be considered merciless, treacherous and unjust. One has a right to pursue sexual happiness with one's spouse. However, when lasting happiness in marriage is achieved it is due not solely to the fact that the spouses are good lovers. It is due to the fact that they are good people who are controlled, loyal, fair-minded and mutually adaptable.[30] Lewis approvingly quotes Johnson, who said, "Marriage is not otherwise unhappy than as life is unhappy."[31]

HEADSHIP IN MARRIAGE

Lewis asserts that it is necessary to have a head if marriage is to be permanent. We may hope that husband and wife will be agreed all the time. When they are agreed, there is no need for a head. However, when they have done all they can to reach agreement and can't, then what are they to do? They cannot decide by majority vote. So someone must have the deciding vote, or else they must go their separate ways. If marriage is to be permanent, then someone must have that casting vote.[32]

Second, Lewis addresses the issue of why the man should be the head. He asks if there is any serious wish for the woman to be the head. He thinks not. He suggests there must be something unnatural about female headship in marriage because wives are half-ashamed of it and despise the husbands whom they rule. In addition, he thinks the headship must fall to the man because the man will be much more just in representing the family to the outside world. The husband should have the last word in order to protect the outside world from the intense family patriotism of the wife.[33]

Lewis recognized that this headship of the husband over the wife in marriage is grounded in Creation. He recognized that all of life is hierarchical.[34] He quotes Paul, who said, "Now I want you to realize that the head of every man is Christ, and the head of the woman is man, and the head of Christ is God" (I Cor 11:3 NIV). He suggests that Paul wants us to picture some divine virtue passing downwards from rung to rung of a hierarchical ladder, and the mode in which each lower rung receives it is through imitation. This is what Lewis takes to be the meaning of Paul's statement that the man is the image and glory of God and the woman is the glory of man (see I Cor 11:7).

Lewis admits in *The Four Loves* that some Christian writers, Milton in particular, have spoken of the husband's headship with a complacency that makes the blood run cold. We must remember that the husband is the head of the wife only in so far as he is to her what Christ is to the church. He is to love her as Christ has loved the church and give up his life for her. This kind of headship is thus embodied most clearly in a marriage that is most like a crucifixion.[35]

JACK AND JOY

Lewis's later ideas on marriage were profoundly influenced by his own marriage, late in life, to fellow writer and friend Helen Joy Davidman Gresham. As an act of charity, Lewis married Joy at the Oxford Registry Office on April 23, 1956, in order to prevent her from being deported to the United States. Jack and Joy had become pen friends during the early 1950s. Then Joy moved from the United States to England with her two sons, David and Douglas, after the breakup of her marriage to William Lindsay Gresham. When Joy was later diagnosed with cancer, Lewis realized that he was in love with her and married her in an ecclesiastical ceremony at her hospital bedside on March 21, 1957. Subsequent to this second marriage ceremony, Joy experienced a miraculous remission of the cancer and went home to the Kilns, where she and Jack lived for another three years as husband and wife. Finally, after a honeymoon in Ireland in 1958 and a physically painful dream trip to Greece in 1960, Joy succumbed to the cancer and died on July 13, 1960.

Lewis's relationship with Joy may have changed his views on divorce and remarriage. As noted earlier, he previously counseled a woman who, like Joy Davidman, had an unfaithful husband. He had told this other woman that she was free to divorce her husband but not to remarry.[36] Obviously Lewis changed his view on this matter, since he married Joy under similar circumstances.[37]

Lewis professes that the most precious gift that marriage gave to him was the constant impact of something close and intimate yet all the time unmistakably other, resistant—in a word, real.[38] He comments that a good wife contains so many persons in herself. In relation to her husband she can be daughter, mother, pupil, teacher, subject and sovereign, mistress, and always, holding all these together, comrade, friend, shipmate and fellow soldier. He asserts that there is a sword between the sexes until an entire marriage reconciles them.[39]

Many in our world today would dismiss Lewis's ideas regarding love and marriage as being outdated. However, to use a Lewisian term, we must ask ourselves whether we are committing "chronological snobbery" by dismissing his views on this subject too hastily. What gives us certainty that Lewis was wrong and that we are correct? Do we have better marriages today to prove our position right? Just because certain ideas belong to a former age and not to our own, it does not immediately follow that those ideas were ever proved wrong. Perhaps we need to investigate Lewis's ideas further, and put them to the test, to see if they might provide some fresh air in what many believe to be this stale culture of ours.

MEN ARE
FROM MARS . . .

C. S. LEWIS WROTE ABOUT GENDER ISSUES long before John Gray ever wrote *Men Are from Mars, Women Are from Venus*.[1] In *Perelandra*, published in 1943, Ransom meets Mars and Venus, or as they are called on their planets, Malacandra and Perelandra, the Oyarses, or archangels of those planets. Lewis asserts that what Ransom saw in them was the real meaning of gender. He insists that our ancestors did not speak about mountains being masculine because they were attributing male characteristics to them. In actuality, Lewis purports, the process works the other way around. Gender is a reality, an even more fundamental reality than sex. Sex is simply the adaptation to biological life of a fundamental polarity that divides all created beings.[2]

MASCULINE AND FEMININE

So what were the ultimate Masculine and the ultimate Feminine like? Malacandra seemed to Ransom to have the look of one standing armed with something like a spear in his hand, his eyes roaming over the whole earth. He shone with cold and morning colors, a little metallic—pure, hard and bracing. Perelandra's eyes opened inward. She glowed with a warm splendor, full of the suggestion of teeming vegetable life. She stood with her hands open and the palms toward Ransom.[3]

The themes of Masculine and Feminine appear again in the third installment of Lewis's cosmic trilogy, *That Hideous Strength*. As mentioned before, Jane Studdock is a thoroughly modern woman, married but trying to maintain her scholarly career by finishing her dissertation on Donne. In order to maintain her career she has put off having children. However, when she begins to have dreams of certain events that start taking place in the real world, she is driven by her fear of the uncontrollable to seek refuge at St. Anne's, a religious community of sorts, where Ransom is the head. For a while, after arriving at St. Anne's, Jane conceives of its spiritual world as something neutral or democratic, a vacuum where differences disappear, where sex and sense are not transcended but taken away. Then the idea begins to dawn on her that there might be differences all the way up the ladder of life, differences that might be richer, sharper, even fiercer, at every higher rung. When she married Mark, Jane had recoiled from the invasion of her being by her husband. But now she begins to realize that the masculinity of her husband may be the easiest form of some shocking contact with reality that she might have to meet in ever more disturbing modes at the highest levels of life.

Ransom tells Jane that there is no escape from the ultimately masculine One. If it were merely a matter of a virgin rejecting a man, he would allow it. Certain souls can bypass the male, on the purely human level, and go on to meet something far more masculine, higher up, to which they must make a yet deeper surrender. Jane's problem is pride. She is offended by the masculine itself—the loud, irruptive, possessive thing. She is disturbed by the very idea of the gold lion or the bearded bull, which breaks through hedges and scatters the little kingdom of her primness. Ransom insists that the One who is above and beyond all things is so masculine that we are all feminine in relation to him.[4]

The ultimately masculine One to whom Ransom refers is God. In "Priestesses in the Church?" Lewis addresses the issue of God language. He asks us to imagine what it would be like if we prayed to our Mother in Heaven. What if God became incarnate as a female, and the second Person of the Trinity was called the Daughter? What if the church was the bridegroom and Christ the Bride? Lewis believes that if all these reversals are carried out, then we will be following a religion different from Christianity. The modernist, feminist reformer may ask, Why can't we speak of God as Mother as well as Father since God has no sex? Lewis responds by saying we ought not to do that because God has taught us how to speak of him, and the Bible is full of masculine imagery for God.[5] God may not be male, but he is certainly masculine.

PRIESTESSES IN THE CHURCH?

This leads to the reason why Lewis did not support the ordination of priestesses in the Church of England. Lewis begins his essay on this subject by quoting Jane Austen's *Pride and Prejudice,* chapter 11, one of his favorite books. "I should like Balls infinitely better," said Caroline Bingley, "if they were carried on in a different manner. . . . It would surely be much more rational if conversation instead of dancing made the order of the day." "Much more rational, I dare say," replied her brother, "but it would not be near so much like a Ball."[6]

Lewis suggests that the proposed arrangement, to ordain priestesses, would make the church much more rational but not near so much like a church. It would be more rational because the church is short of priests. Women are not less capable than men of piety, zeal, learning and whatever else is necessary to the pastoral office. However, while there were women prophets in the Bible, there were no women priests.[7]

Why then, if a woman can preach, can't she be a priest? In answer to this Lewis explains the function of a priest, which is to represent the people to God in prayer and to address the people in God's behalf. Lewis maintains it is appropriate for a woman to do the former but not the latter because only one wearing the masculine uniform can represent the Lord to his church. In Lewis's view we are all feminine in relationship to the ultimately masculine Lord of the universe.[8]

Getting back to Jane Austen, Lewis contends that the church should be more like a ball than like a factory or a political party. The ball exists to stylize courtship. We better not tamper with it. When we come to the church we are dealing with something even closer in to the center of our nature as human beings than a ball. In church "we are dealing with male and female not merely as facts of nature but as live and awful shadows of realities utterly beyond our control and largely beyond our direct knowledge. Or rather, we are not dealing with them but (as we shall soon learn if we meddle) they are dealing with us."[9]

HIERARCHY

The theme of gender is but a subset of a larger theme in Lewis's writing. That is the theme of hierarchy. As we have already seen, Lewis believed in the importance of hierarchy in marriage and in the church. But why did he believe in it? Lewis describes the hierarchical conception in *A Preface to Paradise Lost.* He says that there are degrees of value objectively present in the universe. Everyone except God has a natural superior and everything except unformed matter has a natural inferior. Happiness in life depends upon assuming our rightful role. If we step out of our place in God's system, then we make the very nature of things our enemy.[10]

Granted, Lewis is describing the hierarchical conception that was in the mind of Milton. However, Lewis believed in the importance of hierarchy as well. In his essay entitled "Membership," he asserts that he does not believe that God created an egalitarian world. He believes the authority of parent over child, husband over wife, learned over simple was as much a part of God's original plan as the authority of humans over the animal kingdom. If it weren't for the Fall, patriarchal monarchy would be the sole lawful government.[11] However, since we have fallen, we have had to substitute a legal fiction of equality to remedy the corruption brought on by too much power being held by too few people. Equality is in the same position as clothes—it is a result of the Fall and a remedy for it. But when we come out from the world into the church it is like turning from a march to a dance. It is like taking off our clothes. Lewis says it delights him that there are some moments in the worship services of his church when the priest stands and he kneels. As democracy becomes more complete in the outer world, the refreshment of inequality, which the church offers us, becomes all the more necessary.[12]

LEWIS A MISOGYNIST?

Given Lewis's views on hierarchy and on the masculine and feminine aspects of life, it has been claimed that Lewis was a misogynist. However, one need only look at the facts of Lewis's life to know that he was not a hater of women.

Granted, Lewis lived most of his life in the predominantly male bastion of Oxford. As a Fellow of Magdalen, Lewis voted for limiting the number of women at the university in 1927.[13] And there are some remarks that Lewis made about women, recorded in his letters prior to his conversion, that could lead one to think he was a misogynist.[14]

However, let us also remember that Lewis grew up having happy relationships with his mother, his nurse at home and his matron at school. By choice, he spent a good part of his life with two women, Janie King Moore and her daughter, Maureen Moore. He hosted children in his home during World War II when they were evacuated from London because of the air raids. One of those children was a sixteen-year-old girl, June Flewett, with whom Lewis and his brother maintained a lifelong relationship.[15] Lewis had positive relationships with women writers such as Dorothy Sayers[16] and Ruth Pitter.[17] Most of his correspondence, after his conversion, was with women who wrote to him about his books.[18] He tutored young women at Oxford who have written positively about their experience with him.[19] He married an outspoken woman with a very strong mind and character.[20] Finally, one of the most famous obituaries on Lewis was written by a woman scholar, Dame Helen Gardner.[21] If Lewis had been a hater of women, one of these many women in his life would have made a statement, at some time, reporting the fact. But the record from Lewis's time does not portray him as such.

It seems that in our day, some people can no longer understand a time when men like Lewis saw deep differences between men and women, honored their differing roles and believed in the importance of hierarchy in life.[22] Perhaps we need to more seriously consider Lewis's statement in *The Four Loves* that the sternest feminist need not grudge the male sex the crown offered to it either in the pagan or in the Christian mystery. For the one crown is of paper and the other is made of thorns.[23]

One wonders, if Lewis was a misogynist, how could he write to a woman, and a nun no less, that there ought, spiritually speaking, to be a man in every woman and a woman in every man? He says to Sister Penelope that he can't bear "a man's man" or a "woman's woman."[24] And if Lewis was a misogynist, how could he have written a book like *Till We Have Faces* with such a multidimensional and powerful female character as Orual?

Speaking of Orual leads to a consideration of one more area in which hierarchy was important to Lewis. But it will require another chapter to do that.

I Am the King's Man

WE READ IN *THAT HIDEOUS STRENGTH* that the moment Jane Studdock looks at Ransom for the first time her world is unmade. Why? Because up until that moment Jane believes in a world of total egalitarianism. Now she realizes, once again, in the depths of her soul, that hierarchy holds a deeper truth than the legal fiction of equality. Lewis writes,

> She had (or so she had believed) disliked bearded faces except for old men with white hair. But that was because she had long since forgotten the imagined Arthur of her childhood—and the imagined Solomon too. Solomon—for the first time in many years the bright solar blend of king and lover and magician which hangs about that name stole back upon her mind. For the first time in all those years she tasted the word *King* itself with all linked associations of battle, marriage, priesthood, mercy, and power. At that moment, as her eyes first rested on his [Ransom's] face, Jane forgot who she was, and where . . . her world was unmade; she knew that. Anything might happen now.[1]

With these words Lewis introduces us to the importance of monarchy. It is vital because it reminds us that we do not live in an egalitarian world but rather a world in which hierarchy exists at all levels. In *Miracles* Lewis tells us that if we come to the grand miracle of the Incarnation hoping that it will deliver us from the world of inequality into a transparent and enlightened spirituality where inequality vanishes, we shall be disappointed. Rather we shall find that there is hierarchical inequality all the way up. Through the Incarnation we can learn that this hierarchical inequality holds sway in the realm beyond nature.[2]

As noted in earlier chapters, Lewis believed in maintaining the legal fiction of democracy and equality in society in order to protect human beings from some of the effects of the Fall, namely, what Lord Acton called the tendency of absolute power to corrupt absolutely. But Lewis also believed that we needed reminders in life that equality is not the rock-bottom reality and that hierarchy holds the deeper truth. For this reason he urges that Britons should rejoice in having a legal democracy without losing a ceremonial monarchy. The monarchy satisfies the human craving for inequality. He suggests that a person's reaction to monarchy is a sort of test. Those who debunk the monarchy are people whose taproot in Eden has been cut. They are no longer hearing the music of the Great Dance. To these debunkers, pebbles laid in a row are more beautiful than an arch. Yet even if they say they desire mere equality, they cannot achieve it. Lewis maintains that if people are forbidden to honor a king they will honor millionaires, athletes or movie stars instead. Our true spiritual nature must be served in some way. If we are denied real spiritual food, we will devour poison.[3]

But what of the current state of the monarchy in England? Lewis returns to the Jane Austen metaphor, "Wouldn't conversation be more rational than dancing?" said Miss Bingley. "Yes," replied Mr. Bingley, "but much less like a Ball." Lewis writes that it would of course be much more sensible to abolish the English monarchy. But what if, by taking such an action, Britons would leave out the one element in their state that matters most? What if the monarchy is the one conduit through which all the most important elements of citizenship are channeled, elements such as loyalty, the consecration of secular life, the hierarchical principle, splendor, ceremony, continuity?[4]

Lewis asserts that just because the monarchy is ceremonial doesn't mean it is no longer necessary. England needs the monarchy in order to irrigate, to bring to life, the modern dustbowl of statecraft. Lewis, writing of the coronation of Elizabeth II, told an American correspondent that people in England did not get a fairy-tale feeling about the coronation. He said that what was most impressive was the way in which the queen seemed to be overwhelmed by the sacramental side of the coronation. He professed that the pressing of the huge, heavy crown on Elizabeth's small, young head was to him a sort of symbol of the situation of humanity. As human beings we are called by God to be his representatives on Earth, yet we are so inadequate.

We have all been crowned, and our coronation contains a tragic splendor.[5]

So here is yet another deep truth of which the monarchy reminds us—the dust we are has been crowned with glories and dangers and responsibilities beyond our imagining. God has raised the mere animal creatures that we are to the level of reason and a possible relationship with him. Tragically we have rejected that relationship, floundering backward into a maze of imbecility. Yet all is not lost, for the rightful King of the universe has landed in disguise on this planet and has set about winning us back to himself, that he might raise us to reign with him in the heavenlies (see Eph 2:6). The monarchy is a reminder of all this and more. For it reminds us too that all of life is filled with the glory of hierarchy and that there is a Monarch who is higher than all earthly kings.

The concept of hierarchy is quite important in what some consider to be the most memorable of all C. S. Lewis's writings, *The Chronicles of Narnia*. Narnia is invested with a king and queen from its very founding when Aslan appoints Frank the Cabby and his wife, Helen, to be the first king and queen of that fair land. When Frank tells Aslan he is not up to the job, Aslan asks him a series of questions. He asks Frank if he can be a good gardener, if he can rule other creatures fairly, if he can bring up his children and grandchildren to do the same. Aslan asks if Frank will play favorites or allow injustices. And if enemies come against Narnia, Aslan asks if Frank will be at the head of the battle and the last one in retreat. When Frank answers all of Aslan's questions appropriately Aslan assures him that if he will do these things then he will have done all that a king should do.[6]

The investiture of King Frank reminds us that the king is still under the law of Aslan, who is the son of the Emperor-over-the-Sea, the King above all High Kings in Narnia.[7] Aslan is the one who puts kings in their place and tells them how to rule.[8] There are reminders at other points that the king is not above the law. When Caspian asserts that he is going with Reepicheep to see the World's End, Reepicheep reminds him that he is the king of Narnia and that therefore he cannot please himself with adventures, as though he were a private person.[9] When King Tirian rashly kills two Calormenes who are mistreating a Talking Horse and felling trees in Narnia, he soon realizes his wrongdoing.[10] Tirian realizes that he is not the maker of law but, even as king, he is under the law.

There is also in Narnia a clear delineation of hierarchy and the manner in which commoners should relate to those of royal blood. When Dr. Cornelius tells Prince Caspian that he is the true king of Narnia, the true son and heir of Caspian the Ninth, Cornelius, to Caspian's great surprise, drops down on one knee and kisses his hand.[11] Toward the end of *The Horse and His Boy* it is recognized that there is something different about Shasta. After Shasta tries to rescue Aravis and Hwin from the lion's attack, at the risk of his own life and limb, Bree and Hwin acknowledge that Shasta is the best of them all.[12] A little later, the Lord Darrin, seeing how Shasta takes his seat on a horse, recognizes that there must be noble blood in him.[13] And there *is* noble blood in him, for Shasta is in reality Cor, the son of King Lune and twin of Corin of Archenland.

The proper allegiance to proper kings who rule at Aslan's bidding is modeled throughout *The Chronicles of Narnia*. Perhaps the converted Eustace expresses it best when, at the Parliament of Owls in *The Silver Chair*, he asserts that he is the king's man and that he will have nothing to do with any plots against the rightful sovereign of Narnia.[14]

A similar statement is made by Ransom in *That Hideous Strength*. Merlin asks him whether any help is to be found in the king who sits at Windsor, to which Ransom replies in the negative. Merlin then presses his case and asks if the king can be overthrown. And Ransom says that he has no desire to overthrow him simply because the king is the king and he, Ransom, is the king's man.[15]

Defending the monarchical impulse caused by reading the Narnia stories, Lewis wrote in a letter to an American,

> American children, as I know from the letters they write me, are just as "Aslan-olatrous" as English ones. The world of fairy-tale, as the world of Christianity, makes the heart and imagination royalist in a sense which mere politics hardly [touches]. What my stories do is to liberate—to free from inhibitions—a spontaneous impulse to serve and adore, to have a "dearest dread", which the modern world starves, or diverts to film-stars, crooners, and athletes.[16]

If we are to judge by the sale of Narnia books alone (over one million every year), then Lewis's world of fairy tale is continuing to make many a heart and imagination royalist.

THE SERVANT KING

One more important point in regard to Lewis's concept of hierarchy must be understood. That is that, to Lewis's mind, the proper king is one who acts as a servant. This was Lewis's belief because our divine monarch, the Lord Jesus Christ, had a servant's heart and washed his disciples' feet. Jesus said, "For even the Son of Man did not come to be served, but to serve, and to give his life as a ransom for many" (Mk 10:45 NIV). As we saw earlier, in the chapter on the Person and Work of Christ, Lewis believed that the Son of God came down from Heaven to lift us up.

The humility of the monarch is crucial to Lewis and permeates his fiction. There is a lovely line in *The Lion, the Witch and the Wardrobe* where the great lion Aslan is leading all the talking beasts off to war with the White Witch and he says to the animals, "Those who are good with their noses must come in front with us lions to smell out where the battle is." The other lion immediately picks up on Aslan's words and remarks, "Did you hear what he said? *Us lions.* That means him and me. *Us lions.* That's what I like about Aslan. No side, no stand-off-ishness. *Us lions.* That meant him and me."[17]

In *The Magician's Nephew*, as already noted, the first king of Narnia, Frank, is a cabby in our world before he is transported to Narnia and installed in his new role. And one of the greatest people in Heaven in *The Great Divorce* is the celestial lady who used to be on Earth simply Sarah Smith of Golders Green.[18] In *The Horse and His Boy*, Aravis, who is a great Tarkheena of noble Calormene blood, must learn to have the same humility as Shasta, who also is of noble blood but does not realize it for most of the story. And even when Shasta does realize who his father is, he wears his royalty very lightly. Lewis seems to take great joy, in the same story, poking fun at the pompously hierarchical society of Tashbaan in which you have to bow and scrape before your superiors and constantly be saying, "May he live forever!" whenever the Tisroc, the King of Calormen, is mentioned.

Clearly for Lewis, the greatest in the kingdom is the least of all, the servant of all. The greatest king is the one who is most humble, most serving, most loving.

WAR AND PEACE

C. S. LEWIS BECAME POPULAR as a Christian author and broadcaster during the Second World War.[1] In fact, it has been said that Lewis's voice was the most recognized in all of Great Britain during that war, second only to that of Winston Churchill. This raises the question of what Lewis thought about the Second World War and about war in general. One is not disappointed in finding an answer to that question, for Lewis had quite a bit to say about the subject.

Lewis believed Britain's participation in the Second World War to be a righteous cause, as far as human causes go. Therefore he thought it his duty to support the war effort.[2] This does not mean that he liked war. He participated as a soldier in the First World War out of a sense of obligation to his adopted country of England even though he was under no requirement to serve, since he was an Irish citizen.[3] His memories of his participation in the First World War haunted his dreams for years, and prior to World War II he thought death preferable to living through another war.[4] At the same time, while serving in World War I, Lewis did not seem to spend much time thinking about the war. It would appear that Lewis spent more time reading and thinking about great literature than he did anything else.[5] In fact, his first impression of the war was that he was experiencing what Homer wrote about.[6] As far as the reading of wartime news was concerned, he viewed that activity as he viewed the reading of any newspaper; he considered it to be a colossal waste of time.[7]

LEARNING IN WARTIME

While Lewis spent a good part of World War I serving in the trenches in

France, he spent World War II teaching in Oxford. One of his most famous sermons of the time, delivered to a packed congregation in the University Church of St. Mary the Virgin, was entitled *Learning in War-Time.*[8] In that sermon Lewis suggests that war raises three enemies against the scholarly life. One is excitement, the temptation to be constantly distracted from one's work by news of the war. The best defense against this enemy is to realize that it is not a new one. One must do the best one can to stay focused on one's work. Lewis says the people who will achieve most in the scholarly arena are those who want knowledge so badly that they pursue it even when conditions are unfavorable to that pursuit.

The second enemy of the scholarly life raised by war is frustration, the feeling that one will never have enough time to finish one's work. However, Lewis points out that this is always a possibility, in peacetime as well as in war. Even in middle age a person must face the fact that there are certain projects he or she can no longer take on due to lack of time. It is essential to realize that the present is the only time in which one's duties can be done and grace can be received. It is best not to plan much for the distant future or put off until tomorrow what can be done today.

The third enemy of the scholarly life presented by war is fear. Knowing how Jesus handled fear in the Garden of Gethsemane teaches us that we don't have to try and maintain a stoic indifference to it. In order to handle fear we must realize that war does not make death more frequent, war just makes death more real to us, and that is a good thing. One should be prepared for death and not put too much of one's hope in this life. It is appropriate to look at the scholarly life as one approach to Divine reality. But if one was hoping to build a Heaven on Earth through scholarship, then one must have one's hopes properly dashed by war.

SCREWTAPE ON WAR

One of Lewis's greatest literary creations during the Second World War was *The Screwtape Letters.* In those letters, Screwtape, not unexpectedly, has a great deal to say to his nephew, Wormwood, about war and how it may be used to their advantage.

Screwtape maintains that war and peace are, like sickness and health, age and youth, simply raw material for the devils' work.[9] From the devils' perspective, there are positive opportunities afforded by war as well as great dangers. Ardent pacifism and extreme patriotism can both serve the devils' cause.[10] However, hatred and malice in humans are disappointing when directed against imaginary scapegoats such as "the Germans" rather than being directed against "real persons" in one's immediate vicinity.[11] Screwtape observes that, on the up side, a good deal of cruelty and unchastity can come out of war, but on the down side many humans may turn to God in the midst of war, or at least turn to causes higher than themselves.[12] War can be used to get human beings thinking and worrying about an uncertain future rather than doing their duty in the present;[13] this is a real plus. However, war also affords opportunities for humans to display courage or to be repentant and humble when they fail to display appropriate courage; this is a negative. In summary, war makes human beings more aware of good and evil, and this is definitely not to Screwtape's liking.[14]

THE ATOMIC BOMB

Given that Lewis was alive at the time the atomic bomb was dropped on Hiroshima and Nagasaki, one wonders what he thought of that particular expression of war. In fact, Lewis commented a good bit on the subject.

First, Lewis did not think that the dropping of the atomic bomb on Hiroshima was necessarily or simply wrong.[15] He was less concerned about the actual use of atomic warfare than he was about what thoughts of such warfare were already leading human beings to do. He thought that worries about the atomic bomb were leading too many people to mope and sulk their way through life rather than continuing with their present duties.[16]

Lewis urged that we should not make too much of the atomic bomb. All human beings are going to have to face death someday, with or without the bomb. If we are all to be killed by the bomb, then when that bomb is dropped on us, Lewis believed it would be best if we were found doing sensible things such as praying, working, teaching, reading and parenting, not huddled together waiting anxiously for the final calamity. The bomb may break our bodies, but it need not fill our minds. The whole universe is running down anyway. All that the atomic bomb has done is force us to realize what kind of universe we have been living in all along.

The important thing is not whether the bomb will obliterate civilization but whether there is something beyond nature and civilization. Is there, in fact, a spiritual realm? If nature is all there is, then we have three possible responses. First, we could all commit suicide. Second, we could all go for the gusto and try to get as much pleasure out of this life as possible. Third, we could attempt to defy the universe and seek to be merciful to others in spite of the fact that the universe is manifestly unmerciful. Our tendency to prefer responses two and three shows that our hearts are out of sync with nature as we have come to know it. But why is this the case? Perhaps, Lewis suggests, this is the case because nature is out of sync with its Creator. Perhaps, after all, we are not prisoners of nature, but rather we are meant by our mutual Creator to be colonists of nature. If the supernatural view of life is once accepted, then we can go on, as colonists, to do some good about all the problems of this life, including the atomic bomb. For, as Lewis propounds, those who most desire Heaven have been most useful on Earth.[17]

WHY LEWIS WAS NOT A PACIFIST

All of the foregoing raises the question of why Lewis was not a pacifist. He answers that question in some detail. Lewis gave a talk to a pacifist society in Oxford during the Second World War, sometime in 1940, stating why he was not a pacifist.[18] He declared that in deciding this question one is raising a much larger question regarding how to decide what is good or evil. The usual answer, he says, is that one should decide according to conscience. The problem is that one's conscience can be changed by argument. One should always do what one thinks is right, but mistakes of conscience do need to be corrected. The question is how.

Lewis posits that one way conscience can be corrected is by reason, and a train of reasoning has three elements. First off, there are the facts we are to reason about, which may come from two sources: personal experience and/or authority. Because each of our personal experiences are relatively limited, the second source, authority, is much more reliable. Second, in addition to the mind receiving certain facts to reason about, there is the mental process of perceiving self-evident truth, what Lewis calls intuition. Third, there is the act of arranging facts, which produces intuitions, which in turn yield a proof of the proposition being argued. Lewis claims that one cannot reach the pacifist position by intuition alone. Anyone who asserts that this is possible is mistaking one's opinion or passion for intuition, because one cannot hold by mere intuition a position that is contrary to the position of most of the human race.

From this point Lewis seeks to examine the facts relevant to the pacifist position, the position that it is immoral to obey the civil government when that government commands one to serve in a war. The first fact that all parties agree upon is that war is disagreeable. Pacifists urge, in addition, that war does more harm than good. However, there is no way to prove such a broad historical generalization.[19] Lewis admits that war may never do half the good that the belligerents say it is going to do,[20] but that is not the same as saying it does no good. There have been some useful wars down through history and some useless ones.

Second, Lewis examines the supposed intuition upon which the pacifist position is based. The intuition is that love is good and hatred is bad or that helping is good and harming is bad. Does reason lead us from this intuition to the pacifist position? Lewis holds that before we can answer that question we must further define the intuition, because no one can ever do simple good. One must do *this* or *that* good to *this* or *that* specific person. And if you do good to one person, it may mean you can't at the same time do good to another. Taking this a step further, Lewis argues that if person B is committing some violence against person A, then one can either do nothing (thus disobeying the intuition of beneficence) or one must follow conscience and help A against B.[21] To end with a pacifist conclusion one must either say that it is lawful to do violence to B only in so far as killing is not involved, or one may kill B, but that the mass killing of war is wrong. Lewis admits that the lesser violence that is done to B is always to be preferred, but only provided that it restrains B from harming A. Killing B may be the only effective method of restraint.[22] In regard to capital punishment and the state of the soul of the criminal, Lewis thinks that person B is as likely to make a good end of his life in the execution shed as he might twenty years later in a prison hospital. Lewis admits it is arguable that a criminal could always be dealt with satisfactorily without the death penalty, but it is certain that whole nations cannot be prevented from taking whatever they want without war. The pacifist position presupposes that pain and death are the greatest evils, but Lewis thinks not. He believes that the suppression of a higher religion or society by a lower religion or society would be a much greater evil. Furthermore, Lewis does not see increasing the number of pacifists in a given society as the answer to the evil of war. This would only result in liberal societies who tolerate pacifists being overrun by totalitarian societies who do not.[23]

Third, Lewis examines what authority has to say about the pacifist question. Lewis notes that the specific English society to which he belongs has always decided against pacifism. He maintains that the verdict of general human society is also unequivocal. Homer and Virgil, Plato and Aristotle, Zarathustra and the *Bhagavad-Gita*, Cicero and Montaigne, Iceland and Egypt have all praised righteous war. The third source of authority that Lewis examines in regard to the pacifist question is divine authority as that is expressed in Christianity. Christian pacifism, Lewis points out, is almost exclusively based upon certain statements of Jesus. The rest of Christian authority has traditionally been against the pacifist position.[24] Whether one turns to the Anglican Thirty-Nine Articles or to the Presbyterian Westminster Confession of Faith or to the great doctors of the Roman Catholic Church, Aquinas and Augustine, one receives the same answer, namely, that there is such a thing as a just war.[25]

The entire Christian case for pacifism rests on such statements of Jesus as, "Do not resist an evil person. If someone strikes you on the right cheek, turn to him the other also" (Mt 5:39 NIV). Lewis posits that there are three ways of interpreting this statement. One is the pacifist interpretation that this command imposes the duty of nonresistance on all people in all situations. A second interpretation would view Jesus' statement as hyperbolic. Lewis rejects this position from the start. The third interpretation is that Jesus meant what he said but that there is an understood reservation in favor of obvious exceptional cases. Lewis maintains that if one's neighbor does some simple injury to oneself then one has the obligation, according to Jesus, to mortify the desire to retaliate. But, Lewis argues, Jesus could not possibly have meant that if a homicidal maniac is attempting to kill a third person we should stand by and let it happen. Lewis also thinks it unlikely that Jesus' hearers would have supposed him to be referring to war, since his audience was made up of private people in a disarmed nation. Lewis maintains that any statement should be taken in the sense it would most naturally have had at the time and place of utterance. If one follows this third line of interpretation, then Jesus' statement in Matthew 5:39 also harmonizes better with his unequivocal praise of the Roman centurion who showed faith in him, as well as harmonizing better with the rest of the New Testament. Lewis notes how Paul in Romans 13:4 and Peter in 1 Peter 2:14 approved of the government's right to wield the sword.[26] Lewis concludes,

> This, then, is why I am not a Pacifist. If I tried to become one, I should find a very doubtful factual basis, an obscure train of reasoning, a weight of authority both human and Divine against me, and strong grounds for suspecting that my wishes had directed my decision. As I have said, moral decisions do not admit of mathematical certainty. It may be, after all, that Pacifism is right. But it seems to me very long odds, longer odds than I would care to take with the voice of almost all humanity against me.[27]

What's Love
Got to Do with It?

In *The Four Loves*[1] C. S. Lewis begins by making a distinction between Gift-love and Need-love. Divine love is Gift-love. God has no need to be filled; rather he has plenteousness to give.[2] Human love for God is primarily a Need-love. We need God to forgive us, cleanse us, love us and fill us with himself. Therefore human beings approach God most nearly when they are least like God. What could be less like God than need?

This leads Lewis to make another distinction between what he calls "nearness by likeness" and "nearness of approach." He uses the illustration of hiking on a mountain pass. When you hike to the top of the last mountain between you and the house you are heading for that night, you may be so close to the house that you could throw a stone down on it from the peak of the mountain. That is nearness by likeness. But because you cannot climb down the huge crags to the valley below, you must follow the trail that goes a long way around to get to your final destination. When you are following that trail it may take you miles further away from your destination. Thus, as you follow that trail you are moving further and further away from a "nearness by likeness." Yet, you are gaining a greater "nearness of approach" to your destination as you follow that trail to your house.

Lewis draws the application that each of the loves implanted in us by God give us some nearness by likeness to God. But they do not necessarily give us a nearness of approach. There is only one kind of love that can do that. Lewis says that the likeness of sonship in relation to God is not the likeness of a portrait but the likeness of union. God created us in his image, thus giving us the likeness to him of a portrait. But to gain the likeness of union requires much more.

Lewis quotes with much agreement the statement of Denis de Rougemont, "Love ceases to be a demon only when he ceases to be a god."[3] That theme runs throughout *The Four Loves*. Lewis makes clear that God is love but love is not God. Every human love has this tendency to claim divine authority. The higher the love the more likely this is. Indeed, all those who love greatly are near to God, but it is nearness by likeness, not necessarily nearness of approach.

Our Need-loves do not claim to be gods. They are much humbler. But, as Lewis often repeats, the highest does not stand without the lowest. Lewis notes that our Need-love of God is in a different position than our Need-love of other human beings; our need of him can never die, though our awareness of it can.

LIKINGS AND LOVES FOR THE SUBHUMAN

Lewis goes on to talk of Appreciative love and Appreciative pleasure.[4] Appreciative pleasure is the starting point for our whole appreciation of beauty. Need-love cries to God from our poverty; Gift-love longs to serve or even to suffer for God; Appreciative love thanks God for his glory. Lewis says that when we love anything outside ourselves we take one step away from total spiritual ruin, but we will not achieve full spiritual health until we love God more than anything or anyone else.[5]

Lewis talks about love of nature in *The Four Loves*. He says that nature has given the word *glory* meaning to him. Nature didn't teach him that there exists a God of glory. We must go back to our studies, to church, to our Bibles, to our knees in order to gain an increasing knowledge of God. The problem with our love of nature is that it can set up as a religion and claim to be God. Lewis cites the lives of Coleridge and Wordsworth to show that this doesn't work. Lewis writes,

> Say your prayers in a garden early, ignoring steadfastly the dew, the birds and the flowers, and you will come away overwhelmed by its freshness and joy; go there in order to be overwhelmed by its freshness and joy; go there in order to be overwhelmed and, after a certain age, nine times out of ten nothing will happen to you.[6]

Lewis moves on to talk about love of one's country. In defense of love of country he says that those who don't love their fellow villagers whom they have seen won't get very far toward loving "Man," whom they have not. However, love of country, like all other natural loves, can become a demon in whose name we commit cruelty and treachery against others. Many in the world will not hear of Christianity until Christians disown their inglorious, imperialist past in which they shouted the name of Christ but enacted the service of Moloch.

AFFECTION

Storge,[7] according to the ancient Greeks, is that affection, especially, that parents have toward their children. Affection is the humblest and most widely diffused of loves, for it is even shared with the beasts. It is the least discriminating of loves, though its objects have to be familiar. It is hard to catch affection beginning because it is so subtle in its start and gradual in its growth.

Affection includes both the Need-love of the young for their mother and the mother's Gift-love for her children. But the mother's love is also a Need-love that needs to give, a Gift-love that needs to be needed. Appreciative love is not part of affection; there is the tendency for affection to take its loved ones for granted.

This love often mixes with other loves, such as Eros, and so makes those other loves better, more enduring. In fact, affection, friendship and Eros once had the kiss in common.

Affection also has its drawbacks. It can be deceiving; it can appear to be like charity; it can appear to be humble. But we must not mistake affection for charity.[8] When affection takes the form of a Need-love we can crave the affection of others. But we have no clear right to expect, always, the affection of others. We must elicit it. Lewis quotes Ovid, "If you would be loved, be lovable."

Every kind of love is liable to jealousy, and that includes affection. We can even be jealous of God when he takes away, either through conversion[9] or death, the one for whom we feel great affection. Lewis gives examples of this in the character of the mother who has lost her son in *The Great Divorce*[10] and Orual, who loses Psyche in *Till We Have Faces.* Of course, Lewis comments, churchgoing families seldom react better to one of their number becoming an atheist than do atheists to one of their number becoming a Christian.

Affection, in the form of Gift-love, has its perversions too. Lewis cites the case of Mrs. Fidget, who "lived for her family." Her family seemed so much happier when she died; they no longer had that "hunted look."[11] Lewis notes that the proper aim of giving is to put recipients in a state where they no longer need your gift. But this is not how Mrs. Fidget gave to others. It seems that deep down, she always wanted others to be in her debt, to need her. Lewis suggests that if we try to live by affection alone we will turn bitter.[12] We need a higher love to make us better.

FRIENDSHIP

Friendship[13] is the least natural of loves. We can live and breed without it. Friendship doesn't help us to live, but it does help us to live well.[14] Friendship forms where there is a common interest shared. Thus there is no duty for anyone to be my friend. Lewis's delightful rule of friendship is this: "People who bore one another should meet seldom; people who interest one another, often."[15]

Where lovers are always looking at each other, friends stand shoulder to shoulder looking out toward their common interest. Lewis asserts that you will not find fellow Christians by staring into their eyes but by praying alongside them.

Friendship has a nearness by likeness to Heaven, where the multitude of the blessed increases the fruition that each has of God. Each soul, seeing him in her own way, communicates that unique vision to all the rest. Lewis cites the angels in Isaiah 6:3 as an example of this. They cry, "Holy, holy, holy!" about God to one another.

Lewis maintains that for the Christian there are no accidents. Christ chooses our friends for us, and us for them. God uses friendship as the instrument by which he reveals to each of us the beauties of the others.

We need to be careful not to confuse friendship with companionship. Friendship arises out of the matrix of companionship when two companions suddenly realize that they share a common outlook or interest which they thought all along was unique to them.[16] Friendship often begins with the cry, "You too!"[17] One of the key questions, the answer to which determines whether friendship can exist between two companions, is: Do you see the same truth?

Lewis asserts that every civilized religion begins with a small group of friends. Little knots of friends who turn their backs on the world are also those who transform the world. The early Christians survived in part because they cared so much for the love of the brethren that they stopped their ears to the pagan society around them.

Lewis notes that appreciative love is very active in friendship. One feels highly privileged to have the friends one does. Friendship is also eminently spiritual; it has no ties to biology. Yet Scripture rarely pictures the relationship between God and humanity as one of friendship. The relationship between God and human beings is pictured as one of affection; God is our Father through Christ. It is also pictured as one of Eros; Christ is the Bridegroom of the church.[18] God can safely represent himself as Father or Bridegroom because only a lunatic would mistake him for our physical father or husband. Friendship, however, if used as a symbol for the relationship between God and humanity, can easily be mistaken for the thing symbolized. We can easily mistake nearness by likeness for nearness of approach.

Friendship has its dangers. Friendship can form around a shared evil or hatred, as easily as a shared good. Because friendship is a spiritual love, the danger that besets it is spiritual too. That danger is that friendship has a tendency to engender corporate pride. One is so honored to be part of the "Inner Ring."[19] There may be a tendency to look down on those who don't share the outlook of your friends. In the end, friendship cannot save itself. And in an explicitly religious friendship this is even more important to remember.

EROS

Lewis says that Eros[20] (being in love) can transform a Need-pleasure (for sex) into one of the most appreciative of pleasures. Eros, without diminishing desire, can make abstinence from Venus easier.

God can teach us through Eros to love him and others with a similar prodigality, not counting the cost. Eros helps us to leap over the wall of selfhood, make appetite altruistic and toss personal happiness aside. Without effort, Eros enables us to fulfill the Law by loving our neighbor, at least one neighbor, as ourselves. This is a foretaste of the love we must have toward everyone if Love himself is to guide us.

However, in the grandeur of Eros there are the seeds of danger. In Eros we have nearness by likeness to God but not nearness of approach. Furthermore, Eros can lead two people into the most unsuitable of matches. And, as we have seen in earlier chapters, Eros may sanction unfaithfulness to a spouse. Eros is most prone, of all the loves, to demand our worship. Being "in love" can be turned into a religion. There is the tendency in Eros to idolize one's love.

The bottom line with Eros is that it promises what it can't perform because Eros doesn't last. Lewis proclaims that we must learn to do the works of Eros when Eros is not present. As with all the other natural loves, Eros needs help if it is to become all that it promises to be. Eros needs to be ruled by a higher love.

CHARITY

In *Mere Christianity*[21] Lewis defines charity. It is not just giving alms,[22] and it is not an emotion; charity is not simply liking someone. Charity is love in the Christian sense. It is wishing another's good.[23]

Natural liking makes charity easier. Therefore we need to try to like people as much as we can. Of course, we need to watch out for the liking of one person that makes us uncharitable to another. Liking for a person can also conflict with charity toward that same person. We can see this in the doting mother who gives her child everything he wants but not the charity and discipline he needs.

How do we develop charity in ourselves? Lewis urges that we should act *as if* we love others and then we will end up loving them. Practicing charity can even lead to affection, whereas acting out of dislike makes you dislike people more, as Lewis witnessed in relationships between the English and the Germans during World War I, World War II and their aftermath. He notes how worldly people treat people kindly because they like them. The Christian, trying to treat everyone kindly, ends up liking more people.

Little decisions are infinitely important in this whole process. As we act out love in little, everyday ways, virtue increases at compound interest. But the converse is also true. As we fail to act out love, vice increases at compound interest.

How should we grow in our love for God? Again Lewis insists, act as if you love God and you will love him. God doesn't care about our feelings so much as he cares about our will.[24] And we must remember that though our feelings come and go, his love does not waver.[25]

In the chapter on "Charity" in *The Four Loves*,[26] Lewis reminds us that the natural loves are not self-sufficient. God has planted all of the loves in our life, but our will must dress them as a gardener tends his garden. Grace must shine and rain on the garden of our loves if the loves are to grow properly. Left to themselves the natural loves either vanish or become demons. But when God arrives, these half-gods can remain and be fruitful.

Lewis admits that all of the natural loves are possible rivals to God. Since these natural loves are not sturdy and enduring, Augustine encourages us not to put our goods into these leaky vessels. But Augustine's argument, Lewis counters, is closer to the spirit of Stoicism than the spirit of Christianity. We follow One who wept over Jerusalem and at the grave of Lazarus. We follow One who loved, in a special sense, one disciple above the rest. In one of the most moving passages in all of his writings, Lewis asserts,

> There is no escape along the lines St. Augustine suggests. Nor along any other lines. There is no safe investment. To love at all is to be vulnerable. Love anything, and your heart will certainly be wrung and possibly be broken. If you want to make sure of keeping it intact, you must give your heart to no one, not even to an animal. Wrap it carefully round with hobbies and little luxuries; avoid all entanglements; lock it up safe in the casket or coffin of your selfishness. But in that casket—safe, dark, motionless, airless—it will change. It will not be broken; it will become unbreakable, impenetrable, ir-redeemable. The alternative to tragedy, or at least to the risk of tragedy, is damnation. The only place outside Heaven where you can be perfectly safe from all the dangers and perturbations of love is Hell.[27]

Lewis maintains that God wants us to be uncalculating in our loves. We will draw nearer to him not by trying to avoid the suffering inherent in all loves but by offering that suffering to him.

The real question about the proper order in love is, "Whom do we put first?"[28] Lewis quotes Jesus' statement from Luke 14:26 (NIV), "If anyone comes to me and does not hate his father and mother, his wife and children, his brothers and sisters—yes, even his own life—he cannot be my disciple." Lewis explains that "to hate" in this context means to make no concession to the Beloved when he or she utters the suggestions of the devil. This is how we are to handle all rivals to our love for God. We must put the Lord absolutely first whenever there is a conflict between our loves. We must turn down our nearest and dearest when he or she comes between us and obedience to God. Lewis suggests that every married couple should have an understanding, up front, that God comes first. Then this "hating" of the earthly beloved may never need to happen.

Lewis references 1 John 4:10 (NIV), "This is love: not that we loved God, but that he loved us and sent his Son as an atoning sacrifice for our sins." God is love; he is Gift-love par excellence. There is no hunger in him. He was not under necessity to create us or anything. Rather, God created us simply so that he could love and perfect us. And he did this even though he knew it would cost him the cross.[29]

God implants in us natural Need-loves and natural Gift-loves. We see in Orual, toward the end of *Till We Have Faces*,[30] a natural Gift-love, a self-forgetfulness, that reminds us of God. However, this natural Gift-love, while providing nearness by likeness to God, does not provide nearness of approach. Only Need-love for God can do the latter.

God can also give us supernatural Gift-love, or agape, toward himself and others.[31] This is charity, doing what is best for another. Matthew 25:31-46 links Gift-love toward God and Gift-love toward others. And God can give us a supernatural Need-love of himself and others.[32] If we have a supernatural Need-love of him, then we will truly recognize our own neediness, and we won't think that he loves us because we are lovable.[33] We will be "jolly beggars." Supernatural Need-love of others is hard to come by. How difficult it is to receive a love from others that is not based upon our lovableness!

Our natural loves may have to be renounced, as Abraham was called upon to renounce his love for Isaac in favor of his love for God. But in the end Abraham's love for Isaac did not have to be completely given up. Rather, it was transformed. So too do all of our natural loves need to be transformed. And, as Lewis suggests, the invitation from God to have our natural loves transformed is never lacking.[34] But our natural loves can be raised only if they have shared somehow in Christ's death, just as Abraham's love for Isaac shared mystically in Christ's death.[35] Then in the end, by loving God more than our natural loves, we shall love our natural loves more than we do now.[36] If we love God more than this world, we will love even this world better than those who know no other.[37]

Finally, Lewis points out that God can also awake in us a supernatural appreciative love toward himself. Love for God finds its natural expression in praise. We glorify God most when we enjoy him to the full.[38] Lewis suggests that he has not experienced enough of this love to write more about it, but he does give one suggestion. If we cannot practice the presence of God,[39] it is something to practice his absence, to realize the vacuum in our hearts that only he can fill.

What's love got to do with theology? C. S. Lewis would say, "Everything."

THE CHURCH

C. S. LEWIS PUT FORWARD SEVERAL REASONS why the church is necessary. First, he maintained that religion is not simply what one does
with solitude. The New Testament knows nothing of solitary religion.
The church is already institutional in its earliest documents. And to
make Christianity a private affair while taking away all privacy, as in the
collective, is to eliminate Christianity.[1] Furthermore, we are forbidden
by Scripture to neglect the assembling of ourselves together, though
there may be providential reasons for missing worship services from time
to time.[2]

Second, Lewis's experience was that he at first tried to go it alone as a
Christian but later found that being part of the church and attending services was the only way to "fly his flag."[3] For Lewis, this meant becoming a
target. He suggests that your family may not like the change when you become a Christian; they may not like you getting up early to go to church on
Sundays. However, all Christians are obliged to take the sacrament, and you
can only do this in church.

Third, Lewis suggests that if you are going to fight against the enemy,
then you need to go to church. It is an essential step in conducting spiritual
warfare. He contends that when we go to church our activity is like listening
in to the secret wireless from our friends. Satan is anxious to prevent us from
doing this. He tries to prevent us going to church by playing on our conceit
and laziness and intellectual snobbery.[4]

Fourth, we need to go to church to be reminded of the truths of Christianity. Lewis asserts that once we have accepted Christianity, then we need
to hold some of its main doctrines before our minds every day. Therefore,

daily prayers, religious reading and churchgoing are necessary. We need to be continually reminded of the truth.[5]

Fifth, Lewis declares that we need to go to church because it is in the context of the church that God reveals himself to us. In fact, the only adequate means of learning about God is the whole Christian community as it waits on him together.[6]

In spite of the tremendous value that Lewis attached to the church, or perhaps because of that value, he was against all religious compulsion.[7] He believed that all Christians ought to attend church services and be practicing members of a local parish, but he was against setting down rules for others, and especially against forcing non-Christians to take part in religious observances.

THE MEANING OF MEMBERSHIP

Lewis reminds us that the word *membership* has Christian roots. In the Pauline sense, being a member means nothing like being the member of a club, an interchangeable part, but it means being an organ, something essentially different and yet complementary, part of a body.[8] The society into which the Christian is called at baptism is not a collective. The family is an image of this Body on the natural level. In a family the members are diverse. Yet there is unity within diversity in a good family. In the same way, in the church, the members are diverse. And what could be more diverse than the Head who is immortal and the other members of the Body who are mortal?[9]

Our diversity gives meaning to our love for one another, the communion of saints. If we all experienced God in exactly the same way, then the music of the church would not be a symphony. Heaven itself will be like a body because the blessed souls there will remain eternally different. Each one will have ever-fresh news to tell the others of their unique perspective on God. God wants us to achieve union with him and not mere sameness.[10] As Lewis reminds his fictitious friend Malcolm, it takes all sorts to make a world or a church. If grace must perfect our nature, it must expand all our natures to accommodate the richness of the diversity that God intended when he created us. Heaven will display far more variety than hell.[11]

Lewis believed that in the church we truly become ourselves. In the church we strip off the artificial disguise of equality. We uncover our true inequalities and are thereby refreshed.[12]

Not only that, but the humblest person's position in the church is eternal and cosmic. The church is going to outlive the universe, and in the church the individual is going to outlive the universe as well. Everything joined to the immortal head will share in his immortality.[13] This provides a profound motivation for becoming a member of Christ's Body.

THE PURPOSE OF THE CHURCH

Lewis addressed people who were concerned about the salvation of those who might not hear the message of Christ. He suggests that if Christians are part of Christ's Body, then every addition to that Body enables him to do more. Therefore, if we want to help those outside the Body we must join the body. Lewis wryly remarks that cutting off one of Christ's fingers would be a strange way of helping him reach more people.[14] Usually it is those who know Christ who bring him to others. That is why the church, the whole Body of Christ, showing him to one another is so important.[15]

This gets to the heart of the church's purpose. Lewis saw that purpose to be: drawing people to Christ and making them like Christ. He said that the church exists for no other purpose. If the church is not drawing people to Christ and making people like Christ, then all the cathedrals, clergy, missions, sermons, even the Bible, are a waste of time.[16] There exists in every church something that sooner or later works against the very purpose for which it came into existence.[17] So we must strive very hard, by the grace of God, to keep the church focused on the mission that Christ originally gave to it.

DENOMINATIONS AND MERE CHRISTIANITY

Lewis repeatedly declares that he has no help to offer those choosing between denominations.[18] He states that he is a member of the Church of England, not especially high or low or anything else. He claims that his beliefs are contained in the Book of Common Prayer.[19]

As a child Lewis disliked the church he attended while at Wynyard School. At the time, he wrote to his father saying it was such a high church that it might as well be Roman Catholic.[20] Later, Lewis claimed that it was in this church that he first heard the doctrines of Christianity taught by men who really believed them, and so he became an effective believer there for the first time.[21]

On the converse side, Lewis wrote, at the end of his life, that the low church milieu in which he grew up tended to be too cosily at ease in Zion.[22] Still, he wrote to Sister Penelope that the real distinction is not between high and low church but between religion with supernaturalism and salvationism and all watered-down modernist versions.[23] He asserted that what unites the evangelical and the Anglo-Catholic against the liberal or modernist is the fact that the first two are thoroughgoing supernaturalists who believe in the Creation, the Fall, the Incarnation, the Resurrection, the Second Coming and the four Last Things (death, judgment, Heaven and hell). This unites them not only with each other but also with the Christian religion understood everywhere and by all.[24]

Lewis believed that it is at the center of each communion that the truest Christians dwell. Those who are at the center of their communion are closer to others at the center of theirs than the people who are on the fringes. This suggests that at the center there is a Person who against all differences speaks with one voice.[25]

Lewis wanted to focus on expounding "mere Christianity," borrowing that term from Richard Baxter, the seventeenth-century Puritan divine. Lewis believed that mere Christianity is positive and pungent.[26] He did not present mere Christianity as an alternative to joining a particular communion. Rather, he compared the church with a house. Mere Christianity is like the hall that you enter when you come in the front door of the house and become a Christian, a believer. From there you must choose a room to enter, for it is in the rooms that there are meals to feed you, fires to warm you and furniture to rest on. Each room is like a different denomination in the one church of Jesus Christ. In order to choose which room you should stay in you must keep asking, "Which is the true one?" Don't ask which one you like best for its paint, paneling or its particular doorkeeper (pastor). Don't ask whether you like a particular kind of service, but ask, "Are these doctrines true? Is holiness here?" Lewis also made clear that we must be kind to those who choose other rooms. That is one of the rules common to the whole house.[27]

SCREWTAPE ON THE CHURCH

Screwtape says that one of the demons' great allies at present is the church, not the church spread out through all time and rooted in eternity, but what the humans see of the visible, local church.[28] Screwtape encourages Wormwood to play on his patient's natural disappointment on first becoming a member of the church, mainly his disappointment in the ordinariness and sinfulness of other people in the church. At the same time, Wormwood should keep his patient from examining his own sinfulness and ordinariness.[29]

Screwtape says that the demons want the church to be small, not only so that fewer people find out about the Enemy, but also so that the demons can turn the church into a faction or at least play on the animosities and factions within the church.[30] Wormwood's patient should be encouraged to join a party within the church so that the demons can work up hatred between him and another party.[31] The real problem with Wormwood's patient is that he is associating with *mere* Christians. The patient should be encouraged to devote himself to "Christianity *And*"[32]—for instance, Christianity *and* spelling reform! Screwtape looks forward to having the Pharisees from different parties with him in hell.[33]

Screwtape suggests that if Wormwood's patient can't be cured of churchgoing, then he should be encouraged to go all around the neighborhood looking for a church that "suits" him. The search for a "suitable" church will make Wormwood's patient a critic instead of a learner.[34]

Screwtape recommends to Wormwood what we have come to know as the user-friendly church. He speaks highly of the pastor who has been watering down the faith for so long that it is now he who shocks his parishioners with his unbelief, not they who shock him. This pastor focuses only on his favorite passages of Scripture. Thus his congregation is safe from any new truth reaching them through the Bible.[35]

LEWIS AND THE CHURCH OF ROME

Lewis generally refused to discuss why he was not a Roman Catholic, as well as refusing to discuss the differences between the Roman Catholic Church and the Church of England.[36] However, we do get some hints of his views from his various letters.

In answering one correspondent, Lewis maintained that incense and

Hail Marys are in two different categories. The first is merely a question of ritual that some find helpful and others don't. Hail Marys raise a doctrinal question, whether it is right to address devotions to any creature, however holy. Lewis's view was that a salute to any saint or angel cannot be wrong any more than taking off one's hat to a friend. But such a salute can start one down the road to where the Blessed Virgin Mary is treated as a divinity and even becomes the center of one's religion. Lewis therefore thought such salutes would be better avoided. He suggested that if the Blessed Virgin is a good mother she won't want any attention diverted from her Son to herself anyway![37]

Lewis was most clear about his view of the Roman Catholic Church in a letter to H. Lyman Stebbins written on May 9, 1945. In that letter Lewis draws an analogy between finding the true church and discovering the correct interpretation of Plato's teaching. He asserts that what he is most confident in accepting is that interpretation that is common to all the Platonists down through the centuries. He rejects right away any purely modern views that claim to have discovered for the first time what Plato meant; he rejects out of court any view which says that everyone from Aristotle down has misunderstood Plato. But, Lewis claims, there is something else he would also reject. If there was an ancient Platonic society still existing at Athens and claiming to be the exclusive trustees of Plato's teaching, he affirms that he would approach them with great respect. However, if he found that their teaching was unlike Plato's actual text and unlike what ancient interpreters said about Plato, and furthermore if, in some cases, the teaching of this Platonic society could only be traced back to within a thousand years of Plato's time, then he would reject their exclusive claims. Yet he would still be ready to take any particular thing this society taught on its own merits. Lewis contends that he treats Christianity in the same manner. What most certainly is true Christianity is the vast amount of doctrine agreed upon by Scripture, the early church fathers, the Middle Ages, modern Roman Catholics and modern Protestants. That is true "catholic" or universal Christian doctrine. Mere "modernism" he rejects at once. And he also rejects the Roman Church where it differs from this universal tradition and especially where it differs from apostolic Christianity. What particular Roman Catholic teachings does Lewis reject? He rejects their theology about the Blessed Virgin

Mary, which seems to him utterly foreign to the New Testament; their papalism, which seems equally foreign to the attitude of St. Paul towards St. Peter in the Epistles; and the doctrine of transubstantiation, which insists on defining Communion in a way that the New Testament does not seem to him to countenance.

Therefore, Lewis maintains, he must reject the claim of the Roman Catholic Church to be the one true church, though for him this does not necessarily mean rejecting everything the Church says.[38] Lewis's reasons for not becoming a Roman Catholic seem clear.[39] But, that being said, what were his views about possible reunion between Canterbury and Rome?

REUNION

Lewis wrote to Dom Bede Griffiths, a Roman Catholic, that he had no contribution to make regarding reunion between the Church of England and the Roman Catholic Church. He confessed that reunion was never more needed. A united church would be the answer to the new paganism. But Lewis countered that he didn't see how that reunion was to come about. He thought the immediate task would be vigorous cooperation in areas of agreement, combined with full admission of their differences. An experienced unity on some things might become the prelude to complete unity in all things. Furthermore, Lewis suggested that nothing would give more support to the papal claims than a pope really functioning as the head of Christendom.[40]

In another letter Lewis notes that St. Paul has already told us what to do about divisions in the church. Stronger brothers need to limit their expressions of freedom so as not to cause their weaker brothers to stumble.[41] He declares that the time is always ripe for reunion. Divisions between Christians are a sin and a scandal, and therefore Christians ought to always be working toward reunion, if only by their prayers.[42] Lewis detested the fighting between Protestants and Catholics in Northern Ireland and traced the origin of that conflict to the confusion of religion with politics.[43]

However, Lewis did not believe that the whole cause of schism lay in sin.[44] He urged that we should be distressed and ashamed of divisions in the church. At the same time, he maintained that lifelong Christians may be too easily discouraged by the divisions. Such people do not know what the church looks like from the outside. Seen from that vantage point, what all

Christian denominations have in common, despite their divisions, still presents an immensely formidable unity.[45]

DECLINE IN RELIGION?

On a related subject, Lewis contends that we should not be overly discouraged about the apparent "decline in religion." He maintains that the religion that declined in his day was not Christianity but a vague theism where churchgoing was merely a matter of loyalty, good manners and respectability. Once no one goes to church except to seek Christ, then the number of actual believers can be discovered.[46]

Lewis was firm in preaching to the clergy of his own church that they needed to draw doctrinal boundary lines beyond which they would not go. He maintained that if any member of the clergy were to go beyond those bounds, then that person should give up being a member of the clergy.[47] He believed that we needed to have a standard of "mere Christianity" that would put modern controversies in their proper perspective, and that standard could only be gained from reading the old books.[48] Lewis found the role of missionary to the priests of his church an embarrassing one. Yet he felt it was a job that had to be undertaken. Otherwise, he believed, the future of the Church of England would be very short.[49]

LITURGY

In *Letters to Malcolm* Lewis asserted that laypeople should take what is given them in the liturgy of the church and make the best of it. He thought this would be easier if the liturgy was always and everywhere the same. He was not in favor of innovations. Novelty can only have an entertainment value. We don't go to church to be entertained but to use the service, to enact it. We are better able to worship and focus on God when we are so familiar with the service that nothing distracts our attention from him. Every novelty prevents this; it focuses our attention on the service, or even on the one leading the service, rather than on God. Lewis believed that doctrinal issues should not be settled by a change in liturgy.[50] He claimed that his whole liturgical position boiled down to a plea for permanence and uniformity. He asserted that he would especially appreciate uniformity in the time taken by services. A lengthened service may throw the whole day into hurry and confusion for laypeople, since they have has less control over their hours of business than the clergy do.

Any tendency to have a passionate preference for one type of service must be regarded as a temptation.[51] Lewis regarded a love of religious observances as a merely natural taste.[52] He denied being choosy about services. He claimed any form would do for him so long as he was given time to get used to it.[53] He contended that if we can't lay down our liturgical preferences at the door of the church, along with all other carnal baggage, we should bring them into church with us to be humbled and modified.[54]

As to the words of the service, Lewis believed that if you have a liturgy in the vernacular, then you must have a changing liturgy, because no living language can be timeless. He thought it best if any changes made to the liturgy, however, would be made gradually and almost imperceptibly, with only one obsolete word being changed every century![55] He made the point that prose needs to be very good in a special way in order to stand up to repeated reading aloud. He felt it would be hard for any modern writer to beat Cranmer, the original author of the English prayer book, as a stylist.[56]

Yet, in favor of diversity, Lewis said that what pleased him about an Orthodox mass he once attended was that there seemed to be no prescribed behavior for the congregation. Some stood, some knelt, some sat, some walked, and one person even crawled around on the floor. The beauty of it was that no one took any notice of what anyone else was doing.[57]

Lewis believed that anything the congregation *could* do could also properly and profitably be offered to God in public worship, including such things as sacred dance, so long as the congregation could do it well.[58] He affirmed that the most valuable thing the Psalms did for him was to express that delight in God which made David dance. He thought this spirit to be far superior to that of the mere dutiful church-going and laborious saying of prayers. He wanted to see the Anglican Church recover the same joy seen in the Psalms, but for the Christian, such joy would need to be compatible with the tragic depth of the cross.[59]

MUSIC

Lewis often wrote about how books and music conveyed beauty to him. But, he urges, we must not trust in books or in music because the beauty is not in them. It only comes *through* them, and what comes through them is long-ing.[60] Lewis was a great lover of music, at least in his youth. He especially enjoyed the music of Wagner, for it communicated joy, *sehnsucht*, longing to his soul.[61] Certainly Screwtape expressed the opposite of Lewis's view when he said that he detested music and silence and that he wanted to make the whole universe one noise in the end.[62]

However, Lewis states some caveats regarding the religious importance of music. He writes that we must distinguish between the effect that music has on the musically illiterate, who get only an emotional effect, and the effect that it has on real musical scholars who perceive the structure of the music and get an intellectual satisfaction as well as an emotional one. He asserts that either of these effects is ambivalent from the religious point of view. Emo-tional and intellectual satisfaction can be a preparation for or even a medium for meeting God, but these satisfactions can also be a distraction and imped-iment to meeting God. He goes so far as to suggest that the emotional effect of music may also be a delusion. Some people, feeling certain emotions in church, think they have had a supernatural experience when they have only had a natural one. Genuinely religious emotion is only a servant; no soul is saved by having it or damned by lacking it. The test of music is always the same. We should ask ourselves, "Does this music make me more obedient, more God-centered and neighbor-centered or more self-centered?"[63]

Lewis found hymns to be dead wood in the English church because he thought that the English couldn't sing well and that the art of poetry had developed for two centuries in a private and subjective direction. Yet he felt if the hymnody could be improved then it was his duty, as a layman, to sub-mit to it, whether it would suit his preference or not.[64] Lewis often noted how he disliked hymns, but as he grew in his Christian life he saw that these same hymns were being sung with devotion and benefit by saints very dif-ferent from himself. This, Lewis maintained, helped to peel away his pride and conceit.[65]

Lewis wrote an essay entitled "On Church Music," in which he made the following points. First, nothing should be done or sung or said in church that does not either glorify God or edify the people or both. Second, church music glorifies God by being excellent in its own kind. In the composition and highly trained execution of sacred music we offer our natural gifts, at their highest, to God. Third, as noted above, Lewis was unconvinced that the physical and emotional exhilaration produced by singing hymns had any religious relevance. He asserted that he would like to have fewer, better and shorter hymns, especially fewer! Fourth, he thought the case for abolishing all church music was strong. (Incidentally, Lewis most regularly attended the service without music at his parish church.) But he recognized that the main sense of Christendom would be against him and others if they tried to abolish all church music. Fifth, the highbrows and the lowbrows each assume far too easily the spiritual value of the music they like. Sixth, Lewis maintained, there are two musical situations on which we can be confident that God's blessing rests. One is where the highbrow priest or organist gives the people the humbler and coarser fare that they want, out of a desire to bring them closer to God. The other is where the lowbrow laypeople submit humbly and patiently to the music that they cannot fully appreciate, in the belief that this somehow glorifies God. To both these groups, acting in this way, church music becomes a means of grace. Where the choir and the congregation are on this right road, no insurmountable difficulties will occur. Discrepancies of taste and capacity provide opportunities for charity and humility. What matters most is our *intention* in offering our praise to God through music.[66]

Finally, Lewis believed that our present services are merely attempts at worship. When we attempt to worship God in church what we are doing is tuning our instruments for Heaven, where one day we shall praise God perfectly, with total delight.[67]

PRAYER

IN THE LAST CHAPTER WE EXAMINED what Lewis had to say in *Letters to Malcolm* on the subject of corporate prayer. In chapter 2 of *Letters to Malcolm*[1] he begins to talk about private prayer by dealing with the subject of home-made versus ready-made prayers. Home-made prayers are prayers that we pray using our own words. Ready-made prayers are those that we pray using the words of others, such as the Lord's Prayer. Lewis challenges his fictitious friend Malcolm to broaden his mind and include more ready-made prayers in his devotional life.

HOME-MADE OR READY-MADE?

Lewis claims that he tried to pray without words, with only mental images, when he first became a Christian.[2] He soon realized, however, that he could not do this effectively all of the time. But, Lewis maintains, words are only a secondary aspect of prayer. They are like an anchor or the movement of a conductor's baton. Words canalize worship so that our prayers don't become puddles.

It doesn't matter who first put the words of a prayer together. Our words harden into a formula the more we pray on a regular basis. And if we use ready-made prayers on a regular basis we will find ourselves pouring our meaning into those words.

Lewis says that he uses homemade prayers as a staple, along with a modicum of the ready-made.[3] A ready-made form can't serve for our intercourse with God all of the time any more than we can use ready-made forms to converse with other human beings. However, ready-made forms have a few positive things to be said in their favor. First, they keep us in touch with sound doctrine. Second, they remind us of what things we ought to ask. Third, they provide an element of the ceremonial. When we don't use any ready-made forms we tend to get too cozy with the Almighty. Lewis contends it is important to keep in mind God's transcendence as well as his proximity. We need balance in our prayer life. Fourth, ready-made forms set our devotions free, and they keep our minds from wandering so much in prayer. Finally, ready-made prayers keep us from being too eaten up with the concerns of the moment.[4]

PRAYERS TO AND FOR THE DEAD

Regarding prayers *to* the dead Lewis queries, "If we can ask for the prayers of the living why can't we ask for the prayers of the dead?" If we believe in the communion of the saints, which most Christians confess in the Apostles' Creed, and if that means communion with saints both living and dead, why can't we ask for the prayers of both? The dead are still alive to God in Heaven.

Lewis notes that devotions to saints also have the benefit of reminding us that we are very small compared with them, how much smaller compared with their Master. But there is also a danger in asking for the prayers of the dead. We may end up viewing prayer as a system by which we try to pull the right wires to get what we want from Heaven. Lewis asserted that he had no plans to take up the practice.

However, Lewis maintains that all Christians should be agreed about praying with the saints. As it says in the prayer book, "With angels and archangels and all the company of Heaven." It can be encouraging to think that our little twitter in prayer is being added to the prayers of the great saints. Perhaps their prayers will drown out the ugliness of our own or highlight any tiny value they have.

Lewis answers Malcolm's potential objection that there is not a great difference between praying with the saints and praying to the saints. Lewis claims it is all the better if that is the case because reunion with Rome may then engulf us unaware. Discussions about difference in doctrine usually separate people, whereas actions unite.[5]

Regarding prayers for the dead, Lewis asserts that it is a spontaneous and all but inevitable action on his part since most of the people he loves best are dead![6] He asks how he can even talk to God intimately if the people he

loves most are unmentionable to him. One answer we might give Lewis is
that he could give thanks for his dead loved ones. Even the most rigorous
Protestant could not object to giving thanks for the blessed dead in prayer.

Lewis notes that on the Protestant view, prayer for the dead is useless because their final destination is sealed. But, as Lewis points out, this is an argument against praying for the living as well. He asks, "Isn't their destiny
sealed too?" And besides, can't there be perpetual increase of beatitude in
Heaven, thus making our prayers for the blessed dead helpful?[7]

WHEN AND WHERE TO PRAY

Our chief prayers should not be left to the end of the day, Lewis maintains,
because we need energy and concentration to pray well.[8] He says that he
prays in trains, on park benches, or pacing back streets, anything to keep
from leaving his prayers until bedtime. Churches, however, pose various distractions when we seek to pray there by ourselves during the week. Often in
England, Lewis says, churches are too cold to pray in during most of the
year. Or else cleaning people come along to distract one from praying. He
confesses that one can't kneel to pray in strange places. However, kneeling is
important. The body needs to be active in prayer as well as the soul. But concentration matters more than kneeling.[9]

THE WHY AND WHAT OF PRAYER

Lewis poses the important question, Why pray when God knows all? His
answer: because in prayer we assent with our whole will to be known by God
as persons.

How important must an object be before we can, without sin or folly,
allow our desire for it to become a matter of serious concern to us? And
granted the existence of such a serious concern in our minds, can it always
be properly laid before God in prayer? Lewis answers these questions by
saying that we must aim at ordinate loves in our lives. We must put first
things first and second things second, and so on. But we must also lay before God what *is* in our minds, not only what *ought* to be there. Whatever is
the subject of our thoughts should be the subject of our prayers, whether
in penitence or petition or both. Those who have not learned to ask God
for childish things will have less readiness to ask him for great things. And

God will help us moderate any excess in our prayers; we can ask him to give us ordinate loves.[10]

FESTOONING THE LORD'S PRAYER

Festoonings[11] are the private overtones we give to certain petitions. They are the words we hang on each petition of a ready-made prayer such as the Lord's Prayer.

Lewis's festoonings to the Lord's Prayer are as follows. In *Mere Christianity* he suggests that when we pray "Our Father" we are putting ourselves in the place of children of God. We are dressing up as Christ. This may seem like outrageous cheek, but the Lord has instructed us to do this. It is a good kind of pretense that will lead us to really become children of God in the fullest sense of the phrase.[12] Lewis festoons the petition "Hallowed be thy name" with the prayer-book phrase "with angels and archangels and all the company of Heaven."

To "thy kingdom come" Lewis says that he adds the meaning "may your reign be realized here as it is there." He takes "there" in three senses: as in the sinless world, as in the best human lives we have known, and as in Heaven, among the blessed dead.

Lewis views "thy will be done" as primarily an act of submission,[13] mainly to disagreeable outcomes, just as the Lord prayed in Gethsemane: "Not my will but thine be done." However, he also takes it in the sense of "thy will be done—by me—here and now." Third, he thinks that we may need to submit ourselves to future blessings as well as difficulties, so that we don't look back to different blessings in the past and say "Encore!"

Regarding "Give us this day our daily bread," Lewis suggests that we can use these words to pray for spiritual and physical needs.[14]

In regard to "Forgive us our trespasses as we forgive those who trespass against us," much has already been said in an earlier chapter. Lewis confesses that the hard part about this is to keep on forgiving others every time their offense comes back into our minds.

"Lead us not into temptation" raises the question of whether God is a fiend. Would he ever lead us into temptation? Lewis points out that the word *temptation* in Greek can also mean "trial." He maintains that this adds a caveat to all our other prayers, as if to say, "If I have prayed for anything that would lead to a time of trial, keep me from it and don't give me what I have asked for."

Finally, Lewis notes how he views "the kingdom" as a reference to God's sovereignty de jure; God would deserve our worship whether he was all-powerful or not. "The power" he takes as a reference to God's sovereignty de facto—God *is* all-powerful. And "the glory" refers to the beauty of God that is so old and so new.[15]

PENITENTIAL PRAYER

Lewis claims that he prays for the daily dose of self-knowledge that he can handle. And when his conscience won't come down to brass tacks and convict him of a specific sin, he tells his conscience to be quiet and move on.[16]

Malcolm points out that there are different levels of penitential prayer, and Lewis agrees. There is the lower level at which we are trying to placate an angry deity by our penitence. Then there is a higher level at which we are trying to restore an infinitely valued and vulnerable personal relationship that has been shattered by our sin. Both these levels are valid and needed because it is easy for the higher level to be turned into a mere feeling, whereas the lower level requires sheer action, which is more powerful than feeling.[17]

Lewis does not agree with the Puritans, who suggest that we ought to have a permanently horrified perception of our sin. This is not compatible with the fruit of the Spirit (love, joy, peace, etc.) or with Paul's "forgetting those things behind." Besides, Lewis says, we can't have a permanent program of emotions. Our emotional reactions to our behavior are of limited ethical significance. We need spiritual emetics at certain moments, but not as a regular diet![18]

PETITIONARY PRAYER

Some people ask, Why pray if the future is already certain in God's mind? Lewis reminds us that we must ask God for things because we are taught to petition the Lord by precept, in the Lord's Prayer, and by the example of Jesus,[19] regardless of the chances of our getting what we want. Jesus made a petitionary prayer in the Garden of Gethsemane and didn't get what he asked for.[20]

In his essay on "The Efficacy of Prayer,"[21] Lewis starts out by giving possible examples of prayer's efficacy. One is the incident where he went to see his barber in answer to his barber's prayer. The other is the example of Joy being healed in response to Peter Bide's prayer.[22] But, Lewis asks, what sort of evidence would prove the efficacy of prayer? Empirical proof is not possible—the thing we prayed for may have been going to happen anyway.[23] Invariable success in prayer would prove the efficacy of magic, not of Christian prayer. The assurance that God answers prayer can come only through a relationship with him.[24]

Does prayer work?[25] Lewis suggests that this question puts us in the wrong frame of mind. Does prayer change God? Lewis answers that our prayers don't change God's mind, but his overall purpose may be realized in a different way due to our prayers.[26]

Lewis quotes Pascal: "God instituted prayer in order to lend to His creatures the dignity of causality."[27] Lewis moved a bit beyond Pascal's position between the publishing of "The Efficacy of Prayer" in 1959 and the publishing of *Letters to Malcolm* four years later. By the time of the latter, he asserted that if our prayers are granted at all they are granted from the foundation of the earth. Before all worlds God's providential and creative act takes into account all the situations produced by the acts of his creatures. He takes our petitions as well as our sins into account.[28] And being taken into account matters more, spiritually speaking, than having our prayers answered affirmatively.[29]

THE PRAYER OF FAITH

Lewis asks what we are to do with Jesus' words in Mark 11:24 (NIV), "Therefore I tell you, whatever you ask for in prayer, believe that you have received it, and it will be yours."[30] How do we reconcile this promise with the fact that so many prayers are not answered affirmatively? How do we reconcile Mark 11:24 with Jesus' prayer in Gethsemane?[31]

Lewis answers these questions by saying that obviously the answer to some prayers is no, even when we pray in faith.[32] It is understandable why our petitions are refused when we so often ask for the wrong things. But why then is this great promise made in Mark 11:24? And how can one have perfect faith when one knows refusal is possible?

Lewis concludes that Mark 11:24 contains truth for advanced disciples, not beginners. For most of us, the prayer in Gethsemane, "Not my will but thine be done," is the everyday model to follow.

Furthermore, we should not try to work up a subjective state of faith.[33] The absence of such faith is not necessarily sinful. Our Lord had no assurance that his prayer would be answered affirmatively in Gethsemane. The kind of faith mentioned in Mark 11:24 is a gift. It is given to the person who prays as God's fellow worker; it is given to the apostle, the prophet, the missionary and the healer.[34] But perhaps this gift is given only on special occasions, since Jesus apparently did not receive this gift in the Garden of Gethsemane.

INTERCESSORY PRAYER

Do you ever find yourself praying more easily for others than you do for yourself? Malcolm apparently did. But Lewis contends that praying more easily for others doesn't necessarily mean we are maturing in the Christian life. This is the case for two reasons. First, we often pray for others when we should be doing things for them. As Lewis says, it's easier to pray for a bore than to go and see him! Second, if I pray for your besetting sin, I have no work to do. But if I pray about my besetting sin, then I will have a lot of work to do!

How can we pray effectively for other people when our prayer lists get too long over the years? Lewis suggests fixing our minds upon God, and then the person we should pray for will naturally come to mind. But it doesn't work the other way around.[35]

Lewis believed that we are under orders to pray for our enemies,[36] just as Jesus said.[37] He believed that two things could help us to make these prayers more real. One is realizing that we are joining our voice with the intercession of Christ, who died for these very people,[38] and the other is a recollection of our cruelty that under different conditions could have blossomed into something terrible. At rock bottom, none of us are so different from Hitler or Stalin.[39] Lewis claimed he would sooner pray for God's mercy than for God's justice on his friends, his enemies and himself.[40] And the best thing to do for the person who has hurt you, Lewis maintained, is to pray for him or her and then fill your mind with another subject.[41]

Lewis wrote to one correspondent saying that prayers for the sick are un-

questionably right and can do real good.[42] In addition, our anxiety about un-
believers is most usefully employed when it leads us not to speculation about
their destiny but to earnest prayer for them.[43]

DIFFICULTIES IN PRAYER

Lewis notes numerous obstacles to prayer in his essay "The Seeing Eye."
Many modern obstacles include lack of silence and solitude, the radio, reading the wrong books or reading the newspaper. One could add television,
the telephone and the Internet to the modern list of obstacles to prayer.
There is the perennial list of obstacles: money, sex, status, health, our griev-
ances,[44] the multiple distractions of domesticity.[45] And then there is the
devil himself who tries to distract us.[46]

Regarding the normal difficulty of mental distractions in prayer, Lewis
says that we should make these same distractions the subject of our prayers.
We shouldn't try to keep the distraction out of our minds. Rather, we
should pray about the distraction, and then we may be able to return to our
normal pattern of prayer.[47]

Another difficulty Lewis encountered in prayer was the feeling that he
was talking to himself, performing a soliloquy. Is prayer just a soliloquy? He
answers the question with a poem of his own creation.[48] He affirms: yes,
prayer is a soliloquy; it is God speaking to himself through me![49] Why then
does God involve us in prayer? He does it because he loves to delegate; Creation is delegation through and through.[50]

But how can God hear all of our prayers at once? some people ask. Lewis
responds to this difficulty by pointing out that God is not moving in the
time stream like we are. God exists in an "eternal now." He has infinite attention to devote to each one of us. He does not have to hear our prayers
en masse.[51]

Lewis confesses that prayer is not easy for adult converts from the intel-
ligentsia. It is hard for such people to put themselves in the presence of God.
Lewis contends that if he tries to do this in the simple way he ends up with
two phantoms juxtaposed: the bright blur that stands for God, and the other
is the idea that he calls "me." So for him the first step in preparing to pray
is to banish the bright blur, to break the idol. He claims he does this first by
realizing that matter is not solid. The four walls around him are just a stage-

set. Moreover, his consciousness is just a façade. He asserts that he must come to the point of realizing God as the ground of his being and as the ground of matter. Thinking of the material world around himself as merely being a stage-set and himself as an actor helps him to come to this realization. He argues that we cannot in our flesh leave the stage-set. But we can remember that places, such as backstage, the orchestra and the mezannine, exist. We can remember that as actors we have a real life outside of the stage set. In prayer what is happening is the real I struggling to speak to the Author, the Producer, the Audience, all of whom are God. Lewis urges that the prayer preceding all prayers should be, "May it be the real I who speaks. May it be the real Thou that I speak to."[52]

In *A Grief Observed*, Lewis also notes the difficulty of praying during a time of bereavement. After his wife's death he feels like there are no answers to his prayers, only a locked door, an iron curtain, a vacuum, absolute zero.[53] But as he perseveres in prayer he comes to feel that the door is no longer shut and bolted. Perhaps it never was. It was only his desperation that made it seem that way.[54]

IMAGES USED IN PRAYER

Lewis says that the use for him of outer images, or icons, in prayer is limited, though it does help to focus on a physical object.[55] Icons can be a distraction either by being too well done artistically or by being poorly done. Besides, most icons are of Jesus, and this can lead to mere "Jesus-worship" rather than worship of the triune God. Lewis asserts over and over again that God is the great iconoclast. Every image of him must be shattered.[56]

Lewis claims that meditating on certain biblical scenes works no better for him. Modern archeology has taught us enough to know that we don't picture most biblical scenes accurately. And if we try to picture the crucifixion scene as it was, then it tends to fill us with physical horror rather than devotion.

Yet mental images play an important part in Lewis's prayer life. He affirms that mental images help him most when they are most fugitive. If he tries to focus on them too long they go dead. He must, to quote Blake, "kiss the joy as it flies." Images in his mind become like a spray or mist thrown off by a wave. He finds this happening more in adoration than in petition.

ADORATION AND THANKSGIVING

Malcolm taught Lewis that adoration can start, for example, from a water-fall, which is an exposition of God's glory.[57] The pleasures we get from nature and from other sources are shafts of glory as they strike our sensibility. Lewis professes that he has tried to make every pleasure a channel for adoration, but not simply by giving thanks for it.

"Gratitude exclaims, very properly, 'How good of God to give me this.' Adoration says, 'What must be the quality of that Being whose far-off and momentary coruscations are like this!' One's mind runs back up the sunbeam to the sun."[58] Pleasures can become "patches of Godlight" in the woods of our experience.

The contrast between adoration and thanksgiving is similar to another contrast Lewis often draws in his writings. It is like the difference between "looking at" and "looking along." When we give thanks we are looking at a pleasurable or beautiful object and thanking God for it. When we adore we are looking along that object back up to God. We get the idea, from *Letters to Malcolm* and from Lewis's real correspondence, that he used this method of prayer during his daily walks. He found that he could take every bird song, every flower, every tree, every shaft of sunlight, and turn each one into a cause for thanksgiving as well as an opportunity for adoration. Lewis believed that by spending time in God's creation every day we reconstitute our souls. And in chapter 17 of *Letters to Malcolm* he teaches us how he did it.

THE DUTY OF PRAYER

Lewis refreshingly and humbly admits that prayer is irksome! Admitting that praying is something we must do, we rush on through the exercise of prayer so that we can get on to the things that we want to do.[59] Why is this the case? Lewis says it is so for two reasons: because of sin[60] and because of the difficulty of concentrating on something that is concrete yet immaterial like God. The irksomeness of prayer doesn't prove that when we are praying we are doing something we weren't created to do. If we were perfected creatures, prayer would not be a duty but a delight. We must remember that we are still in the school of prayer; we haven't graduated yet. And what seem to be our worst prayers may be our best; being performed by sheer willpower, such prayers come from the depths.[61]

In conclusion one might ask, "Why should we read Lewis on prayer?" The answer: because in his writings we find a compassionate fellow traveler on the road to God, one who never imposes his view but who shares his experience in such a way as to keep us out of the common ruts and on the main road to our destination.

21

THE SACRAMENTS

THOUGH C. S. LEWIS DOES NOT WRITE AT LENGTH about the sacraments, what he does write shows that they are important to him. The sacraments, for Lewis, are the avenue to the real.[1] They rank in importance with prayer and showing charity to others. Thus Screwtape counsels Wormwood concerning his human patient, to make the world an end, and faith merely a means to that end. If Wormwood can lead his patient to see meetings, pamphlets, policies, movements, causes and crusades as more important than prayers and sacraments and charity, then the patient will be in his possession.[2] And if Wormwood can get his patient to worry more about what his fellow Christians call the sacrament of bread and wine, rather than being concerned with the true meaning of it, it will be all the better.[3]

THE MEANING OF THE SACRAMENTS

How did Lewis view the Christian sacraments? Are the sacraments rituals that always effect God's grace, *ex opere operato,* by the working of the works? Or did he view the sacraments as mere ordinances of God, commands to be obeyed? Or was his view somewhere in between?

In *Mere Christianity* Lewis wrote that there are three things that spread the Christ life to us: baptism, belief, and Holy Communion. He says, in effect, that we shouldn't be surprised that the new life in Christ is spread by physical as well as mental actions, for when the New Testament speaks of Christians being in Christ, or Christ being in them, it means that Christ is operating through them. The growth of the new life in Christ is not merely the spreading of an idea; it is more like evolution—a biological or superbiological fact. We are not meant to be merely spiritual creatures but composite creatures with soul and body. Lewis affirms that is why God uses things like bread and wine to put the new life into us.[4]

This passage in *Mere Christianity* makes it sound like Lewis identified the sacraments with the grace of God and that the sacraments always spread his grace to the recipients. But a passage in *Reflections on the Psalms* makes it clear that this is not what he believed.

Lewis speaks of Old Testament Jewish worshipers not being aware of any dualism between seeing the Lord and seeing the festival in the temple. He proposes that a modern person who wished to "dwell in the house of the Lord all the days of [his] life, to gaze upon the beauty of the LORD" (Ps 27:4 NIV) would mean that this person hoped to receive frequent moments of spiritual vision and the "sensible" love of God. The modern person may depend upon the sacraments and other services to accomplish this end but won't confuse the two. The psalmist, by contrast, would have drawn no distinction between seeing the beauty of the Lord and the acts of worship.

Lewis asserts that when a person becomes capable of abstract thinking, an old unity breaks up. As soon as it is possible to distinguish the rite from the vision of God, then there is the danger of the rite becoming a substitute for or a rival to God. Lewis then gives the example of the child, who, at a certain stage in life, cannot separate the religious from the merely festal character of Christmas or Easter. He tells the story of a very small and "very devout boy" who was heard murmuring to himself on Easter morning, "Chocolate eggs and Jesus risen." Lewis finds the boy's piety and poetry admirable for his age. But, Lewis contends, the time will soon come when that child will no longer be able to effortlessly and spontaneously enjoy that unity. He will begin to distinguish the spiritual from the ritual and festal aspect of Easter; chocolate eggs will no longer be sacramental. Now once the boy has distinguished between the two he must put one or the other first. If he puts the spiritual first, he can still taste something of Easter in the chocolate eggs. If he puts the eggs first, they will soon mean no more than any other candy.[5]

When we apply this line of thought to the Christian sacraments we can see fairly quickly what Lewis was getting at. Children are able to think only in concrete terms. So up to a certain age a child does not see any distinction between eating the bread and drinking the wine of the sacrament, on the one hand, and feasting on the body and blood of Christ, on the other.

When the child becomes a youth and is able to think in abstract terms, then he will realize that the bread and wine are not literally the body and blood of Christ. But if the young person puts the spiritual first and desires to have the benefits of the death of Christ sealed to his life, he can still use the sacrament to experience this. If the young person puts the sacrament, the physical ritual of eating and drinking, first in his life, he may become a very religious person, but he will have missed the higher reality to which the sacrament is pointing.

THE SACRAMENTS IN LEWIS'S FICTION

In *The Pilgrim's Regress* and *Perelandra*, Lewis suggests that to participate in the sacraments is to participate in a mythology. In *Perelandra*, Ransom comes to perceive that the triple distinction of truth from myth and of both from fact is an earthly trichotomy, part and parcel of that unhappy division between soul and body which resulted from the Fall. Lewis argues that the sacraments exist on Earth as a permanent reminder that the division is neither wholesome nor final.[6] In other words, the sacraments join physical actions with spiritual ones.

In *The Pilgrim's Regress*, when John finally comes to cross the Grand Canyon (created by sin), he must undergo a kind of baptism. John is told by Mother Kirk that he must take off his rags and dive into the water at the bottom of the canyon. John protests that he has never learned to dive. And Mother Kirk responds by saying that there is nothing to learn but something to unlearn. John must cease trying to preserve himself. He has to let himself go.

After many moments of reflection John rubs his hands, shuts his eyes, despairs and lets himself go. It is not a good dive, but at least he reaches the water head first.

While John is under the water, swimming through an underground tunnel, he learns many things and dies many deaths. A voice speaks to John in the tunnel explaining what is happening to him by diving under the water. The voice tells him that it *is* mythology. It is truth, not fact, an image, not reality. But it is the veil under which the Person behind the voice has chosen to appear. Finally the voice asks John if there is any age in any land when people did not know that corn and wine were the body and blood of a dying yet rising God.[7]

Thus the voice (of God) declares to John that the sacraments of baptism and Holy Communion (corn and wine) are his mythology. These sacraments are the veil under which he has chosen to appear. It is for this end that our senses and imagination were made, that through these sacraments we might see the face of God and live.

THE SACRAMENTS AS INSTANCES OF TRANSPOSITION

Another way that Lewis has of describing the sacraments is in terms of transposition. He notes that when something is transposed from a higher medium into a lower one this can be done only by giving each element in the lower medium more than one meaning. And then what is happening in the lower medium can be understood only if we know the higher medium. He goes on to distinguish between the concept of transposition and that of developmentalism. Developmentalism says that things obviously natural slowly turn into things claiming to be spiritual. Lewis maintains this is not what happens in a sacrament. The natural act of eating, after millions of years, hasn't somehow turned into the Eucharist. What Lewis believes is that the spiritual reality behind Communion, which existed before there were any creatures who ate, gives to a natural act a new meaning. In a certain context, this spiritual reality makes the natural act to be a different thing. He draws an analogy to paintings of landscapes. He asserts that real landscapes enter into pictures; pictures don't sprout real trees and grass.[8]

Sometimes the element in the lower, natural medium bears little or no resemblance to the element that is transposed from the higher, spiritual medium. In *A Grief Observed*, Lewis asks whether it is in some ways an advantage that a little round, thin, cold, tasteless wafer can't pretend the least resemblance to that with which it unites him. He professes that he needs Christ, not merely something that resembles Christ.[9]

Lewis contends that belief in the sacraments should keep us from having a purely negative spirituality. In *Miracles* he contrasts the traditional versus the modernist approaches to spirituality. The traditionalist, looking into the future, sees gleams of gold, whereas the modernist sees only the mist— white, featureless, cold and motionless. Lewis maintains that this kind of negative spirituality is forbidden to Christians. Of all people, Christians should know that the physical and the spiritual need not be separated in this way. The Christian God is the God of corn and oil and wine. He is the glad Creator. He has become incarnate in Christ. The sacraments have been given to us. In fact, certain spiritual gifts are offered us only on condition that we perform certain bodily acts. To step back from all this physicality into negative spirituality would be like running away from horses instead of learning to ride them.[10]

In other words, we cannot pull all the physical elements out of Christianity and still be Christian. Christianity affirms the goodness of the body as God created it to be. As Lewis says in *Mere Christianity*, God likes matter; he invented it![11] And so he communicates spiritual realities to us through physical substances like water, bread and wine.

BAPTISM

What did baptism mean to Lewis? He was baptized as an infant and was never rebaptized after his adult conversion, so he obviously believed in infant baptism. He referred in one place to the Baptists as an extreme Protestant sect.[12] But what was the meaning of the rite to him?

He affirms that baptism symbolizes our calling to be part of the Body of Christ.[13] The Christian life begins when one is baptized into the death of Christ.[14] And baptism into his death is a remedy for the Fall. Only he who loses his life will save it, as Jesus said.[15]

But does baptism make a person a Christian? Did Lewis believe in baptismal regeneration? His answer to a correspondent suggests not. He argues that when we talk about being made Christians by baptism we are saying it in the same way we might say that a man is made a soldier when he joins the army. It may not be until six months later that the man's instructors say they have actually "made a soldier of him." Lewis contends that we must be careful to understand the different uses of phrases such as these.[16]

For Lewis, baptism was a powerful symbol, as we have already seen in *The Pilgrim's Regress*. In *The Voyage of the Dawn Treader*, Eustace undergoes a baptism when Aslan transforms him from a dragon back into a boy. After tearing off Eustace's dragon skin, Aslan catches hold of him and throws him into the water. It smarts for a moment; then Eustace realizes the pain is gone and he has become a boy again. Afterwards, Aslan dresses Eustace in new clothes, symbolic of being clothed in the righteousness of Christ.[17]

For Lewis one important "baptism" took place in his life when he read George MacDonald's *Phantastes* as a teenager. He says that upon reading that book his imagination was baptized, but that the rest of him, not unnaturally, took a little longer![18]

CONFIRMATION

So far as I know, Lewis never referred to confirmation as a sacrament. He did write very briefly about his confirmation in *Surprised by Joy*. He claimed it was one of the worst acts of his life. Because his relationship with his father was so strained, he allowed himself to be prepared for confirmation, and confirmed, and to take his first Communion in total disbelief, acting a part, eating and drinking his own condemnation, as he later viewed it.[19] He claimed he did this because it seemed impossible to tell his father that he was an atheist.

CONFESSION

Lewis began a practice of weekly confession to a priest at the end of October 1940, but I know of no place where he refers to confession, or penance, as a sacrament. He wrote to Sister Penelope that the decision to go to confession for the first time was one of the hardest he ever made.[20] But afterwards he realized that it wasn't so bad. As has already been mentioned in a previous chapter, Lewis's spiritual director was Father Walter Adams, one of the priests of the Anglican Society of Saint John the Evangelist in Cowley, a suburb of Oxford.

Lewis also mentioned confession numerous times in his letters. On January 4, 1941, he tells a correspondent that if he wants confession and absolution he will be happy to find him a spiritual director. He encourages his correspondent not to look at the confessional experience as some sort of psychoanalysis. The confessor, Lewis maintains, is the representative of our Lord and declares his forgiveness. The confessor's advice or understanding is of secondary importance.[21]

To another correspondent Lewis writes that talking about interpersonal problems to someone they approach as a confessor is no more disloyal than revealing one's body to a doctor is indecent exposure. Confessing sin to a trained confessor is a disinfectant situation.[22]

And in another letter Lewis professes that there is a gain in self-knowledge

through confession. Most people, he contends, never face the facts about themselves until they speak them aloud in plain words, calling a spade a spade.[23]

I know of no place where Lewis refers to anything except baptism and
Holy Communion as Christian sacraments. While he writes at some length
about marriage, I have yet to find a reference to it as a sacrament. He touches
on the subject of holy orders in "Priestesses in the Church?" but he does not
refer to ordination as a sacrament. Lewis did receive the last rites, also
known as extreme unction or simply anointing with oil, when he went into
a coma during the last year of his life.[24] But again, he does not refer to the
last rites as a sacrament.

HOLY COMMUNION

Lewis usually refers to Holy Communion as *the* sacrament. And, in fact, it is
the sacrament that he writes most about. He declares that if there is anything
in the teaching of the New Testament that is a command, it is that Christians are obligated to take the sacrament, and we can't do it without going
to church.[25] He claims it is the only rite that we know has been instituted by
our Lord. He quotes two Scriptures in support of this: "Do this in remem-
brance of me" (Lk 22:19) and "If ye do not eat the flesh of the Son of man
and drink his blood, ye have no life in you" (Jn 6:53-54). Lewis reiterates
that these are orders that must be obeyed.[26] Communion is holy, for in it
Christ is truly hidden.[27]

Lewis did not think it important to take Communion every week when
he first became a Christian. But he changed his mind about this later on in
his life and became a weekly communicant.[28] He received private communion during Joy's illness and found it "extraordinarily moving" to the point
where he thought he was in danger of preferring private communion to communion in church.[29] The most important thing about Holy Communion to
Lewis, however, was not the location of receiving it but the fact that in this
rite God communicates himself to humanity.[30]

Lewis gave some advice to his goddaughter, Sarah, before her first Communion. He wrote,

> Don't expect (I mean, don't *count on* and don't *demand*) that when you are con-
> firmed, or when you make your first Communion, you will have all the *feelings*

you would like to have. You may, of course: but also you may not. But don't
worry if you don't get them. They aren't what matter. The things that are happening to you are quite real things whether you feel as you w[oul]d wish or
not, just as a meal will do a hungry person good even if he has a cold in the
head which will rather spoil the taste. Our Lord will give us right feelings if
He wishes—and then we must say Thank you. If He doesn't, then we must
say to ourselves (and Him) that He knows us best. This, by the way, is one
of the very few subjects on which I feel I do know something. For years after
I had become a regular communicant I can't tell you how dull my feelings
were and how my attention wandered at the most important moments. It is
only in the last year or two that things have begun to come right—which just
shows how important it is to keep on doing what you are told.[31]

LETTERS TO MALCOLM ON COMMUNION

Lewis comments to Malcolm that his ideas about the sacrament would
probably be called "magical" by many modern theologians. One result of
this view is that the more one believes in a strictly supernatural event taking
place in the sacrament, the less importance one attaches to the dress, ges-
tures and position of the priest administering the Sacrament.[32]

It is in *Letters to Malcolm*[33] that Lewis writes most extensively about Holy
Communion. He says that he hasn't written about Holy Communion before
for two reasons: because he is not good enough at theology and because certain doctrines regarding Holy Communion have a negative effect on him,
and in explaining this he does not want to upset the faith of some. But he
denies that he admits rather than welcomes the sacraments. They are much
more important to him than that.

Lewis wishes that no definitions of Holy Communion had ever been
necessary and that none had been allowed to divide the churches. He goes
on to share his understanding of Communion. He says he can't imagine
what the disciples understood our Lord to mean at the Last Supper. Lewis
sees no connection between eating a man and entering into spiritual one-
ness with him. He agrees with neither transubstantiation (the Roman
Catholic view that the bread and wine become the actual body and blood
of Christ when consecrated by a priest) nor the memorial view (the view
of some Baptists and others who say that in the Lord's Supper we are

merely remembering Christ's sacrifice for our sins on the cross).[34]

Lewis states his view in these words:

> Yet I find no difficulty in believing that the veil between the worlds, nowhere else (for me) so opaque to the intellect, is nowhere else so thin and permeable to divine operation. Here a hand from the hidden country touches not only my soul but my body. Here the prig, the don, the modern in me have no privilege over the savage or the child.[35]

Lewis is thankful, in any event, that Jesus' command was "Take, eat," not "Take, understand." Being tormented by wondering what the wafer and wine are stops one from receiving what God wants to give. He says it is like taking a red coal out of the fire to examine it; it goes dead. Overanalysis of Communion leads to paralysis in the reception of it.

A PICTURE OF COMMUNION

Toward the end of *The Voyage of the Dawn Treader*[36] there is a beautiful picture of Holy Communion. The sacrament is pictured in the stone table on Ramandu's Island. The table is laid with a rich crimson cloth, and on it lays a knife that the White Witch once used to kill Aslan. Filling the table is food of all sorts. The smell of fruit and wine from the table blows toward the voyagers like a promise of all happiness. Around the table are sitting three of the seven lost lords of Narnia, fast asleep. We are told that they fell asleep because they would not eat of the feast, and also because they got into a fight with one another and one of them grasped the knife that had killed Aslan. Faithful and valiant Reepicheep is the first to dare to eat of the table's fare, but once he leads the way the other voyagers join in as well. When Eustace asks how the food keeps, he is told by Ramandu's daughter that it is eaten and renewed every day.

What could be a better picture of Holy Communion, in Narnian terms, than this? The rich crimson represents the blood of Aslan shed for traitors like Edmund. The presence of the knife makes it clear that this table is like unto the Stone Table upon which Aslan was killed. There is rich food and wine to be had upon this table. And in the three sleepers there is an echo of Paul's warning in I Corinthians 11:27-30 (NIV):

Therefore, whoever eats the bread or drinks the cup of the Lord in an unworthy manner will be guilty of sinning against the body and blood of the Lord. A man ought to examine himself before he eats of the bread and drinks of the cup. For anyone who eats and drinks without recognizing the body of the Lord eats and drinks judgment on himself. That is why many among you are weak and sick, and a number of you have fallen asleep.

Lewis knew what it was like to eat from that "magic" table without recognizing the body of the Lord. But he also knew the joy of waking from that enchanted sleep of judgment and feasting upon all the delights of the Lord's Table. For Lewis, Holy Communion became *the* sacrament through which a hand from the hidden country touched not only his soul but his body. And that touch eventually became so real to Lewis that he wanted to experience it as often as possible. For as he found, the sacrament of Holy Communion is a foretaste of Heaven.[37]

22

HELL

C. S. LEWIS WARNS US THAT TO THINK much of Heaven or hell apart from God corrupts the doctrine of both and corrupts us while we think that way. God's nature is the sanction of his commands. Union with that nature is Heaven; separation from it is hell.[1] Therefore anyone who turns to this chapter or the next two out of pure curiosity before reading the earlier chapters should read the rest of this book first!

HEAVEN AND HELL IN THE OLD TESTAMENT

Lewis notes that in most parts of the Old Testament there is little or no belief in a future life. The word often translated as "hell" in the Old Testament is *Sheol*, the place of the dead, of good and bad alike. The Jewish religion did not encourage one to think about Sheol. The Old Testament speaks of Sheol very much as a modern person who has no belief in a future life would speak of death or the grave. Lewis presents how the Jews, like many other nations, had believed that a person possessed a soul, separable from the body, which went at death into this shadowy world called Sheol. For the Jew, Sheol was a land of forgetfulness and imbecility where none could call upon the Lord any more. From Sheol ghosts could return and appear to the living, as Samuel's ghost had done at the command of the witch of Endor.[2] Lewis cites many examples of this type of belief in Sheol in the Psalms.[3] However, Judaism greatly changed in this respect by the time of Jesus. The Sadducees still held to the old view, while the Pharisees and others believed in the life of the world to come.

Why did God, who revealed so much else to the Jews, not reveal the existence of Heaven and hell? Lewis notes that the Egyptians were too concerned with the afterlife. God may not have wanted his chosen people to follow their example. When one is concerned only with one's place either in Heaven or hell, God is not at the center of one's thinking. An effective belief in Heaven and hell, coming too soon in one's spiritual development, may render impossible the development of an appetite for God. Lewis mentions how he was allowed for a whole year to believe in God and tried to obey him without any belief in a future life. And he says that year was of very great value.[4]

The Jews of the Old Testament period may not have believed in Heaven and hell as the later Christians came to believe in both. But this should not be construed in such a way as to suppose that Heaven and hell did not exist during the Old Testament period or that these realities came into existence only after the Incarnation. Progressive revelation by God is different from progressive creation by God of wholly new realms.

WHAT IS HELL?

Lewis defines hell as banishment from the presence of him who is present everywhere, erasure from the knowledge of him who knows all. To be in hell is to be left totally outside—repelled, exiled, estranged and absolutely ignored.[5] Hell is the cold and dark of utmost space.[6] It is eternal starvation.[7] Hell is that which is outside of all self-giving;[8] it is the place where love is absent.[9] All your life an unattainable ecstasy has hovered just beyond your reach. Hell will be to awake and realize that you have lost forever that ecstasy.[10] Hell will be the inevitable result of one's bad temper or other sins gradually getting worse and worse.[11] All our lives, by each of our innumerable choices, we are turning the central core of ourselves either into something heavenly or something hellish.[12] And if we are turning into hellish creatures, it means we are moving gradually into nonentity, being absorbed into the evil one. As Lewis says in *Perelandra*, there is a confusion of persons in damnation; in hell bad people are melted down into their master, just as a lead soldier slips down and loses his shape in the ladle held over the gas ring.[13]

In *The Great Divorce*, Lewis pictures hell as a gray city, always in the rain and always in evening twilight, full of dingy lodging houses, small tobacconists, billboards from which posters hang in rags, windowless warehouses and goods stations without trains. The town is empty of people because all the people are so quarrelsome that they constantly keep moving further and further away from each other. The worst sinners, people like Genghis Khan, Julius Caesar, Henry the Fifth and Napoleon, are millions of miles away from other people in hell. Consequently, hell doesn't even afford the pleasure of meeting interesting historical personages. It's easy for these people to move apart from each other because all they have to do is think a house and there it is.[14] The problem with these imaginary houses is that they don't keep the rain out![15]

In his preface to *The Screwtape Letters*, Lewis says that hell is a place where everyone is perpetually concerned about his or her dignity and advancement, where everyone has a complaint, and where everyone lives out the deadly serious passions of envy, self-importance, and resentment.[16]

In *The Pilgrim's Regress* Lewis describes hell as a tourniquet. He says that the Landlord (God) does not make the blackness of hell. The blackness is there already wherever the taste of mountain-apple (sin) has created the rebellious will. Hell is a hole, something that ends. Hell is a black hole—in other words, blackness enclosed, limited. The Landlord has made hell only in the sense that he has enclosed it. He has allowed a worst thing to exist in the world. However, Lewis maintains, evil of itself would never reach a worst point. If evil could reach a worst point on its own, it would no longer be evil because form and limit belong to the good. Lewis suggests that the walls of hell are the tourniquet on the wound through which a lost soul would otherwise bleed to death forever. Hell is God's final service to those who will let him do nothing better for them.[17]

HELL AS A STATE OF MIND

Is hell a state of mind? In a letter to Arthur Greeves written in 1946 Lewis says that the New Testament plainly implies the possibility of some people finally being left in "the outer darkness."[18] Whether this means a purely mental existence or whether there is still some sort of environment, Lewis does not pretend to know. However, he insists he would not put the question in the form, Do I believe in an actual hell? One's own mind is actual enough. If it doesn't seem fully actual now that is because one can always escape from it into the physical world by looking out of a window, smoking a cigarette or even by going to sleep. When there is nothing for us but our minds (no body to go to sleep, no books or landscape, no sounds, no drugs) our minds will be as actual as coffins are actual to people buried alive.[19]

Lewis gives a picture of hell in *The Last Battle*. Some bad dwarfs get into Aslan's country through a stable door, as do Eustace, Jill, Tirian and Jewel the Unicorn. But the difference is that the dwarfs still think they are in a stable. Try as they might, the children, and Tirian, and even Aslan cannot enable the dwarfs to see their error or to see Aslan's real country around them. Finally Aslan concludes about the dwarfs, "They will not let us help them. They have chosen cunning instead of belief. Their prison is only in their own minds, yet they are in that prison; and so afraid of being taken in that they can not be taken out."[20]

George MacDonald confirms this line of thinking in *The Great Divorce*. He says that hell is indeed a state of mind. And every state of mind, left to itself, every shutting up of a creature within the dungeon of its own mind is, in the end, hell.[21]

ANSWERING OBJECTIONS TO THE DOCTRINE OF HELL

Lewis's most extensive teaching on the doctrine of hell appears in *The Problem of Pain*.[22] In a chapter entitled simply "Hell," he starts out by making the point that hell exists because of free will.[23] He claims that there is no doctrine he would more willingly remove from Christianity than the doctrine of hell, but it has the full support of Scripture, of Jesus' words, of Christendom and of reason. He notes that the sayings of Jesus regarding hell are addressed to our conscience and will, not to our intellectual curiosity. These statements are meant to rouse us into the action of obedience to him.[24]

Lewis notes that the problem of hell, within the Christian system of doctrine, is not simply that of a God who consigns people to hell. That is the problem of the Islamic religion. The Christian doctrine is more complex. In Christianity we hear of a God so full of mercy that he becomes a man and dies on a cross in the place of sinners but who refuses to remove the possibility of hell by sheer power. So much mercy, but hell still exists.

Lewis answers several objections against the doctrine of hell. First, there is an objection in many minds to the idea of retributive punishment as such. In answer to this objection he asks us to picture a man who has risen to wealth and power by a continued course of evil. Having attained success, the man uses that success for the gratification of lust and hatred and in the end betrays his accomplices. Imagine further that this man has not the slightest trace of remorse. Lewis asks if we can really desire that such a man, remaining what he is, should be confirmed forever in his present happiness.[25] The obvious answer to this question is "No." Lewis posits that it is better, in a sense, for this man, even if he never becomes good, to know that he was a failure, a mistake. In this sense, hell as a retributive punishment is just. But Lewis also notes how judgment consists in people preferring darkness to light.[26] The bad person's consignment to hell is not so much a sentence imposed as it is an inevitable result of being what he or she is.[27]

Second, Lewis answers the objection that there seems to be a disproportion between eternal damnation and transitory sin. He says that if we think of eternity as the mere prolongation of time, then it is disproportionate to transitory sin. But he suggests another way of thinking about eternity. If we think of time as a line, then we ought to think of eternity as a plane or solid. That solid would be mainly the work of God, but human free will contributes the base line, in time. If we draw our base line askew, then the whole solid will be in the wrong position. Lewis suggests that the fact that we are only allowed to contribute one little line, the fact that life is short, is really a divine mercy.[28] What a mess we might have made of things if we were allowed to draw more than just the base line!

Lewis also answers the simpler form of this same objection. Some people say that death ought not to be final, that we ought to have a second chance after death to do things God's way. Lewis insists that the idea of a second chance ought to be distinguished from the doctrines of Purgatory and of Limbo. Purgatory is for those already saved, and Limbo is for those already lost. Lewis believes that if a million chances were likely to do good, then God would give them to us. But God is like a good teacher who knows when giving his pupil another chance at an exam is likely to do good and when it is not. Finality must come sometime, and God in his omniscience knows when that time has come.

A third objection has to do with the frightful intensity of the pains of hell. Lewis points out how Jesus speaks of hell under three symbols: punishment (Mt 25:46), destruction (Mt 10:28) and privation—banishment into "the darkness outside," as in the parables of the man without a wedding garment or of the wise and foolish virgins (Mt 22:1-14; 25:1-13). Lewis rules out the possibility of mere annihilation of the soul. The destruction of one thing always means the emergence of something else. Burn a log and you have gases, heat and ash.[29] The damned go to a place never prepared for them; hell was originally prepared for the demons (Mt 25:41). To enter hell is to be banished from humanity; that which is cast into hell is not a person but merely "remains."[30]

A fourth objection that Lewis deals with is that no charitable person could be blessed in Heaven while he or she knew that even one human soul was in hell. Behind this objection lies the conception of Heaven and hell co-existing at the same time.[31] However, Lewis points out that Jesus, while emphasizing the terror of hell, does not talk about its duration. Rather, he speaks of its finality. Consignment to the fires of hell is usually treated as the end of the story, not the beginning of a new story. Hell is the outer rim where being fades away into nonentity.

MacDonald gives a wonderful answer to this objection to hell in *The Great Divorce*. MacDonald points out that it sounds grand to say that you won't accept a salvation that leaves even one creature in hell. But, warns Mac-Donald, we must watch such a line of thinking or else we will make "a Dog in a Manger the tyrant of the universe." After saying this, MacDonald shows Lewis a tiny crack in the ground of Heaven and informs him that this is the crack through which he came up from hell. Lewis questions whether this is really true, and MacDonald tells him that hell is smaller than even one atom of Heaven.[32]

A final objection Lewis deals with is the idea that the ultimate loss of a human soul means the defeat of Omnipotence. Lewis agrees with this. However, he maintains that Omnipotence has voluntarily limited himself by creating beings with free will. Lewis calls it miracle, not defeat. For God to create human beings, who are not part of himself and who can resist his will, is, according to Lewis, one of the most astonishing accomplishments of Deity.

CHRIST'S DESCENT INTO HELL

Lewis believed in the reality of Christ's descent into hell and preaching to the dead, suggested by 1 Peter 3:19 and confessed by most Christians in the Apostles' Creed. He believed that this action took place outside of time and included those who died long before the Son of God's Incarnation, as well as those who died long after it.[33]

In *The Great Divorce*, Lewis asks MacDonald whether anyone can ever reach the damned souls in hell. MacDonald says that only God can make himself small enough to enter hell. The higher something is, the lower it can go down. Lewis asks whether God will ever go to hell again. MacDonald tells Lewis that God doesn't need to do this because all moments were present in the moment of his descending. There is no spirit in prison to whom Christ did not preach.[34]

WHY BELIEF IN HELL IS IMPORTANT

In *Letters to Malcolm*, Lewis says that belief in the reality of hell is important because people who disbelieve in hell cannot have a life-giving belief in Heaven.[35] Second, he suggests that belief in hell is important because, apart from Christ, we are destined to go there. We need to wake up and do something to change our destiny to Heaven.[36]

While some evangelical Christians may have areas of disagreement with Lewis's teaching on hell, especially with its leanings toward annihilationism, we need to see Lewis's views in the context of his time. We can be most grateful for the fact that Lewis believed, taught and wrote about his belief in a literal Heaven and hell in an age that has tried to water down these realities almost into nonexistence.

23

PURGATORY

C. S. LEWIS'S FIRST REFERENCE TO PURGATORY is in *The Problem of Pain*, where he mentions in a footnote that the conception of a "second chance" must not be confused with the concept of Purgatory, which is for souls already saved.[1] But he doesn't tell us, in this place, whether or not he believes in Purgatory.

The next hint of the doctrine of Purgatory in Lewis's writings comes at the end of *The Screwtape Letters*, where Screwtape is talking to Wormwood about the death of his patient. Screwtape describes the moment at which the patient was snatched from Wormwood's clutches. He describes what the patient must have felt at that moment. It is like a scab falling from an old sore or like the shuffling off for good of a defiled, wet, clinging garment—a final stripping and complete cleansing, or like the extraction of a tooth that hurts more and more until finally the tooth is out.[2] Lewis doesn't use the word *Purgatory* in this context, but the images he uses to describe what happens to the Christian patient after death are similar to images he uses to describe Purgatory in his later writings.

The first definite suggestion of Lewis's belief in Purgatory comes in *Beyond Personality*, published in 1944. The suggestion of Purgatory comes in the chapter where Lewis talks about counting the cost of becoming a Christian. He contends that Christ plans to make us perfect. The moment we put ourselves in his hands, that is what we are in for. He insists that whatever suffering it may cost us in our earthly life and whatever inconceivable purification it may cost us after death, Christ will not rest until we are literally perfect.[3]

THE GREAT DIVORCE

Lewis elaborates on this idea of purification after death in *The Great Divorce*. One of the bright, solid people from Heaven tells one of the ghosts from the Grey City that he has been in hell. But if he chooses not to go back he may call the Grey City Purgatory.[4] A few pages later, the same solid person encourages the Episcopal Ghost to remain in Heaven by telling him how quickly any pain involved in purification will all be over; one pull and the tooth will be out.[5] This is the same image of purification after death that Lewis uses in *Screwtape*.

Later in the story, George MacDonald confirms what this bright person had said to the Episcopal Ghost.[6] Lewis questions whether there is a real choice after death. But MacDonald encourages Lewis not to occupy himself with such questions because he cannot fully understand the relation of choice and time until he is beyond both.[7] This exchange tells us two things. It suggests that Lewis was trying to find a via media between the Roman Catholic doctrine of Purgatory and the Protestant exclusion of Purgatory. It also reveals that *The Great Divorce*, as a story, is not so much about what Heaven, hell and Purgatory will be like as it is about choice in this life. Lewis begs readers in his preface to remember that the story is a fantasy. He maintains that the conditions of the afterlife are solely an imaginative supposal not intended to arouse factual curiosity about the details of the afterworld.[8]

LETTERS

References to Purgatory appear a few times in Lewis's published letters. In one letter Lewis again distinguishes between the doctrine of "a second chance" and Purgatory. The latter he describes as a process by which the work of redemption continues, and first begins to be noticeable after death.[9]

In a letter to Mary Willis Shelburne, Lewis again uses the image of tooth pulling to describe Purgatory. He talks about having one of his teeth pulled by the dentist. He wonders whether the moment of death may be like that moment when one realizes that the tooth is out and the dentist says, "Rinse your mouth out with this." The mouthwash, Lewis says, will be Purgatory.[10] In another letter to the same person he fancies that one stage in Purgatory might take place in a kitchen where things are always going wrong. The purifying task, Lewis says, will be for the women to learn to sit still and mind their own business while the men have to learn to jump up and do something about the problems! When both sexes have mastered the exercise, they get to move on to the next stage of Purgatory.[11]

A couple of months before his death, Lewis even writes to Sister Penelope and asks her to come down and look him up in Purgatory when she dies. That is if "prison visiting" is allowed![12]

LATER WRITINGS

There is a brief mention of Purgatory in *Reflections on the Psalms*. Lewis queries whether in Purgatory we shall see our own faces and hear our own voices as they really were on Earth.[13]

There are a couple of references to Purgatory in *A Grief Observed*. Reflecting on the encouragement of many people who tell Lewis after his wife's death that she is "at rest," he questions why they are so sure. He mentions that more than half the Christian world and millions in the East believe in some kind of pain after death. And if there is the pain of separation for the lover left behind, why wouldn't there be pain for the lover who departs?[14] In book 3 of *A Grief Observed*, Lewis says he never believed before that even the most faithful soul could leap straight into perfection and peace after the moment of death. To start believing so now would only be wishful thinking in regard to his dead wife. He mentions how splendid Joy was. He calls her a straight soul, bright and tempered like a sword. But she was not a perfected saint. Lewis surmises that the sword will be made even brighter now that she has died.[15]

LETTERS TO MALCOLM

Lewis's most definitive statement regarding Purgatory is in the last book that he prepared for publication, *Letters to Malcolm*. He states categorically there that he believes in Purgatory. He admits that the Protestant Reformers had good reasons for throwing out Rome's doctrine of Purgatory as it had become degraded by the sixteenth century. He points out how Purgatory had gone from being a place of cleansing for people already saved, in Dante's *Purgatorio*, to being a temporary hell in Thomas More's *Supplication of Souls*.[16] Lewis notes how Fisher has lost sight of the very etymology of the word *Purgatory*.[17] In Fisher's writings Purgatory has become simply a place of punishment, and no longer a place of purification. Lewis believes that the right view returns magnificently in Newman's *Dream*, where the saved soul upon entering Heaven begs to be taken away and cleansed before approaching the throne. Lewis believes that in this sense our souls demand Purgatory. He assumes that purification in Purgatory will involve suffering. He bases this partly on tradition and partly on life experience. Most of the good he has experienced in life, he insists, has come from suffering. But the suffering of Purgatory will have nothing to do with earning merit before God. Purification will be the only purpose of any suffering we will have to endure.[18]

Most Protestants find themselves uncomfortable upon encountering Lewis's teaching on Purgatory, and I must admit that I do not agree with all of his thinking in this regard. However, we must be very careful to note what Lewis does and does not say about Purgatory. He does not say that we can pay for our sins in Purgatory or that anything can be added to the sacrifice of Christ. The purpose of Purgatory, to Lewis's mind, is entirely one of cleansing and purification, as the etymology of the word *Purgatory* suggests. Even the most ardent Protestant, while not agreeing with Lewis that our souls demand Purgatory, can agree that our souls demand purgation (see 1 Jn 1:10; Phil 3:12). And Lewis's picture of Purgatory being like rinsing with mouthwash after having your tooth pulled at the dentist is much more like the Protestant understanding of instantaneous glorification at death than it is like the Roman Catholic insistence upon prolonged purgation in a place separate from Heaven or hell (see also Rom 8:30; Lk 23:43; 2 Cor 5:6-8). So while I may not fully agree with Lewis's thinking on Purgatory, I am grateful for the way Lewis challenges and stretches my own thinking on this point. And reading Lewis makes me long for the purging of sin from my own soul that alone will prepare me for the joy of Heaven.

24

HEAVEN

C. S. LEWIS REALIZED THAT MANY PEOPLE in his day, did not want to speak of Heaven. Lewis lived at the tail end of the modern age, when many people, at least in Oxford, believed that the physical realm was all that existed. In this postmodern age perhaps many more people are likely to believe in Heaven; at least many more are interested in spirituality today than in Lewis's time in Oxford. But those who are interested are likely to have unorthodox notions of what Heaven is like. The writings of Lewis function as a good apologetic for Heaven in our day, just as they did in his time.

In his sermon "Learning in War-Time," preached in Oxford on October 22, 1939, Lewis mentioned that many people don't like to mention Heaven or hell even in a sermon. But since the source of Christian teaching on the subject is Jesus, Heaven must be reckoned with.[1]

TOUCHY SUBJECT

It is impossible to remove talk of Heaven from the Bible, or from Christianity in general, without changing the one into a different book or the other into a different religion. So why were people in Lewis's time reluctant to speak of Heaven? Lewis suggests that people are very shy of even mentioning Heaven because they are afraid of the jeer about pie in the sky. They are afraid of being told that they are trying to escape from reality. Lewis tackles this problem head-on. He responds that there is either pie in the sky or there isn't. If there is not, then Christianity is false and can be disregarded, for the doctrine of Heaven is woven into its very fabric. If there is pie in the sky, then the truth of Heaven must be faced.[2]

Lewis recognized that even Christians in his day were shy of talking about

Heaven. Many wanted to make Christianity more palatable to non-Christians by downplaying talk of it. Perhaps that is why Lewis asks his fictitious friend Malcolm how the next world can loom less large if it is believed in at all. If it exists then it is an extremely important factor to be considered in one's whole worldview.[3]

DEFINITION

Part of the problem for some people in accepting the reality of Heaven comes in understanding exactly what Christians are talking about when they speak of it. Many people outside the church perhaps believe that Christians have a naive notion of Heaven being up in the sky somewhere. Lewis has a lovely response to this idea. He suggests that looking for God, or Heaven, in outer space is like reading all of Shakespeare's plays in the hope that you will find Shakespeare as one of the characters or Stratford as one of the places. Shakespeare is in a sense present throughout every play. But he is never present in the same way as one of his characters, nor is Shakespeare diffused throughout the play like a gas.[4] The same is true of God in relation to his creation.

In *Miracles*, Lewis clarifies what Christians mean when they talk of Heaven. We examined this definition in an earlier chapter where we explored the meaning of the Ascension of Christ. Heaven can mean the life of God beyond this universe. Or it can mean blessed participation in that life by one of God's creatures. It can mean the whole nature in which redeemed human beings can enjoy such participation fully and forever. Or the word *Heaven* can refer to the physical Heaven, the sky, the space in which our earth moves. In the biblical idea of Heaven all these meanings were latent, ready to be brought out by later analysis. Lewis claims that when the early followers of Christ looked up at the sky, they never doubted that it was the home of God. But when they thought of Christ ascending to Heaven, they never doubted he was ascending in what we would call a spiritual sense.[5]

HEAVEN ON EARTH?

It is important to note that Lewis rejected from the start any possibility of Heaven on Earth, at least Earth as it now is. He insists this is not a live option for the Christian. For Lewis, tribulation is necessary to redemption, and we should not anticipate an end to that tribulation until God's work of redemption is complete. Therefore Christians should ignore those who promise that Heaven on Earth will be ushered in if only some reform in our economic, political or hygienic system is made.[6]

Lewis depicts Screwtape as trying to entice people to worldliness by causing them to think that they can create a Heaven on Earth. Screwtape says that the devils' best method of attaching human beings to Earth is to make them believe that it can be turned into Heaven by politics or eugenics or science or psychology or what not.[7] Lewis notes elsewhere how the popular philosophies of his day were attempting unsuccessfully to create Heaven on Earth.[8]

Perhaps it is easy for the younger generation today to imagine that Heaven on Earth is possible because it has not had to live through a world war. Lewis maintains that war helps us to see the sort of universe we have been living in all along. War shatters any foolish un-Christian hopes about human culture. War brings disillusion, in this sense, and not a moment too soon.[9] As Lewis insists in one of his letters, true security is in Heaven; Earth only provides imitations.[10]

BIBLICAL IMAGES OF HEAVEN

One difficulty that some people have when it comes to believing in Heaven stems from the biblical images of it. What are we to make of them? Lewis wrestled with this question. In *Mere Christianity* he wrote that all scriptural images (harps, crowns, gold, etc.) are symbolic attempts to express the inexpressible. Musical instruments are mentioned because music suggests ecstasy and infinity. Crowns are mentioned to suggest splendor and power and joy. Gold is mentioned to suggest the timelessness of Heaven and the preciousness of it. Lewis contends that those who take these symbols literally might as well think that when Jesus told his disciples to act like doves, he meant for them to lay eggs![11]

So we do not have to take the biblical images of Heaven literally. And at this many of us want to breathe a collective sigh of relief. But what are we to do with the biblical images when they speak so poorly to our imagination? Lewis admits in *The Weight of Glory* that he relates to this feeling. He confesses that the appeal of the biblical imagery is to him, at first, very small. But that, he claims, is what we ought to expect. If Christianity can tell us no more of

Heaven than our imaginations surmise already, then Christianity is no higher than us. But, Lewis maintains, if Christianity has more to tell us, then we must expect it to be less immediately attractive than our own ideas.[12] Once we have awakened more to our new life in Christ, perhaps the biblical images of Heaven will become more interesting to us.

THE DANCE OF HEAVEN

In the meantime Lewis offers to those of us not stimulated by the biblical images some images of his own, in an effort to awaken our desire for Heaven. One of those images is of Heaven as the place of the Great Dance. Heaven is the place where the Master of the dance leads in the revelry, giving himself eternally to his creatures and back to himself in the sacrifice of the Word. This eternal dance makes Heaven drowsy with its harmony. The pleasure of the Great Dance is strictly incomparable with the sufferings of this present time. As we draw nearer to its uncreated rhythm, pain and pleasure sink out of sight. There is joy in the dance, but the dance does not exist for the sake of joy. Rather, it exists for the sake of God.[13]

As we have seen in the chapter on the three-personal God, Lewis answers the objection of those who say that this image of the Great Dance is too frivolous to describe Heaven. He counters that it is only in our time off, only in our moments of festivity, that we find a proper analogy to Heaven. Dance and game *are* frivolous on Earth, for this is not their proper place. On Earth, dance is but a moment's rest from the life we were placed here to live. But we must remember that we live in a world where everything is upside-down. The joy of the Great Dance is the serious business of Heaven.[14]

ETERNAL MORNING

Another image that Lewis uses repeatedly to describe Heaven is that of the eternal morning. He uses this image in *The Pilgrim's Regress*. After John, the pilgrim, dives into the water and comes up on the other side, thus symbolizing his conversion to Christ and the church, he gets a glimpse of the island that he has desired his whole life long. It is early in the morning when John comes to the island and hears the sound of the waves. The morning wind brings to him the sweet smell of orchards. The smell conveys the purity of early air and is mixed with a little sharpness of the sea.[15]

It seems that Lewis chose morning as the time of day for his descriptions of Heaven because thoughts of morning communicate freshness to our minds and hearts. Eternal morning appears again as a picture of Heaven in *The Great Divorce*. In that book, Lewis, as a character in the story, describes his first exposure to Heaven upon disembarking the bus from hell. His first thought is that the light and coolness drenching him are like those of summer morning, early morning, a minute or two before the sunrise.[16]

One of Lewis's most delightful vignettes in *The Great Divorce* is the story of the ghost with the lizard of lust upon his shoulder. Once the ghost submits to having the angel kill the lizard, he is transformed into a real, solid man, and the lizard is transformed into a winged horse. Then they ride off together into that everlasting morning.[17] Clearly for Lewis, Heaven is like morning, full of the promise of a new day, a fresh start, sunrise not sunset.

THE REAL WORLD

Another image Lewis gives us of Heaven is a Platonic one. It is of Heaven as the real world. He maintains that as Christians we should think of ourselves as seeds patiently waiting in the earth, waiting to come up as flowers into the real world.[18]

In *The Great Divorce*, Lewis pictures the hard reality of Heaven by making the grass, flowers, water, in fact all the physical objects of Heaven, so utterly real and hard that they hurt the ghosts who are new arrivals there from hell.[19] Heaven will be so real that once there, we will taste truth as though it is honey, and we will be embraced by it as by a bridegroom. Our thirst will be quenched.[20]

In *The Last Battle*, Digory, Polly, Peter, Edmund and Lucy experience a railway accident and suddenly find themselves in a new country, which in some parts reminds them of Narnia and in other parts reminds them of England. Finally it begins to dawn on them where they are. Digory explains that when Aslan said they could never go back to Narnia, he meant the old Narnia. But that was not the real Narnia. The old Narnia had a beginning and an end. It was but a shadow, a copy of the real Narnia. In the same way, Digory says, our world is only a shadow or a copy of something in the real world. All that really matters in the old Narnia is drawn into the real Narnia. Of course this real Narnia is different, as different as waking from dreaming.[21]

DESIRE FOR HEAVEN

Lewis's descriptions of Heaven probably go a long way toward creating a desire for Heaven in the hearts of many of his readers. He wrote frequently of the desire for Heaven. And he defended this desire as a right and proper one, at least in the right context. For Lewis admitted that Heaven is too often desired chiefly as an escape from hell.[22] And that is not the right motive for wanting Heaven.

However, Lewis maintained that the proper desire for Heaven is not simply a form of escapism or wishful thinking. Rather, it is one of the things a Christian is meant to have. He points out that those Christians down through the ages who have thought most of the next world are also the ones who have done the most for this world. He cites as examples the apostles, who instigated, by the power of the Holy Spirit, the conversion of the Roman Empire. He also cites the great men of the Middle Ages and the English evangelicals, like William Wilberforce, who abolished the slave trade. All of these people left their mark on Earth, mainly because their minds were focused on Heaven. Lewis posits that it is because Christians have stopped thinking of Heaven that they have become so ineffective on Earth. Aim for Heaven, and you will get Earth along with it; aim for Earth, and you will get nothing.[23]

But what of those who don't think they desire Heaven? Lewis explains why many of us find it difficult to desire Heaven. He believes this is because our whole education tends to fix our minds on this world. Another reason is that when we really desire Heaven, we do not recognize it. Most people, if they really looked into their hearts, would know that they do want, and want deeply, something that cannot be had in this world. There are all sorts of things in this life that promise to give it to us, but they never quite keep their promise. The longings that arise in us when we first fall in love, or first think of some foreign country, or first take up some subject that excites us, are longings which no marriage, no travel, no learning can ever fully satisfy.[24]

Lewis notes that there are three ways of dealing with this longing: the fool's way, the way of the disillusioned "sensible man" and the Christian way. The fool chases one dream after another hoping it will satisfy his or her desire, but it never does. The sensible man realizes that his desires will never be satisfied, and he gives up hope of even having his desires satisfied in another world. The Christian properly recognizes that creatures are not born with desires unless satisfaction exists for those desires. A baby feels hunger, and there is such a thing as food. A duckling wants to swim, and there is such a thing as water. People feel sexual desire, and there is such a thing as sex. If we find in ourselves a desire that this world cannot satisfy, perhaps it is because we were made for another world. Lewis urges that we must keep alive in ourselves the desire for our true country, the one we will not find until we die. We must make it our main purpose to press on to that other country and to help others to do the same.[25]

In *The Problem of Pain*, Lewis wonders whether we have ever wanted anything other than Heaven. He talks about beloved books being bound together by a secret thread. We know their common quality but can't put it into words. Sometimes we stand before a landscape and seem to feel that it embodies what we have been looking for all our lives.[26] Hobbies and friends may also embody this longing for Heaven.

Lewis goes on to explain the reason for these desires that are unique to each one of us. He says that we have these unique desires because our souls each have a curious shape. There is a hollow in each soul that is made to fit a particular swelling in the infinite contours of God's being. Alternatively, your soul is like a key that will unlock one of the many rooms in the Father's house (Jn 14:2). Lewis postulates that your place in Heaven will seem to be made for you and you alone, because you were indeed made for it—stitch by stitch just as a glove is made for a hand.[27] Lewis here echoes the truth of Revelation 2:17 (NIV), where the glorified Lord Jesus Christ says to the church, "He who has an ear, let him hear what the Spirit says to the churches. To him who overcomes, I will give some of the hidden manna. I will also give him a white stone with a new name written on it, known only to him who receives it."

The problem is that though we have this desire for Heaven in each one of our hearts, the desire is often misdirected. Lewis argues that often our desire for Heaven is not yet attached to the right object. The object our desires are attached to will sometimes even appear as a rival to Heaven.[28] He gives the example of a boy who steals time away from his proper studies in Greek to read Shelley. The boy doesn't realize that learning Greek will lead him to more joys like reading Shelley, and even better joys. In the same way we desire certain things and people in this life because they remind us of Heaven.

But many of us shun religion because it seemingly has no relation to our true desires, just as the boy reading Shelley shuns his Greek studies because it seemingly has no relation to his true desire. But that is where we are mistaken. If we would only pursue God through the Bible and through his church, we would find the satisfaction of our deepest desires, which are now only partially satisfied through our present activities.

The desire for Heaven should also lead the Christian to have a different attitude toward death. Lewis professes that the times he most desires death are when there seems to be most of Heaven already present in this life. Such experiences are like a lively introduction to a book that whets one's appetite to read the whole story. All joy awakens our desire for Heaven.[29] If this life is really a "wandering to find home," why should we not look forward to our arrival?[30]

THE GLORY OF HEAVEN

What will life in Heaven be like? Lewis asserts that the promises of Scripture regarding Heaven may very roughly be reduced to five areas. Scripture promises that we will be with Christ; that we will be like him; that we will have glory; that we will in some way be fed or feasted or entertained; and that we will have some sort of official position in the universe.[31]

But what is meant by glory? Lewis explains that glory means good report with God, acceptance by God, response, acknowledgment and welcome into the heart of things. He contends that the door on which we've been knocking all our lives will finally be opened.[32] "At present we are on the outside of the world, the wrong side of the door. We discern the freshness and purity of morning, but they do not make us fresh and pure. We cannot mingle with the splendours we see. But all the leaves of the New Testament are rustling with the rumour that it will not always be so. Some day, God willing, we shall get *in*."[33]

Who will get to enter into this glory? What are the requirements? Lewis claims it is not as though God will refuse you admission to Heaven if you have not got certain character qualities. The bottom line is that if you don't have the beginning of these qualities then you won't want Heaven, and then nothing will make you happy with the deep, strong, unshakable kind of happiness God intends for you.[34]

WORSHIP IN HEAVEN

What will we do in Heaven? The book of Revelation does seem to suggest that the main activity of Heaven will be worship. Lewis addresses the feeling most people tend to have when told that they will spend eternity in worship. Won't it be boring? Lewis says that just because we will spend eternity praising God does not mean that Heaven is going to be like some of our dismal church experiences. The problem is that our worship services on Earth are merely attempts at worship, attempts that are never fully successful, and sometimes 99.9 percent failures, or else total failures! We must remember that in earthly worship we are merely tuning our instruments. We must ask ourselves, if even one experience of tuning our instruments is glorious, what will the symphony be like?[35]

A PLACE OF PERPETUAL GIVING

Lewis also suggests that Heaven will be a place of perpetual giving, a place where only those who have learned the art of giving will reside. Heaven will be the place where our wills are perfectly offered back in delighted and de-lighting obedience to God.[36] Lewis notes that there will be no ownership in Heaven.[37] We shall cast all our crowns at the feet of the One who once wore a crown of thorns.

Lewis has a delightful little piece where he contemplates whether or not there will be books in Heaven. He surmises that there *will* be books in Heaven, but only the ones from our libraries that we have given away on Earth. And the dirty thumbprints left by our book's borrowers will be turned into beau-tiful illustrations, just as the scars of the martyrs will be turned into stars.[38]

PEOPLE IN HEAVEN

The fact that Heaven will be a place of perpetual giving leads Lewis in *The Great Divorce* to picture the people of Heaven as those who literally have love flowing out of them. Lewis purports that the people of Heaven have love shining out from their faces and all their limbs as though they had just bathed in some liquid.[39] The heavenly residents are bright, and the earth shakes with their every footstep. Some are naked, some robed. However, the naked ones do not seem any less adorned, and the robes on those wearing them reveal rather than disguise the massive grandeur of muscle and the radiant smoothness of their flesh. Some are bearded, but no one in the group strikes Lewis as being of a certain age.[40]

When asked if there are no famous men in Heaven, one of the heavenly people responds that they are all famous. They are all known by the only One who can render a perfect judgment.[41]

Lewis also pictures the Heaven-*bound* person in *The Chronicles of Narnia*. In a letter to a child, Lewis writes that anyone in our world who devotes his whole life to seeking Heaven will be like Reepicheep.[42] Reepicheep the mouse is the perfect picture of the Heaven-bound person, for he is determined to sail to Aslan's country at all cost.

PAIN IN HEAVEN?

Lewis had the curious notion that there might be pain in Heaven.[43] This ties into his belief in Purgatory and to his belief that there may be different levels in Heaven that the blessed can progressively move through. Remember, in *The Great Divorce* the ghosts when they first arrive on the "outskirts" of Heaven experience pain as the grass there pierces their unsubstantial feet.

However, Lewis claims, even if there are pains in Heaven, all who understand will desire that kind of pain.[44] As Screwtape says of Wormwood's dead patient, he may still have to encounter pain, but it will be a pain that he embraces.[45]

Why might we have to endure pain in Heaven, according to Lewis? In *The Great Divorce*, he suggests that some might have to endure the pain of shame in Heaven. One of the ghosts on the outskirts of Heaven is afraid of having people see through him.[46] And one of the bright, solid people tells the ghost that he will find shame nourishing if he will accept it.[47]

In another place Lewis suggests that the perfected humility of a saved soul in Heaven may bear the shame of sin forever, rejoicing in the occasion that sin furnished for God's mercy to work and glad that the sin should be common knowledge to the universe. Lewis admits that such joy in Heaven will be "an acquired taste," and certain ways of life on Earth may render the taste impossible to acquire. He admits he doesn't know for certain if this is true, but he thinks the possibility worth keeping in mind.[48] One wonders what scriptural basis Lewis would find for such an idea. And one wonders why we should experience unending shame, especially in Heaven, the place of total beatitude.

Sex in Heaven?

Some people ask, Will there be sex in Heaven? To this Lewis responds
that Scripture forbids us to think of life in Heaven as a sexual life. Thus
our imagination is reduced to two unpleasant alternatives: either we will
have very unearthly bodies in Heaven, or there will be a perpetual sexual
fast. As regards the fast, Lewis draws the analogy, mentioned earlier, that
our present outlook might be like that of a small boy who, on being told
that the sexual act was the highest bodily pleasure, should immediately
ask whether you ate chocolates at the same time. Lewis asserts that we
are in the same position. We know the sexual life; we do not know, except
in glimpses, the other thing which, in Heaven, will leave no room for
sex.[49]

A Sensory Life?

But will our life in Heaven be a sensory life? Lewis says we do not know. He
surmises that our life in Heaven will differ from our sensory life here, not
as emptiness differs from water or water from wine but as a flower differs
from a bulb or a cathedral from an architect's drawing.[50]

Lewis uses the illustration of a mother, who happens to be an artist, living with her son in a dungeon. The mother has seen the outside world and
continually tries to describe it to her son, who has only known life in the
dungeon. She draws pictures for her son that for quite some time seem to
satisfy his curiosity about the outside world. Then one day, the boy makes
a comment that gives his mother pause to think. She says, "But you don't
think that the real world is full of lines drawn with lead pencil?" And he
suddenly asks her, "What, no pencil lines there?" The boy conceived the
outside world as being literally like that two-dimensional drawing which
his mother had made for him. He could not imagine what the three-di-
mensional outside world could really be like. Lewis suggests that our natural experiences are like the drawing, pencil lines on flat paper. If those
natural experiences vanish in Heaven, they will vanish only as pencil lines
vanish when replaced by a real landscape. In Heaven our experience will
not be that of a candle flame put out but that of a candle flame that becomes invisible because someone has pulled up the blinds and let in the
blazing light of the sun.[51]

FULLY HUMAN

Lewis posits that Heaven will be the place where we become fully human, where we will discover all that we were created to be.[52] That is why we know so much more about Heaven than about hell, because Heaven is the home of humanity.[53] Heaven is the place where everything becomes more and more itself.[54] In that sense, Heaven will be truly home, as Jewel the Unicorn suggests when he reaches the real Narnia at the end of *The Last Battle.*[55]

NO MORALITY

Because we will have already become fully human in Heaven, there will be no more need for law or morality. Lewis maintains that is why Dante's Heaven is so right and Milton's, with its military discipline, so ridiculous. This is why we must picture Heaven in terms that seem almost frivolous. In this world our most momentous actions are impeded. We can picture unimpeded, and therefore delighted, action only by the analogy of play and dance. Thus we get the mistaken notion that if life in Heaven is as free as all that then it will matter as little as play and dance do in this life. In Heaven the law will vanish, but the results of having lived faithfully under it will not.[56] As Peter suggests at the end of *The Last Battle,* Heaven will be the place where everything is allowed because everything we will want to do there will be good.[57]

REUNION

Someone might ask, Will I be reunited with my loved ones in Heaven? Will I recognize them there? Lewis provides a multifaceted answer.

In a letter written in 1952, he notes that Heaven is presented to us under the symbols of a dinner party, a wedding, a city and a concert. It would be grotesque to suppose that the guests or citizens or members of the choir won't know each other![58]

In *The Four Loves,* he develops his answer further. He says that whether we will know our loved ones in Heaven may depend upon the way in which our love was developing for them on Earth. Someone we had a merely natural love for on Earth might not even be interesting to us in Heaven. Meeting such a love again in Heaven might be like meeting an old friend from school

at a class reunion. All of our common interests and occupations will probably have changed. In Heaven, Lewis argues, a love that never embodied Love
himself will be irrelevant. All that is not eternal will be eternally out of
date.[59]

Furthermore, Lewis makes clear that reunion with the loved dead is not
the goal of the Christian life. He quotes Augustine with approval: "Thou
hast made us for thyself, and our heart has no rest till it comes to Thee."[60]

Lewis is most negative in his reaction to the idea of reunion in *A Grief Observed.* Perhaps it was his grief that clouded his thinking at this point. Or
maybe he didn't want to hope too much for the possibility of reunion with
his dead wife. At any rate, Lewis asserts that all the stuff about family reunions "on the further shore," pictured in earthly terms is unscriptural, all
out of bad hymns. It doesn't ring true. Lewis argues that it couldn't be like
that because reality never repeats.[61]

He contends that Heaven will not be the happy past restored; there will
not be reunion in this sense. But this does not rule out completely the idea
of reunion in Heaven. Lewis writes about such reunions in his fiction. There
are some unpleasant reunions in *The Great Divorce* as well as some very pleasant ones in *The Last Battle.* One of the most meaningful reunions recounted
in the latter book is that between King Tirian and his dead father.

> But before he [Tirian] had had much time to think of this, he felt two strong
> arms thrown about him and felt a bearded kiss on his cheeks and heard a
> well-remembered voice saying:
>   "What, lad? Art thicker and taller since I last touched thee?"
>   It was his own father, the good King Erlian: but not as Tirian had seen him
> last when they brought him home pale and wounded from his fight with the
> giant, nor even as Tirian remembered him in his later years when he was a
> grey-headed warrior. This was his father young and merry as he could just
> remember him from very early days, when he himself had been a little boy
> playing games with his father in the castle garden at Cair Paravel, just before
> bedtime on summer evenings. The very smell of the bread-and-milk he used
> to have for supper came back to him.[62]

The prerequisite to reunion in Heaven, which Lewis pictures for us in *The
Last Battle,* is to recognize that "all the *real* countries—are only spurs jutting
out from the great mountains of Aslan. We have only to walk along the

ridge, upward and inward, till it joins on."[63] Reunion with our loved ones in Heaven can happen only when Aslan, the Lord, is put at the center. If we are moving toward him who is at the center of all realities, then in him we shall also meet all the others who are moving toward that center. But in Heaven the loves that never embodied Love himself will be irrelevant.

THE RESURRECTION OF THE BODY

Another doctrine related to Heaven that people often question is the Christian doctrine of the resurrection of the body. What did Lewis think about it? Did he conceive of Heaven as only a place for disembodied spirits? Numerous remarks throughout his writings show that Lewis believed in the resurrection of the body.

He believed in the resurrection of the body so much that he could write very simply to a friend, at a time when they were both experiencing illness, that they must look forward to the fine new machines (latest resurrection model) that would be waiting for them in the Divine garage![64]

Lewis contends that the remark so often made that "Heaven is a state of mind" bears witness to the wintry and deathlike culture in which we are now living. He points out that Christianity is the one great religion that teaches that the body is good.[65] Christianity teaches that Heaven is not merely a state of the spirit but a state of the body as well.[66]

Lewis admits that there is difficulty in reconciling the ideas that Heaven is, on the one hand, a life in Christ, and that it is, on the other hand, a bodily life. In some of our most spiritual experiences on Earth the body seems irrelevant. And if we try to think of Heaven as life in a body, our minds introduce some vague dream of Platonic paradises instead of the mystical vision of God that we feel (Lewis says rightly) to be more important. But if the discrepancy between life in Christ and life in a body were final, then it would follow that God was originally mistaken when he gave us bodies. We must conclude that the discrepancy is precisely one of the disorders that Heaven will come to heal.[67]

Lewis claims that our present bodies were not given us so that they could one day be done away with. Rather, they were given us for training purposes, just as ponies are given to schoolboys in order to train them how to ride horses.[68] As we have already seen, Lewis works out this analogy to its final and stunning denouement in *The Great Divorce* and the story of the lizard of lust that becomes a great winged horse.

There are problems with the physical universe and our bodies now. These problems—sickness, old age, pollution, and so on—were introduced by the Fall. But that doesn't mean that the physical universe must be erased to correct these problems. On the contrary, Lewis declares that nature will be cured, not tamed nor sterilized.[69]

Lewis admits that no one can imagine what life in the glorified body will be like. However, he points out that we can picture very few things we believe in—will, thought, time, atoms, astronomical distance, places we have never been or even faces we haven't seen for a long time.[70]

What about the idea that some people have, seemingly based upon Scripture, that we will reassume the same bodies we had on Earth? Lewis believes it is a foolish fancy, not justified by Scripture, that we will recover those particular units of matter that we ruled before. There won't be enough to go around, for we all live in secondhand bodies. Lewis contends there are atoms in his chin that probably have served many another man, dog, eel or dinosaur. We don't even retain the same particles in this life; we are constantly shedding some cells and gaining others.[71] While Jesus reassumed the same body that had died only days before on the cross, this does not necessarily mean that we will do the same. What I Corinthians 15 and Jesus' resurrection teach us is that there will be elements of continuity and discontinuity between our earthly bodies and our resurrection bodies.

Lewis's most extensive reflection on the resurrection of the body comes in his final book prepared for publication before his death, *Letters to Malcolm*. In the final chapter of that book he makes several points.

First, he argues that the doctrine of the resurrection of the body is not concerned with matter as such; it is not concerned with waves and atoms and all that. He theorizes that what the soul cries out for is the resurrection of the senses. He makes the point that even in this life matter would mean nothing to us if it were not the source of sensations.

Second, Lewis suggests that we have already experienced some feeble and intermittent power of raising dead sensations from their graves. What he is talking about is the power of memory. But Lewis does not mean that we will merely have excellent memories in Heaven of our sensuous experience on

Earth. He means that memory is a dim reflection of a power that the soul will exercise in Christ in Heaven. He gives as an example the fact that he can now communicate to his friends the fields of his boyhood only imperfectly, by words. He suggests that in Heaven, perhaps, he will be able to take his friends for a walk through those fields.

Third, Lewis points out how at present we think of the soul as being inside the body. But the glorified body of the resurrection, as he conceives it—the sensuous life raised from its death—will be inside the soul, just as God is not in space but space is in God. This image suggests a dominance of the soul over the body after the resurrection, as opposed to a dominance of the body over the soul such as we often experience it in this life. As Jesus said to his disciples in the Garden of Gethsemane, when they fell asleep while he was praying: "The spirit is willing, but the body is weak" (Mt 26:41 NIV). In the resurrection there will be no weakness of the body to impede, in any way, the activities of the soul. Rather, the soul will perfectly exercise itself through the resurrected sensuous life that the soul will contain.

Lewis denies that this "resurrection of the body" will be mere illusion. Memory is not illusion. Memory is just as real as the original events we remember.

Lewis anticipates Malcolm's protest that this is no resurrection of the body but merely a dream world filled with dream bodies, not real. Lewis protests that the type of resurrection body he conceives of is neither more nor less real than the bodies we have always known. The so-called real world of our present experience has no place in the world described by physics or even by physiology. He points out how physical things enter our experience only by becoming sensation or conception, that is, by becoming something spiritual. And when the soul or spirit is raised and glorified, it will eventually transform everything in the physical realm.

When will this resurrection happen? Lewis recognizes that there is an intermediate state during which the soul, at death, goes to be with the Lord in Heaven, while the body rests in the grave. And he recognizes that the resurrection will take place at the end of the age when Christ returns to the earth.[72] (More on that in the next chapter.)

THE ULTIMATE CHOICE

If we want to be like God and one day see him as he is, Lewis makes clear that we must make a choice. He quotes William Law with approval: "If you have not chosen the Kingdom of God, it will make in the end no difference what you have chosen instead."[73] If we insist upon holding on to hell, or anything other than God in this life, then we shall not see Heaven; if we accept Heaven, we shall not be able to keep even the smallest souvenirs from hell.[74]

But won't that choice, even if it requires plucking out our right eye, be worth it? If only one day we can hear those wonderful words of Aslan spoken to us: "The term is over: the holidays have begun. The dream is ended: this is the morning."[75]

25

THE WORLD'S LAST NIGHT

AS WE HAVE ALREADY SEEN, C. S. Lewis held that belief in the Second Coming of Christ is one of the things that unites the evangelical and Anglo-Catholic against the liberal or the modernist.[1] But what did Lewis believe about the Second Coming of Christ and the end of the world?

In his last official interview Lewis recognized that the world might stop at any time, but meanwhile, he insisted, we should go on doing our duty. The most important thing is to be found at our post when Christ returns. We should live every day as though it might be our last, but we should also plan as though the world might last a hundred years.[2]

Lewis tried to follow his own advice, seeking to live each day as if it might be his last. He was a bold witness for Christ to the end of his life, in his everyday conversation as reported by friends and in his daily correspondence that is available for all to read. At the same time, Lewis planned as though the world might last another hundred years. Up to the last days of his life he was preparing new books for publication, books that would encourage and instruct many over the coming years.

WHY THE DELAY?

Some people ask, Why has Christ delayed his return to the earth? Lewis answers in very biblical fashion[3] that Christ is delaying because

> He wants to give us the chance of joining His side freely. I do not suppose you and I would have thought much of a Frenchman who waited till the Allies were marching into Germany and then announced he was on our side. God will invade. But I wonder whether people who ask God to interfere openly and directly in our world quite realise what it will be like when He

does. When that happens, it is the end of the world. When the author walks on the stage the play is over. God is going to invade, all right: but what is the good of saying you are on His side then, when you see the whole natural universe melting away like a dream and something else—something it never entered your head to conceive—comes crashing in; something so beautiful to some of us and so terrible to others that none of us will have any choice left? For this time it will be God without disguise; something so overwhelming that it will strike either irresistible love or irresistible horror into every creature. It will be too late then to choose your side. There is no use saying you choose to lie down when it has become impossible to stand up. That will not be the time for choosing: it will be the time when we discover which side we really have chosen, whether we realised it before or not. Now, today, this moment, is our chance to choose the right side. God is holding back to give us that chance. It will not last for ever. We must take it or leave it.[4]

THE LAST BATTLE

Lewis believed that God is one day going to return to this world in person and that there will be a physical end to this universe as we know it. Lewis pictured the end of the world using traditional biblical imagery in *The Last Battle* mixed with some of his Narnian imagery. Thus when Narnia comes to an end all the stars fall out of the sky,[5] but true to the ethos of Narnia, the stars are people, and they join Aslan in his new Narnia. Next, all the creatures of Narnia pass through the stable door and come right up to Aslan. As each one looks Aslan in the face, either their expression turns to one of fear and hatred and then they pass into the shadow on Aslan's left, or they look into Aslan's face and love him and thus pass to his right into the new Narnia.[6] We are not told what happens to the creatures who pass into Aslan's shadow. After this the great dragons and giant lizards of Narnia start tearing and crunching all the vegetation of the land until the whole country is only bare rock and earth.[7] When the sun comes up for the last time in the old Narnia it is a huge red sun, such as Digory and Polly saw in the land of Charn during its last days. In the reflection of that sun the waters look like blood, and the moon also looks red.[8] The sun begins to shoot out flames; the moon and sun are rolled together in one huge ball like a burning coal, with great lumps of fire dropping out of it into the sea from which clouds of steam rise up.[9] Finally, at the word of Aslan, Father Time puts an end to

Narnia by reaching out and grabbing the sun, squeezing it like an orange until there is total darkness.[10]

THE WORLD'S LAST NIGHT

Lewis's most extensive treatment of the doctrine of Christ's Second Coming is given in an article he wrote for the winter 1952 volume of *Religion in Life*. That article was originally titled "The Christian Hope—Its Meaning for Today" and later retitled "The World's Last Night." The essay is included in Lewis's collection of essays under the same title. In that essay he posits that there are many reasons why the modern Christian and theologian might hesitate to give to the doctrine of the Second Coming that emphasis which it was given by our ancestors. However, he asserts that it is impossible to retain belief in the divinity of Christ and the truth of Christian revelation while abandoning or neglecting this doctrine. It is part of the Apostles' Creed, it is foretold in Acts 1:11, and Jesus promised during his trial that he would come again on the clouds of Heaven (see Mt 26:64). Lewis maintains that if the Second Coming is not an integral part of the faith once given to the saints, he does not know what is.[11]

In this essay Lewis tries to deal with some of the ideas that keep modern people from a firm belief in, or keep them from giving due attention to, the return of Christ. He posits that the reasons for modern embarrassment about this doctrine fall into two groups: the theoretical and the practical.

Lewis deals with the theoretical issues first. He notes that many people are shy of this doctrine because of the overemphasis put upon it by theologians such as Dr. Albert Schweitzer. According to this school of thought, Jesus' apocalyptic emphasis was the core of his teaching. But, Lewis reasons, because this aspect of Jesus' teaching was overemphasized by Schweitzer and others, we might be in danger of overreacting and falling into the opposite and equally bad error of overlooking this doctrine.

Lewis admits that we can dismiss Jesus' apocalyptic emphasis as being merely part and parcel of the thinking of his age, but to do so is really begging the question. How are we to know that the thinking of Jesus' time was wrong on this point? We are assuming that the thought of our age, that there will not be a sudden, catastrophic end to history, is correct. No one would reject Jesus' apocalyptic simply because it was common to first-century Palestine unless he had first concluded that such apocalyptic thinking was wrong. But on what basis can we justifiably conclude that? There is no basis. So we must approach Jesus and his teaching about the end of the world with an open mind.

A more severe objection to Jesus' teaching on this point is presented by people who say, "But Jesus was wrong. He said that the end of the world would happen within his own generation, and it didn't." Lewis answers this objection by pointing out that Jesus confessed his ignorance about the day and the hour of his return (Mk 13:32). Lewis contends that Jesus' statement in Mark 13:30-31 proves that he *was* ignorant.[12]

Lewis notes another theoretical objection to the doctrine of the Second Coming. That is that this doctrine is uncongenial to the whole evolutionary or developmental character of modern thought. Moderns like to think that the world is slowly growing toward perfection, but Jesus' apocalyptic teaching suggests the opposite, that there will be a sudden, violent end to the universe brought about from the outside. Lewis's answer to this objection is to point out that the modern concept of progress or evolution, as popularly conceived, is a myth. We have already explored Lewis's thinking on this point in the chapter on Creation. Lewis thinks that this myth distracts us from our central duties. How are we to guess what act of the world play we are in? Lewis maintains that we cannot know when the world drama will end. It is none of our business. Our job is to play our individual parts to the hilt. That is what matters most.[13]

From here Lewis moves on to deal with the practical objections to the doctrine of the Second Coming. He admits that this doctrine has led some Christians in the past into great follies. Many have tried to guess the date of Christ's return or have accepted as certain the dates that many quacks have proposed. He cites the example of William Miller, who claimed that Christ would return on March 21, 1843. Lewis urges that the answer to such hysteria is to point people back to Jesus' teaching, which consists of three points: He will certainly return, we cannot know the date, and therefore we must be ready for his return at all times. Lewis asserts that Donne's question, "What if this present were the world's last night?" should be equally relevant to us at all times.[14]

Another practical reason why some people have rejected this doctrine is because some Christians have pressed it upon the minds of others with the purpose of exciting fear. But, Lewis argues, this is not its right use. Religious fear can have a proper use, but the problem with perpetual excitement about the Second Coming is that it is impossible. Such a feeling of crisis is only transitory. Such excitement cannot be our regular spiritual diet. Lewis maintains that what is important is not perpetual fear or hope about the end, but that we should always take it into account. He draws an analogy with the case of a seventy-year-old man. Such a man need not always be feeling or talking about his approaching death. But he should always take it into account. He would be foolish to embark on projects that might require twenty more years of life. He should long since have drawn up his own will. Lewis contends that what death is to the individual, the Second Coming is to the whole human race. We must constantly remember that the whole of humanity is in the same precarious situation as the seventy-year-old man. Empires and civilizations are transitory. All worldly achievements and triumphs will come to an end. The earth will not always be habitable. Humanity is as mortal as individual people are.

If we take these considerations by themselves, we might think that our efforts for the good of posterity are worthless. But we must remember that we are not just facing the end of the world at any moment. We are facing the possibility of the coming judgment that could happen at any time. It is essential that we should be at our posts doing God's will when the inspection comes, whether God's will for us involves the simple labor of feeding pigs or the more complex labor of devising good plans to deliver humanity from some potential calamity one hundred years from now.

Lewis insists that we need to think of the coming judgment not just in terms of the punishment that may follow it but in terms of the verdict. One day the only perfect Judge will render a perfectly correct verdict on each of us. Lewis doesn't find the biblical pictures of physical catastrophe help one so much as the naked idea of judgment. We cannot always be excited, but we can train ourselves to ask how the thing which we are saying or doing, or failing to do, every moment will look in the light of that final judgment. Lewis draws an analogy to women who sometimes have the problem of trying to judge by artificial light how a dress will look in the daylight. We all have a similar problem in the spiritual realm. We must dress our souls not for the artificial light of this present world but for the daylight of the next world. The good soul is the one that can face the light of eternity.[15]

While Lewis didn't write much about the Second Coming of Christ, the end of the world or the final judgment, what he did write is typical of his entire work. Christians of differing end-time persuasions might wish to add a great deal to what Lewis had to say. But in handling the doctrine of the Second Coming Lewis accomplished the same thing he did in teaching so many other Christian doctrines so well—he focused on mere Christianity. He emphasized the most important truths that all true Christians have always agreed upon. He defended the doctrine in the midst of a liberalizing, modernist age, and he presented for our edification the truths we most need to hear. What could be more important than to be found at our posts doing our duty when Christ returns? And what question could be more vital to ask ourselves every day than the question which Donne and Lewis ask: "What if this present were the world's last night?"

CONCLUSION

C. S. LEWIS WROTE TO PROFESSOR WILLIAM KINTER on March 28, 1953: "It's fun laying out all my books as a cathedral. Personally I'd make *Miracles* and the other 'treatises' the cathedral school: my children's stories are the real side-chapels, each with its own little altar."[1]

To get a feel for what Lewis was talking about one should visit Westminster Abbey. It matches the type of cathedral Lewis was referring to in his letter. When one visits the abbey, one is almost overwhelmed by the elaborate scheme of it. On a tour one progresses from the nave to the choir to the high altar. Then one can walk through a little door behind the high altar into another chapel, where King Edward VII is buried. Then from there one moves all the way to the opposite end of the abbey, into the Lady Chapel, with its delicate fan vaulting, and the two great queens, Mary Queen of Scots and Elizabeth I, buried on either side. Making one's way back to the main entrance, one can visit several side chapels. And, of course, there is Poet's Corner, where many of the famed writers of Great Britain are buried and/or memorialized. Outside the main structure of the cathedral itself there are numerous buildings and rooms such as the Jerusalem Room, where the Westminster Confession of Faith was penned.

Lewis's work as a whole does bear some resemblance to a cathedral. His work is rather elaborate when considered in its entirety—forty books published during his lifetime, not to mention numerous articles, poems and countless letters. Each of the Narnia books functions like a little side chapel with an altar pointing out our need for redemption through the blood of Aslan (Christ). The books of the cathedral school—*Miracles, Mere Christianity, The Problem of Pain, The Abolition of Man, The Four Loves, Reflections on the Psalms, Letters to Malcolm, The Weight of Glory* and *The World's Last Night*—all address the mind as well as the heart, preparing one to accept Christ or to grow in knowledge of and a relationship with Christ. Lewis's autobiographical works—*The Pilgrim's Regress, Surprised by Joy* and *A Grief Observed*—take us, in a manner of speaking, into the most intimate part of the cathedral, where they reveal Lewis sometimes wrestling with, sometimes worshiping the triune God. Lewis's novels—*Out of the Silent Planet, Perelandra, That Hideous Strength* and *Till We Have Faces*—all point to the high altar of the mystery of Christ crucified. Lewis's poetry and literary criticism certainly function as "The Poet's Corner" of his life's work. And even those works, in subtle and not-so-subtle ways, point us to the ultimate reality of God in Jesus.

Like Westminster Abbey, Lewis's work grew over the years as he grew, adding a transept here, a side chapel there. His books are the product of a fertile, alive, growing and variegated mind. They are the product of an imagination engaged in the Great Dance. Thus they can provide years of delighted exploration, even to the most expert reader.

People who look for greater uniformity, a single plan, might think a structure like Westminster Abbey imperfect. But I find such a cathedral to be intriguing, the way it has grown over the centuries, displaying a unity in diversity. In the same way, I find the diverse aspects of Lewis's singular work to be fascinating. Like a great cathedral, Lewis's theology is a work of art. Is his work a perfect theological structure? No. But is it one that points, as the spire of every cathedral should, to the King of Heaven, Jesus Christ? Yes. And what could be more important than that?

NOTES

Introduction

[1] C. S. Lewis, *The Problem of Pain* (New York: Macmillan, 1986), p. 10.

[2] C. S. Lewis, *Mere Christianity* (New York: Macmillan, 1984), p. 135.

[3] C. S. Lewis, introduction to *The Incarnation of the Word of God* (London: Bles, The Centenary Press, 1944), p. 6.

Chapter One: Defending the Faith

[1] Sheldon Vanauken, *Encounter with Light*, Marion E. Wade Collection, Wheaton College, Wheaton, Ill., p. 18. This booklet was later revised and republished as one chapter in *A Severe Mercy* (New York: Bantam, 1979).

[2] C. S. Lewis, *The Weight of Glory* (New York: Macmillan, 1980), p. 35.

[3] C. S. Lewis, *The World's Last Night and Other Essays* (San Diego: Harcourt Brace, 1987), p. 26.

[4] C. S. Lewis, *God in the Dock* ed. Walter Hooper (Grand Rapids, Mich.: Eerdmans, 1994), p. 103. See also Lewis's poem "The Apologist's Evening Prayer" in C. S. Lewis, *Poems* (San Diego: Harcourt Brace, 1992), p. 129.

[5] C. S. Lewis, *The Pilgrim's Regress* (Grand Rapids, Mich.: Eerdmans, 1981), pp. 202-3.

[6] Ibid., p. 8.

[7] Lewis, *Weight of Glory*, pp. 6-7.

[8] C. S. Lewis, *The Lion, the Witch and the Wardrobe* (New York: Macmillan, 1970), pp. 64-65.

[9] C. S. Lewis, *Surprised by Joy* (New York: Harcourt Brace Jovanovich, New York, 1955), pp. 17-18.

[10] Ibid., p. 238.

[11] Lewis, *Pilgrim's Regress*, pp. 204-5.

[12] Vanauken, *Encounter with Light*, pp. 18-19.

[13] Lewis, *Mere Christianity*, p. 19.

[14] Ibid., p. 37.

[15] C. S. Lewis, *Miracles* (New York: Macmillan, 1978), p. 15.

[16] George Sayer, *Jack: A Life of C. S. Lewis* (Wheaton, Ill.: Crossway, 1994), p. 307.

[17] C. S. Lewis, *Miracles* (London: Geoffrey Bles, 1947), p. 27.

[18] Walter Hooper, "Oxford's Bonny Fighter," in *C. S. Lewis at the Breakfast Table*, ed. James Como (New York: Harcourt Brace, 1992), pp. 162-63.

[19] Sayer, *Jack*, p. 307.

[20] Hooper, "Oxford's Bonny Fighter," p. 164.

[21] A. N. Wilson, *C. S. Lewis: A Biography* (New York: W. W. Norton, 1990), pp. 214-15.

[22] Sayer, *Jack*, p. 308.

[23] Lewis, *Mere Christianity*, p. 46.

[24] Lewis uses these phrases in his essay "On Obstinacy in Belief." See *World's Last Night*, p. 30.

[25] Lewis, *Mere Christianity*, p. 45.

[26] Ibid., pp. 46-48.

[27] Ibid., p. 48.

[28] Ibid., p. 49.

[29] Ibid., p. 52.

[30] Ibid., p. 55.

[31] See Josh McDowell, *More Than a Carpenter* (Wheaton, Ill.: Tyndale House, 1977), chap. 2.

Chapter Two: Scripture

[1]C. S. Lewis, *The Problem of Pain* (New York: Macmillan, 1986), p. 71.

[2]Ibid., p. 80.

[3]C. S. Lewis, *Miracles* (New York: Macmillan, 1960), p. 33.

[4]C. S. Lewis, *God in the Dock*, ed. Walter Hooper (Grand Rapids, Mich.: Eerdmans, 1994), p. 42.

[5]Lewis, *Miracles*, pp. 133-34 n. 1.

[6]Lewis, *Problem of Pain*, p. 77.

[7]Lewis, *Miracles*, p. 134.

[8]C. S. Lewis, *The Weight of Glory* (New York: Macmillan, 1980), p. 84.

[9]Lewis, *God in the Dock*, pp. 158-59.

[10]C. S. Lewis, *Surprised by Joy* (New York: Harcourt Brace Jovanovich, 1955), p. 236.

[11]C. S. Lewis, *Christian Reflections* (London: Geoffrey Bles, 1967), p. 155.

[12]C. S. Lewis, *The World's Last Night and Other Essays* (San Diego: Harcourt Brace, 1987), pp. 98-99.

[13]Lewis, *Christian Reflections*, p. 145.

[14]C. S. Lewis, *Reflections on the Psalms* (San Diego: Harcourt Brace Jovanovich, 1958), p. 19.

[15]Ibid., p. 22.

[16]W. H. Lewis, ed., *Letters of C. S. Lewis* (New York: Harcourt Brace Jovanovich, 1975), pp. 286-87 (May 7, 1959).

[17]Lewis, *Reflections on the Psalms*, p. 119.

[18]Lewis, *Weight of Glory*, p. 51.

[19]Lewis, *God in the Dock*, pp. 134-35.

[20]Lewis, *Christian Reflections*, pp. 162-63.

[21]Ibid., pp. 163-64.

[22]C. S. Lewis, *The Literary Impact of the Authorized Version* (Philadelphia: Fortress, 1967), pp. 4-5.

[23]Ibid., pp. 32-33.

[24]W. H. Lewis and Walter Hooper, eds., *Letters of C. S. Lewis*, rev. and enl. ed. (San Diego: Harcourt Brace, 1993), p. 432 (August 3, 1953).

[25]Ibid., p. 434.

[26]Ibid., p. 428 (November 8, 1952).

[27]Ibid., p. 423 (June 20, 1952).

[28]Ibid., p. 422 (May 28, 1952).

[29]Ibid., p. 502 (December 28, 1961).

[30]Quoted in Clyde S. Kilby, *The Christian World of C. S. Lewis* (Grand Rapids, Mich.: Eerdmans, 1964), pp. 153-54.

[31]See Mt 22:32, 43 (where Jesus bases his argument on the tense of a word in Scripture); Jn 10:34; Mt 19:4 in reference to Gen 2:24; and Jn 16:13-15.

[32]See 1 Pet 1:12; 2 Tim 3:16; 2 Pet 1:21; 3:16.

[33]It should be noted that though Lewis viewed the accounts of Creation and the Fall as being written in a mythical genre, there is some evidence to suggest that Lewis still believed in an historical Adam. See A. N. Wilson, *C. S. Lewis: A Biography* (New York: W. W. Norton, 1990), p. 210.

[34]See Mt 12:39-41; 16:4; Lk 11:29-32; Mt 24:37-38; Lk 17:26-27; 3:36; Heb 11:7; 1 Pet 3:20; 2 Pet 2:5; Lk 3:38; Rom 5; 1 Cor 15:22, 45; 1 Tim 2:13-14; Jude 1:14; Jas 5:11.

[35]For a more extended examination of Lewis's view of Scripture see Michael J. Christensen, *C. S. Lewis on Scripture* (Waco, Tex.: Word, 1979).

Chapter Three: The Three-Personal God

[1]C. S. Lewis, *Christian Reflections* (London: Geoffrey Bles, 1967), p. 5.

[2]See C. S. Lewis, *God in the Dock*, ed. Walter Hooper (Grand Rapids, Mich.: Eerdmans, 1994), p. 185, and Lewis's letter to Dom Bede Griffiths of August 1962 in W. H. Lewis, *Letters of C. S. Lewis* (New York: Harcourt Brace &

World, 1966), p. 305.

[3]See C. S. Lewis, *Miracles* (New York: Macmillan, 1978), p. 76 nn. 2-4.

[4]Ibid.

[5]Ibid., p. 79.

[6]C. S. Lewis, *The Weight of Glory* (New York: Macmillan, 1980), p. 75.

[7]C. S. Lewis, *Mere Christianity* (New York: Macmillan, 1977), p. 142. See also Lewis, *Miracles*, p. 85, and Lewis, *Christian Reflections*, p. 79.

[8]Lewis, *God in the Dock*, p. 182.

[9]Lewis, *Mere Christianity*, pp. 142-43.

[10]Ibid., p. 143.

[11]J. N. D. Kelly, *Early Christian Doctrines* (San Francisco: Harper & Row, 1978), p. 277.

[12]Lewis, *Mere Christianity*, p. 151.

[13]Kelly, *Early Christian Doctrines*, p. 277.

[14]Lewis, *Mere Christianity*, pp. 151-52. See also C. S. Lewis, *The Problem of Pain* (New York: Macmillan, 1986), pp. 29, 91; C. S. Lewis, *The Screwtape Letters* (New York: Macmillan, 1977), p. 82, and Lewis, *Christian Reflections*, p. 80.

[15]Lewis, *Mere Christianity*, pp. 152-53.

[16]Lewis, *Problem of Pain*, p. 153.

[17]C. S. Lewis, *Letters to Malcolm: Chiefly on Prayer* (New York: Harcourt Brace Jovanovich, 1964), pp. 92-93.

[18]C. S. Lewis, *Perelandra* (New York: Macmillan, 1965), p. 217.

[19]Ibid., p. 210.

[20]Walter Hooper, *C. S. Lewis Companion and Guide* (New York: HarperCollins, 1996), p. 438.

[21]C. S. Lewis, *The Horse and His Boy* (New York: HarperCollins, 1994), pp. 163-66.

Chapter Four: God's Sovereignty and Human Responsibility

[1]C. S. Lewis, *The Problem of Pain* (New York: Macmillan, 1986), p. 51.

[2]Ibid., p. 66.

[3]See the following Scriptures, which are often cited in support of the doctrine of total depravity: Gen 6:5; Jer 13:23; 17:9; Rom 3:9-18; Eph 2:1; Col 2:13; Tit 1:15.

[4]Lewis, *Problem of Pain*, p. 127.

[5]C. S. Lewis, *The Screwtape Letters* (New York: Macmillan, 1977), p. 128.

[6]C. S. Lewis, *Mere Christianity* (New York: Macmillan, 1977), p. 52.

[7]Ibid., p. 64.

[8]C. S. Lewis, *Perelandra* (New York: Macmillan, 1965), p. 149.

[9]Lewis, *Mere Christianity*, pp. 148-49.

[10]Tony Lane, *Exploring Christian Thought* (Nashville: Thomas Nelson, 1984), p. 80.

[11]Walter Hooper, *C. S. Lewis Companion and Guide* (New York: HarperCollins, 1996), p. 752.

[12]Lewis, *Mere Christianity*, p. 179.

[13]C. S. Lewis, *The Great Divorce* (New York: Macmillan, 1979), p. 125.

[14]Lewis, *God in the Dock*, p. 221.

[15]Lewis, *Miracles*, p. 124.

[16]Ibid., p. 179.

[17]Lewis, *Mere Christianity*, p. 146. Lewis borrows this analogy from G. K. Chesterton, *Orthodoxy* (Wheaton, Ill.: Harold Shaw Publishers, 1994), p. 81.

[18]C. S. Lewis, *The Lion, the Witch and the Wardrobe* (New York: Macmillan, 1970), p. 135.

[19]For this insight I am indebted to Clyde S. Kilby, *Images of Salvation* (Wheaton, Ill.: Harold Shaw Publishers, 1978), p. 63.

[20]C. S. Lewis, *The Silver Chair* (New York: Macmillan, 1973), pp. 18-19.

[21]W. H. Lewis and Walter Hooper, eds., *Letters of C. S. Lewis* (San Diego: Harcourt Brace, 1993), p. 426.

[22]Perhaps it is true that one should not generalize about conversions, but Lewis does in his preface to Joy David-man's *Smoke on the Mountain*, where he writes: "For of course every story of conversion is the story of a blessed defeat." See Joy Davidman, *Smoke on the Mountain* (London: Hodder & Stoughton, 1955), p. 8.

[23]Lewis and Hooper, *Letters of C. S. Lewis*, pp. 432-34.

[24]C. S. Lewis, *English Literature in the Sixteenth Century* (Oxford: Oxford University Press, 1973), pp. 33-34.

[25]*The Book of Common Prayer of the Protestant Episcopal Church* (1945), p. 606.

[26]Lewis, *English Literature in the Sixteenth Century*, p. 43.

[27]C. S. Lewis, *Surprised by Joy* (New York: Harcourt Brace Jovanovich, 1955), pp. 227-29.

[28]Ibid., p. 237.

[29]C. S. Lewis, *The Four Loves* (San Diego: Harcourt Brace Jovanovich, 1960), p. 172. Though the Old Testament says nothing of Esau's eternal destiny, Paul's comments on this in Romans 9 are taken by some interpreters of Scripture as pertaining to Esau's eternal destiny.

[30]C. S. Lewis, *A Grief Observed* (New York: Bantam, 1976), pp. 36-37.

[31]C. S. Lewis, *Letters to Malcolm: Chiefly on Prayer* (New York: Harcourt Brace Jovanovich, 1964), pp. 49-50.

[32]Austin Farrer, *The Glass of Vision* (Westminster: Dacre Press; printed by Robert MacLehose and Co., University Press, Glasgow, 1948), pp. 32-33.

[33]C. S. Lewis, *God in the Dock*, ed. Walter Hooper (Grand Rapids, Mich.: Eerdmans, 1994), p. 261.

[34]Austin Farrer, *Lord, I Believe*, 2nd ed. (London: The Faith Press, 1958), p. 47.

Chapter Five: Creation

[1]C. S. Lewis, *Miracles* (New York: Macmillan, 1960), p. 33.

[2]C. S. Lewis, *Reflections on the Psalms* (San Diego: Harcourt Brace Jovanovich, 1958), pp. 110-11.

[3]C. S. Lewis, *Mere Christianity* (New York: Macmillan, 1977), p. 45. See also C. S. Lewis, *A Preface to Paradise Lost* (New York: Oxford University Press, 1961), pp. 89-90.

[4]Heb 11:3; Ps 33:6.

[5]C. S. Lewis, *The Magician's Nephew* (New York: Collier, 1973), p. 107.

[6]C. S. Lewis, *Christian Reflections* (London: Geoffrey Bles, 1967), p. 6.

[7]W. H. Lewis and Walter Hooper, eds., *Letters of C. S. Lewis* (San Diego: Harcourt Brace, 1993), p. 371.

[8]C. S. Lewis, *Letters to Malcolm: Chiefly on Prayer* (New York: Harcourt Brace Jovanovich, 1964), p. 44.

[9]C. S. Lewis, *The Four Loves* (San Diego: Harcourt Brace Jovanovich, 1960), pp. 175-76.

[10]Lewis, *Problem of Pain*, p. 48.

[11]Lewis, *Letters to Malcolm*, pp. 17-18.

[12]*The Westminster Confession of Faith* (Atlanta: The Committee for Christian Education and Publications, 1990).

[13]Lewis, *Problem of Pain*, p. 69.

[14]For some insights on Lewis's enjoyment of nature, listen to Ken Myers's interview with Clyde Kilby, *Mars Hill Tapes*, vol. 30 (January/February 1998). To order call 1-800-331-6407.

[15]See Clyde S. Kilby and Marjorie Lamp Mead, eds., *Brothers and Friends: The Diaries of Major Warren Hamilton Lewis* (San Francisco: Harper & Row, 1982).

[16]Lewis, *Reflections on the Psalms*, pp. 78-80.

[17]C. S. Lewis, *God in the Dock*, ed. Walter Hooper (Grand Rapids, Mich.: Eerdmans, 1994), p. 336.

[18]Ibid., p. 46. See also letter to Captain Bernard Acworth, September 23, 1944, published in *C S L: The Bulletin of the New York C. S. Lewis Society*, vol. 27, no. 9-10 (July-August 1996), p. 30.

[19]Lewis, *Problem of Pain*, p. 133.

[20]One problem with viewing the creation days of Genesis 1 as six twenty-four-hour days is that the sun is not created until the fourth day. How can you have twenty-four-hour days without the earth revolving around the sun?

[21]Lewis, *Reflections on the Psalms*, p.115. It is humorous to note how some Christians object to the idea that humanity came from apes as being undignified. After all, what could be more undignified than the idea that humanity came from dirt (Gen 2:7)?

[22]Lewis, *Problem of Pain*, p. 77. See also Lewis's letter to Sister Penelope of January 10, 1952, in Lewis and Hooper, *Letters of C. S. Lewis*, p. 417.

[23]See again A. N. Wilson, *C. S. Lewis: A Biography* (New York: W. W. Norton, 1990), p. 210.

[24]Lewis, *Problem of Pain*, p. 79.

[25]Lewis, *Miracles*, p. 138.

[26]Lewis, *God in the Dock*, p. 39.

[27]Ibid., p. 44.

[28]Lewis, *Mere Christianity*, p. 35.

[29]Lewis, *God in the Dock*, pp. 39, 44, 92.

[30]Ibid., pp. 79, 211.

[31]Quoted in Walter Hooper, *C. S. Lewis Companion and Guide* (New York: HarperCollins, 1994), p. 608.

[32]Interestingly enough, Merlin the magician is brought back from the dead in *That Hideous Strength* to conquer the scientism of the N.I.C.E. Merlin's sort of magic can still be used to conquer the more hideous magic of scientism because Merlin's magic hails from a more innocent age, according to Lewis.

[33]See C. S. Lewis, *The Abolition of Man* (New York: Macmillan, 1978), pp. 86-90. See also *Miracles*, p. 150, where Lewis notes that lawless applied science is Magic's son and heir.

[34]Lewis, *Christian Reflections*, p. 82.

[35]C. S. Lewis, *The World's Last Night and Other Essays* (San Diego: Harcourt Brace, 1987), pp. 101-3. See also C. S. Lewis, *The Weight of Glory* (New York: Macmillan, 1980), p. 89, and Lewis, *Christian Reflections*, pp. 58, 82-93.

[36]Lewis, *Miracles*, p. 177.

[37]Lewis and Hooper, *Letters of C. S. Lewis*, p. 409 (April 23, 1951).

[38]Lewis, *Mere Christianity*, p. 185.

Chapter Six: The Fall

[1]C. S. Lewis, *The Problem of Pain* (New York: Macmillan, 1986), p. 69.

[2]Ibid.

[3]Ibid., p. 70.

[4]Ibid.

[5]Ibid., p. 86.

[6]Ibid., p. 71.

[7]See the footnote in C. S. Lewis, *Miracles* (New York: Macmillan, 1960), p. 134.

[8]Lewis, *Problem of Pain*, pp. 71-72.

[9]Ibid., pp. 72-74.

[10]Ibid., pp. 74-76.

[11]Ibid., p. 78.

[12]Ibid., pp. 78-79.

[13]Ibid., p. 80.

[14]Ibid.

[15]Ibid., p. 81.

[16]Aurelius Augustinus, *The Nicene and Post-Nicene Fathers*, ed. Philip Schaff, vol. 5, *Saint Augustine: Anti-Pelagian Writings* (Grand Rapids, Mich.: Eerdmans, 1956), p. 266.

[17]Lewis, *Problem of Pain*, p. 82 n. 1.

[18]Ibid., p. 83.

[19]For more information on the Augustinian-Pelagian controversy see Van A. Harvey, *A Handbook of Theological*

Terms (New York: Macmillan, 1964), pp. 177-78, for a very brief summary, or see Williston Walker, *A History of the Christian Church,* 4th ed. (New York: Charles Scribner's Sons, 1985), pp. 206-11, for a more detailed summary.

[20]Lewis, *Problem of Pain,* p. 83.

[21]Ibid., p. 84.

[22]Lewis, *Miracles,* p. 126.

[23]Ibid., pp. 129-30.

[24]C. S. Lewis, *The Weight of Glory* (New York: Macmillan, 1980), pp. 113-14.

[25]C. S. Lewis, *Mere Christianity* (New York: Macmillan, 1977), p. 59.

[26]C. S. Lewis, *The World's Last Night and Other Essays* (San Diego: Harcourt Brace, 1987), p. 89.

[27]C. S. Lewis, *God in the Dock,* ed. Walter Hooper (Grand Rapids, Mich.: Eerdmans, 1994), p. 149.

[28]Ibid., p. 284.

[29]Ibid., p. 336.

[30]C. S. Lewis, *Christian Reflections* (London: Geoffrey Bles, 1967), p. 79.

[31]C. S. Lewis, *Letters to an American Lady,* ed. Clyde S. Kilby (Grand Rapids, Mich.: Eerdmans, 1967), p. 107 (November 8, 1962).

[32]W. H. Lewis and Walter Hooper, eds., *Letters of C. S. Lewis* (San Diego: Harcourt Brace, 1993), p. 354 (July 16, 1940).

[33]Ibid., pp. 392-93.

[34]Ibid., p. 503 (March 21, 1962).

[35]C. S. Lewis, *The Allegory of Love* (New York: Oxford University Press, 1967), p. 15.

[36]C. S. Lewis, *A Preface to Paradise Lost* (New York: Oxford University Press, 1961), pp. 70-71.

[37]C. S. Lewis, *Poems* (San Diego: Harcourt Brace, 1992), p. 98.

[38]C. S. Lewis, *Perelandra* (New York: Macmillan, 1965), pp. 143-44.

[39]John Milton, *Paradise Lost,* book 9.

[40]See Gen 3:1-24; Is 14:12 (KJV); Rev 12:7-17. The Genesis account never makes any connection between Satan and the serpent. For this connection we must turn to Rev 12:9. Though Is 14:12 was thought to refer to Satan by the translators of the Vulgate and the King James Version, it is now thought that it refers to Nebuchadnezzar. Various interpretations of Rev 12:7-9 have been offered: (1) that it refers to the expulsion of Satan from Heaven prior to the Fall of humanity; (2) that it refers to Satan's fall at the time of Christ's ministry; (3) that it refers to a future expulsion of Satan from Heaven shortly before Christ's Second Coming.

[41]Lewis, *Problem of Pain,* pp. 133ff.

[42]Gen 2:9.

[43]C. S. Lewis, *The Magician's Nephew* (New York: Macmillan, 1973), p. 160.

[44]Ibid., p. 175.

[45]Lewis, *Perelandra,* p. 197.

Chapter Seven: The Person and Work of Christ

[1]C. S. Lewis, *Surprised by Joy* (New York: Harcourt Brace Jovanovich, 1955), p. 236.

[2]Ibid., p. 237.

[3]C. S. Lewis, *Mere Christianity* (New York: Macmillan, 1977), pp. 150-51.

[4]C. S. Lewis, *Christian Reflections* (London: Geoffrey Bles, 1967), pp. 4-6; W. H. Lewis and Walter Hooper, eds., *Letters of C. S. Lewis* (San Diego: Harcourt Brace, 1993), p. 364 (December 21, 1941).

[5]Lewis and Hooper, *Letters of C. S. Lewis,* p. 428.

[6]Lewis, *Christian Reflections,* p. 6.

[7]Ibid., pp. 382-83. See also his letter to Sister Penelope, July 29, 1942, in Lewis and Hooper, *Letters of C. S. Lewis,* p. 368.

[8]C. S. Lewis, *Miracles* (New York: Macmillan, 1978), pp. 110-11.

[9]Ibid., p. 123.

[10]C. S. Lewis, *Reflections on the Psalms* (San Diego: Harcourt Brace Jovanovich, 1958), p. 134.

[11]Ibid., pp. 123-24.

[12]Ibid., p. 68.

[13]C. S. Lewis, *The Four Loves* (San Diego: Harcourt Brace Jovanovich, 1960), p. 17.

[14]Lewis, *Mere Christianity*, p. 190.

[15]Lewis, *Miracles*, p. 108; C. S. Lewis, *God in the Dock*, ed. Walter Hooper (Grand Rapids, Mich.: Eerdmans, 1994), p. 80.

[16]Lewis, *Miracles*, pp. 109-10, 119, 137; Lewis, *God in the Dock*, p. 86.

[17]Lewis, *Miracles*, pp. 111-12; see also Lewis, *God in the Dock*, p. 82

[18]Lewis, *Mere Christianity*, p. 154.

[19]Ibid., p. 155.

[20]C. S. Lewis, *The World's Last Night and Other Essays* (San Diego: Harcourt Brace, 1987), p. 86.

[21]C. S. Lewis, *Letters to Malcolm: Chiefly on Prayer* (New York: Harcourt Brace Jovanovich, 1964), pp. 70-71.

[22]Lewis, *Christian Reflections*, p. 171-72.

[23]Lewis, *Mere Christianity*, p. 148.

[24]Ibid., p. 147.

[25]Lewis, *Problem of Pain*, p. 134.

[26]Lewis, *World's Last Night*, p. 99.

[27]Lewis, *Miracles*, p. 118.

[28]Lewis, *Reflections on the Psalms*, p. 127.

[29]Ibid., p. 135.

[30]C. S. Lewis, *The Screwtape Letters* (New York: Macmillan, 1977), pp. 106-8.

[31]Lewis and Hooper, *Letters of C. S. Lewis*, p. 411 (June 13, 1951).

[32]Lewis, *Miracles*, p. 47.

[33]Ibid., p. 59. See also Lewis, *Miracles*, pp. 137-39; Lewis, *God in the Dock*, pp. 26, 31-32, 72-73, 100 for further comments on the Virgin Birth.

[34]Lewis, *God in the Dock*, pp. 96-97.

[35]C. S. Lewis, *The Weight of Glory* (New York: Macmillan, 1980), p. 115.

[36]Ibid., p. 117.

[37]Lewis, *Mere Christianity*, p 147.

[38]Ibid., p. 156.

[39]Ibid., p. 57.

[40]See ibid., p. 157; Lewis and Hooper, *Letters of C. S. Lewis*, pp. 363-64.

[41]For more insight on Anselm's theory of the Atonement see Eugene R. Fairweather, ed., *A Scholastic Miscellany: Anselm to Ockham* (Philadelphia: Westminster Press, 1956), pp. 100-183.

[42]Lewis makes it clear in a letter to Dom Bede Griffiths dated October 13, 1942, that he does not believe Anselm's theory of the Atonement is to be found either in the New Testament or most of the early church fathers. See Lewis and Hooper, *Letters of C. S. Lewis*, p. 369.

[43]Lewis, *Mere Christianity*, p. 59.

[44]Ibid., pp. 60-61. What Lewis is restating here is Irenaeus's recapitulation theory, sometimes called the physical theory of the Atonement. For more information on this theory see J. N. D. Kelly, *Early Christian Doctrines* (San Francisco: Harper & Row, 1978), pp. 170-74. I am indebted to Bishop Kallistos Ware for pointing this out to me.

[45]Lewis and Hooper, *Letters of C. S. Lewis*, p. 411 (June 13, 1951).

[46]Lewis, *Mere Christianity*, p. 155.

[47]Lewis, *Miracles*, pp. 111-12.

[48]Ibid., p. 143.

[49]Ibid., p. 145.

[50]Ibid., p. 147.

[51]Ibid., pp. 147-48.

[52]Ibid., p. 145.

[53]Ibid., pp. 148-49.

[54]Ibid., pp. 155-56.

[55]Ibid., pp. 156-57.

[56]C. S. Lewis, *The Lion, the Witch and the Wardrobe* (New York: Macmillan, 1970), pp. 74-76.

[57]Ibid., pp. 159-60.

[58]C. S. Lewis, *The Horse and His Boy* (New York: HarperCollins, 1994), p. 158.

[59]C. S. Lewis, *The Last Battle* (New York: Macmillan, 1970), p. 148.

Chapter Eight: The Holy Spirit

[1]Leanne Payne, *Real Presence: The Holy Spirit in the Works of C. S. Lewis* (Westchester, Ill.: Cornerstone Books, 1979), p. 15.

[2]C. S. Lewis, *Mere Christianity* (New York: Macmillan, 1977), pp. 64-65.

[3]C. S. Lewis, *The Problem of Pain* (New York: Macmillan, 1986), p. 87.

[4]C. S. Lewis, *Letters to an American Lady*, ed. Clyde S. Kilby (Grand Rapids, Mich.: Eerdmans, 1967), p. 37 (February 20, 1955).

[5]C. S. Lewis, *The Weight of Glory* (New York: Macmillan, 1980), p. 54.

[6]Lewis, *Mere Christianity*, p. 152.

[7]Lewis, *Problem of Pain*, p. 29.

[8]Lewis, *Letters to an American Lady*, p. 37 (February 20, 1955).

[9]W. H. Lewis and Walter Hooper, eds., *Letters of C. S. Lewis* (San Diego: Harcourt Brace, 1993), pp. 421-22 (May 15, 1952).

[10]C. S. Lewis, *Reflections on the Psalms* (San Diego: Harcourt Brace Jovanovich, 1958), p. 126.

[11]Douglas Gresham, lecture on *The Chronicles of Narnia*, October 1998, from the author's library.

[12]Lewis, *Weight of Glory*, pp. 54-55.

[13]Lewis, *Letters to an American Lady*, p. 21 (November 6, 1953).

[14]C. S. Lewis, *Letters to Malcolm: Chiefly on Prayer* (New York: Harcourt Brace Jovanovich, 1958), pp. 67-68.

[15]Lewis and Hooper, *Letters of C. S. Lewis*, p. 423 (June 20, 1952).

[16]C. S. Lewis, *God in the Dock*, ed. Walter Hooper (Grand Rapids, Mich.: Eerdmans, 1994), p. 264.

[17]Unpublished letter quoted by Payne in *Real Presence*, p. 105.

Chapter Nine: Forgiveness of Sins

[1]C. S. Lewis, *Mere Christianity* (New York: Macmillan, 1977), p. 38.

[2]C. S. Lewis, *God in the Dock*, ed. Walter Hooper (Grand Rapids, Mich.: Eerdmans, 1994), pp. 95-96.

[3]Ibid.

[4]C. S. Lewis, *A Grief Observed* (New York: Bantam, 1976), p. 31.

[5]Lewis, *Mere Christianity*, p. 37.

[6]Ibid., p. 55.

[7]C. S. Lewis, *The Weight of Glory* (New York: Macmillan, 1980), p. 122.

[8]C. S. Lewis, *The Problem of Pain* (New York: Macmillan, 1986), p. 61.

[9]Heb 9:22.

[10]Lewis, *Problem of Pain*, p. 122.

[11]Lewis, *Weight of Glory*, p. 121.

[12]W. H. Lewis and Walter Hooper, *Letters of C. S. Lewis* (San Diego: Harcourt Brace, 1993), p. 410 (June 5, 1951).

[13]Martin Moynihan, ed., *The Latin Letters of C. S. Lewis* (South Bend, Ind.: St. Augustine's Press, 1998), p. 69.

[14]C. S. Lewis, *Letters to An American Lady*, ed. Clyde S. Kilby (Grand Rapids, Mich.: Eerdmans, 1967), pp. 71-72 (April 15, 1958).

[15]Ibid., p. 74 (July 21, 1958).

[16]A. N. Wilson, *C. S. Lewis: A Biography* (New York: W. W. Norton, 1990), pp. 233-34.

[17]Moynihan, ed., *Latin Letters*, p. 69.

[18]Lewis, *Weight of Glory*, p. 121.

[19]Lewis, *Mere Christianity*, pp. 105-7.

[20]Lewis, *Letters to an American Lady*, p. 115 (June 25, 1963).

[21]Lewis, *Weight of Glory*, p. 125.

[22]C. S. Lewis, *Reflections on the Psalms* (San Diego: Harcourt Brace Jovanovich, 1958), p. 25.

[23]C. S. Lewis, *Letters to Malcolm: Chiefly on Prayer* (New York: Harcourt Brace Jovanovich, 1964), pp. 27-28.

[24]Ibid., pp. 106-7.

[25]Lewis, *Letters to an American Lady*, p. 117 (July 6, 1963).

[26]Lewis, *Surprised by Joy*, pp. 22-41.

[27]Lewis and Hooper, *Letters of C. S. Lewis*, p. 116.

[28]Ibid., p. 431.

[29]Walter Hooper, *C. S. Lewis Companion and Guide* (New York: HarperCollins, 1996), p. 32.

[30]George Sayer, *Jack: A Life of C. S. Lewis* (Wheaton, Ill.: Crossway, 1994), pp. 274-75.

[31]Moynihan, ed., *Latin Letters*, p. 71.

[32]Wilson, *C. S. Lewis*, p. 239.

[33]C. S. Lewis, *The Four Loves* (San Diego: Harcourt Brace Jovanovich, 1960), pp. 184-85.

Chapter Ten: Faith and Works

[1]C. S. Lewis, *Surprised by Joy* (New York: Harcourt Brace Jovanovich, 1955), p. 226.

[2]C. S. Lewis, *The Problem of Pain* (New York: Macmillan, 1986), p. 65.

[3]C. S. Lewis, *Mere Christianity* (New York: Macmillan, 1977), p. 125.

[4]Ibid., p. 128.

[5]C. S. Lewis, *God in the Dock*, ed. Walter Hooper (Grand Rapids, Mich.: Eerdmans, 1994), pp. 172-73.

[6]Lewis, *Mere Christianity*, pp. 128-29.

[7]C. S. Lewis, *Letters to An American Lady*, ed. Clyde S. Kilby (Grand Rapids, Mich.: Eerdmans, 1967), p. 21.

[8]Ibid., p. 36.

[9]Ibid., p. 46.

[10]C. S. Lewis, *The Weight of Glory* (New York: Macmillan, 1980), p. 119.

[11]Ibid., p. 132.

[12]C. S. Lewis, *Reflections on the Psalms* (San Diego: Harcourt Brace Jovanovich, 1958), p. 13.

[13]C. S. Lewis, *The Four Loves* (San Diego: Harcourt Brace Jovanovich, 1960), pp. 180-81.

[14]Lewis, *Mere Christianity*, p. 129.

[15]Ibid., pp. 129-30.

[16]W. H. Lewis and Walter Hooper, eds., *Letters of C. S. Lewis* (San Diego: Harcourt Brace, 1993), pp. 432-33.

[17]Ibid., p. 428.

[18]Lewis, *Four Loves*, p. 178.

[19]Lewis, *Mere Christianity*, p. 65.

[20]C. S. Lewis, *The Last Battle* (New York: Macmillan, 1970), pp. 159-66.

[21]Lewis, *Mere Christianity*, p. 64.

Chapter Eleven: Satan and Temptation

[1] C. S. Lewis, *The Screwtape Letters* (New York: Macmillan, 1977), p. 3.

[2] Ibid., pp. 32-33.

[3] See also W. H. Lewis and Walter Hooper, eds., *Letters of C. S. Lewis* (San Diego: Harcourt Brace, 1993), p. 446 (February 2, 1955); C. S. Lewis, *God in the Dock*, ed. Walter Hooper (Grand Rapids, Mich.: Eerdmans, 1994), p. 56.

[4] C. S. Lewis, *Surprised by Joy* (New York: Harcourt Brace Jovanovich, 1955), pp. 58-60.

[5] Lewis and Hooper, *Letters of C. S. Lewis*, pp. 122-26 (March 14 and March 21, 1921).

[6] Lewis, *Surprised by Joy*, pp. 175-78.

[7] Walter Hooper, ed., *C. S. Lewis Collected Letters*, vol. 1 (London: HarperCollins, 2000), pp. 605-6 (April 22, 1923); Walter Hooper, ed., *All My Road Before Me* (Orlando, Fla.: Harcourt Brace Jovanovich, 1991), pp. 201-19, 221.

[8] C. S. Lewis, *Miracles* (New York: Macmillan, 1960), p. 170; C. S. Lewis, *The Four Loves* (San Diego: Harcourt Brace Jovanovich, 1977), p. 15.

[9] Lewis, *Screwtape Letters*, p. vii; Lewis, *God in the Dock*, p. 24; C. S. Lewis, *Mere Christianity* (New York: Macmillan, 1977) p. 181.

[10] Lewis, *Mere Christianity*, p. 50.

[11] Lewis and Hooper, *Letters of C. S. Lewis*, p. 440 (November 1, 1954); p. 501 (December 20, 1961).

[12] Lewis, *Mere Christianity*, p. 53.

[13] Ibid., p. 109.

[14] Lewis, *Screwtape Letters*, p. ix.

[15] C. S. Lewis, *Out of the Silent Planet* (New York: Simon & Schuster, 1996), p. 123.

[16] See also Rev 12:7-9.

[17] Lewis points out in this regard that temptation is not the only mode in which the devil can corrupt and impair; see *God in the Dock*, p. 169.

[18] C. S. Lewis, *The Problem of Pain* (New York: Macmillan, 1986), pp. 133-36; Lk 13:16.

[19] Lewis, *Out of the Silent Planet*, p. 111.

[20] Ibid., pp. 120-21.

[21] Lewis and Hooper, *Letters of C. S. Lewis*, p. 322 (July 9 [August], 1939).

[22] Lewis, *Screwtape Letters*, pp. 86-87.

[23] Ibid., p. 4.

[24] Lewis, *Problem of Pain*, p. 84.

[25] C. S. Lewis, *Christian Reflections* (London: Geoffrey Bles, 1967), p. 33.

[26] Lewis, *Miracles*, p. 121.

[27] Lewis, *Problem of Pain*, p. 89 n.

[28] W. H. Lewis, ed., *Letters of C. S. Lewis* (New York: Harcourt Brace & World, 1975), pp. 189-90 (undated letter after August 11, 1940).

[29] Lewis, *Miracles*, pp. 128-29.

[30] C. S. Lewis, *Reflections on the Psalms* (San Diego: Harcourt Brace Jovanovich, 1958), p. 133.

[31] Lewis, *Mere Christianity*, p. 54.

[32] Lewis, *Screwtape Letters*, p. ix.

[33] Lewis, *Screwtape Letters*, p. 95.

[34] Ibid., pp. 13-14.

[35] C. S. Lewis, *The Weight of Glory* (New York: Macmillan, 1980), p. 129.

[36] Lewis, *Problem of Pain*, p. 60.

[37] Lewis, *Mere Christianity*, p. 160.

[38] Lewis, *Screwtape Letters*, p. 33.

[39]Lewis, *Weight of Glory*, pp. 129-31.

[40]Lewis, *God in the Dock*, p. 173.

[41]However, it is interesting to note that all but the first of the *Screwtape Letters* deal with Wormwood's temptation of a patient who is already a Christian. Apparently, to Lewis's mind, Satan and his cohorts spend more time tempting Christians than non-Christians. Perhaps little need be done about the non-Christian, from the devils' perspective, since the non-Christian is already in Satan's camp. The majority of demonic effort in *Screwtape Letters* is expended on wooing the Christian back into Satan's camp.

[42]Lewis and Hooper, *Letters of C. S. Lewis*, p. 406 (March 5, 1951); Lewis, *Screwtape Letters*, p. 172.

[43]Lewis, *Surprised by Joy*, pp. 68-69.

[44]Lewis, *Mere Christianity*, p. 89.

[45]Lewis, *Screwtape Letters*, letter 18, pp. 80-84; Lewis, *Four Loves*, pp. 156-57.

[46]Lewis, *Screwtape Letters*, p. 79.

[47]Lewis, *Mere Christianity*, p. 124.

[48]Lewis, *Screwtape Letters*, pp. 90-91; see also Lewis, *Mere Christianity*, p. 92.

[49]Lewis, *Screwtape Letters*, pp. 40-41.

[50]Lewis, *Mere Christianity*, pp. 112-13.

[51]Lewis, *Screwtape Letters*, pp. 158-59.

[52]C. S. Lewis, *Perelandra* (New York: Macmillan, 1965), p. 116.

[53]See also Lewis, *Problem of Pain*, pp. 80-81.

[54]Lewis, *Mere Christianity*, p. 92.

[55]Lewis, *Christian Reflections*, p. 43; see also C. S. Lewis, *The Pilgrim's Regress* (Grand Rapids, Mich.: Eerdmans, 1981), pp. 50-53.

[56]Lewis, *Screwtape Letters*, p. 5.

[57]Ibid., p. 132; W. H. Lewis and Walter Hooper, eds., *Letters of C. S. Lewis* (San Diego: Harcourt Brace, 1993), p. 365 (January 20, 1942); Lewis, *Mere Christianity*, p. 94; Lewis, *Weight of Glory*, p. 132.

[58]Hooper and Lewis, *Letters of C. S. Lewis*, pp. 422-23 (May 28, 1952).

[59]Lewis, *Reflections on the Psalms*, p. 136; Lewis, *Screwtape Letters*, pp. 53-54, 156-57.

[60]Lewis, *Mere Christianity*, p. 129.

[61]Lewis, *Screwtape Letters*, pp. ix-x.

[62]Ibid., pp. xi, 26, 38, 81, 141, 145.

[63]Lewis, *Four Loves*, p. 160.

[64]Lewis, *Screwtape Letters*, pp. 4, 56.

[65]Ibid., pp. 53-54.

[66]Lewis, *Weight of Glory*, p. 102.

[67]C. S. Lewis, *Letters to Malcolm: Chiefly on Prayer* (New York: Harcourt Brace Jovanovich, 1964), p. 17; Lewis, *God in the Dock*, p. 217; C. S. Lewis, *Letters to an American Lady*, ed. Clyde S. Kilby (Grand Rapids, Mich.: Eerdmans, 1967), p. 108 (November 26, 1962).

[68]C. S. Lewis, *Reflections on the Psalms* (San Diego: Harcourt Brace Jovanovich, 1958), pp. 71-74; Lewis, *Screwtape Letters*, letter 10, pp. 45-48.

[69]Lewis, *Screwtape Letters*, letter 17, pp. 76-79.

Chapter Twelve: The Tao

[1]C. S. Lewis, *The Abolition of Man* (New York: Macmillan, 1978), p. 28.

[2]In *Mere Christianity* and *Abolition of Man*.

[3]C. S. Lewis, *Mere Christianity* (New York: Macmillan, 1977), pp. 70-73.

[4]C. S. Lewis, *Christian Reflections* (London: Geoffrey Bles, 1967), p. 79.

[5]See the appendix to *Abolition of Man*, where Lewis demonstrates the similarity in morals among all major human

cultures of all time.

[6]See Rom 2:14-15.

[7]See Lewis, *Abolition of Man*, pp. 67-91. For an illustration of the abolition of man, read C. S. Lewis, *That Hideous Strength* (New York: Macmillan, 1974). Lewis also notes in *The Magician's Nephew* (New York: Macmillan, 1973), p. 159, that commands like "Do not steal" were hammered harder into boys' heads in Digory's time than at present.

[8]See Peter Kreeft's essay "Can the Natural Law Ever Be Abolished from the Heart of Man?" in his *C. S. Lewis for the Third Millennium* (San Francisco: Ignatius Press, 1994).

[9]C. S. Lewis, *God in the Dock*, ed. Walter Hooper (Grand Rapids, Mich.: Eerdmans, 1994), pp. 264-65.

[10]C. S. Lewis, *Reflections on the Psalms* (San Diego: Harcourt Brace Jovanovich, 1958), p. 65.

[11]Lewis, *Mere Christianity*, p. 72.

[12]Ibid., pp. 78-83.

[13]Lewis, *God in the Dock*, p. 318.

[14]Lewis, *Mere Christianity*, pp. 83-87.

[15]For an insightful comparison of the lives and thought of C. S. Lewis and Sigmund Freud, see Armand Nicholi, *The Question of God* (New York: The Free Press, 2002).

[16]C. S. Lewis, *The Problem of Pain* (New York: Macmillan, 1986), p. 65.

[17]For an illustration of this, see C. S. Lewis, "History's Words," in *The Pilgrim's Regress* (Grand Rapids, Mich.: Eerdmans, 1981), pp. 145-50 (book 8, chap. 8).

[18]C. S. Lewis, *Letters to Malcolm: Chiefly on Prayer* (New York: Harcourt Brace Jovanovich, 1964), pp. 114-15; W. H. Lewis and Walter Hooper, eds., *Letters of C. S. Lewis* (San Diego: Harcourt Brace, 1993), p. 467 (July 18, 1957).

[19]Lewis, *Mere Christianity*, pp. 161-62.

[20]Ibid., p. 165.

[21]C. S. Lewis, *Letters to an American Lady*, ed. Clyde S. Kilby (Grand Rapids, Mich.: Eerdmans, 1967), p. 46 (November 9, 1955).

Chapter Thirteen: Venus

[1]C. S. Lewis, *The Four Loves* (San Diego: Harcourt Brace Jovanovich, 1960), p. 132.

[2]See Eph 5:32 in context.

[3]C. S. Lewis, *God in the Dock*, ed. Walter Hooper (Grand Rapids, Mich.: Eerdmans, 1994), p. 238.

[4]Lewis, *Four Loves*, pp. 145-47.

[5]Ibid., pp. 138-42.

[6]C. S. Lewis, *Letters to an American Lady*, ed. Clyde S. Kilby (Grand Rapids, Mich.: Eerdmans, 1967), p. 19 (August 1, 1953).

[7]Walter Hooper, ed., *C. S. Lewis Collected Letters*, vol. 1 (London: Harper Collins, 2000), p. 974 (October 1, 1931).

[8]C. S. Lewis, *Out of the Silent Planet* (New York: Simon & Schuster, 1996), pp. 72-74.

[9]C. S. Lewis, *Letters to Malcolm: Chiefly on Prayer* (New York: Harcourt Brace Jovanovich, 1964), p. 90; C. S. Lewis, *Perelandra* (New York: Macmillan, 1965), p. 48.

[10]C. S. Lewis, *Miracles* (New York: Macmillan, 1960), p. 91.

[11]C. S. Lewis, *Surprised by Joy* (New York: Harcourt Brace Jovanovich, 1955), p. 170.

[12]C. S. Lewis, *Present Concerns* (San Diego: Harcourt Brace Jovanovich, 1986), pp. 18-19.

[13]Lewis, *Letters to Malcolm*, p. 14.

[14]C. S. Lewis, *The Allegory of Love* (New York: Oxford University Press, 1967), p. 8.

[15]Lewis, *God in the Dock*, p. 321.

[16]Lewis, *Mere Christianity*, p. 53.

[17]W. H. Lewis and Walter Hooper, eds., *Letters of C. S. Lewis* (San Diego: Harcourt Brace, 1993), pp. 338-39 (February 11, 1940).

[18]Lewis, *Mere Christianity*, pp. 88-95.

[19]C. S. Lewis, *The Weight of Glory* (New York: Macmillan, 1980), p. 98.

[20]See C. S. Lewis, *The Great Divorce* (New York: Macmillan, 1979), pp. 98-105.

[21]C. S. Lewis, *The Abolition of Man* (New York: Macmillan, 1978), p. 68.

[22]C. S. Lewis, *That Hideous Strength* (New York: Macmillan, 1974), p. 14.

[23]Ibid., pp. 278-79.

[24]Sheldon Vanauken, *A Severe Mercy* (New York: Bantam, 1979), pp. 210-12.

[25]Lewis, *Surprised by Joy*, p. 89.

[26]Ibid., p. 101.

[27]Ibid., pp. 108-9.

[28]Lewis, *Four Loves*, pp. 90-94.

[29]See Jn 9:1-3.

[30]Vanauken, *A Severe Mercy*, pp. 146-47.

[31]Lewis and Hooper, *Letters of C. S. Lewis*, p. 281 (February 1, 1958).

[32]Ibid., p. 292 (May 17, 1960).

[33]For more information on Lewis's relationship to Arthur Greeves, the best resource is to read Walter Hooper, ed., *They Stand Together: The Letters of C. S. Lewis to Arthur Greeves* (New York: Macmillan, 1979). Though *They Stand Together* is out of print, these letters are now being included in the three volume series: *C. S. Lewis Collected Letters*, also edited by Walter Hooper.

[34]See Jesus' statement in Mt 22:30.

[35]Lewis, *Miracles*, pp. 159-60.

[36]Lewis, *Perelandra*, pp. 32-33.

[37]C. S. Lewis, *The Weight of Glory* (New York: Macmillan, 1980), pp. 3-4.

Chapter Fourteen: Marriage and Divorce

[1]W. H. Lewis, ed., *Letters of C. S. Lewis* (New York: Harcourt Brace Jovanovich, 1975), p. 55.

[2]See C. S. Lewis, *Letters to an American Lady*, ed. Clyde S. Kilby (Grand Rapids, Mich.: Eerdmans, 1967), p. 99 (January 17, 1962); pp. 106-7 (November 8, 1962).

[3]C. S. Lewis, *Mere Christianity* (New York: Macmillan, 1977), p. 91; C. S. Lewis, *God in the Dock*, ed. Walter Hooper (Grand Rapids, Mich.: Eerdmans, 1994), p. 147. See also C. S. Lewis, *Studies in Medieval and Renaissance Literature* (Cambridge: Cambridge University Press, 1996), p. 117; C. S. Lewis, *English Literature in the Sixteenth Century* (Oxford: Oxford University Press, 1973), p. 35, where Lewis says that the exaltation of marriage is a Protestant and specifically Puritan trait.

[4]C. S. Lewis, *Reflections on the Psalms* (San Diego: Harcourt Brace Jovanovich, 1958), p. 129; see also Lewis, *God in the Dock*, p. 238.

[5]Lewis, *God in the Dock*, pp. 284-85.

[6]W. H. Lewis and Walter Hooper, eds., *Letters of C. S. Lewis* (San Diego: Harcourt Brace, 1993), pp. 347-48 (April 18, 1940).

[7]Lewis, *Mere Christianity*, p. 95.

[8]C. S. Lewis, *The Screwtape Letters* (New York: Macmillan, 1977), p. 83.

[9]Sheldon Vanauken, *A Severe Mercy* (New York: Bantam, 1979), p. 207.

[10]Ibid., p. 211.

[11]C. S. Lewis, *The Four Loves* (San Diego: Harcourt Brace Jovanovich, 1960), p. 174.

[12]C. S. Lewis, *A Grief Observed* (New York: Bantam, 1976), p. 13.

[13]Ibid., p. 39.

[14]Ibid., p. 59.

[15]Ibid., p. 64.

[16]Lewis, *Mere Christianity*, p. 96.

[17]Ibid.

[18]Lewis, *Letters of C. S. Lewis*, pp. 218-20 (September 2 and 6, 1949).

[19]Ibid., p. 240 (May 13, 1952).

[20]Lewis, *Mere Christianity*, pp. 96-97.

[21]Ibid., pp. 101-2.

[22]Lewis, *Four Loves*, pp. 137-38; see also 1 Cor 7:32-35.

[23]Lewis, *Mere Christianity*, pp. 97-98.

[24]Ibid., p. 98.

[25]Ibid., pp. 98-101.

[26]Vanuaken, *A Severe Mercy*, p. 184.

[27]C. S. Lewis, *The Screwtape Letters* (New York: Macmillan, 1977), p. 13.

[28]See also Lewis's letter of November 8, 1931, to Arthur Greeves in Walter Hooper, ed., *They Stand Together: The Letters of C. S. Lewis to Arthur Greeves* (New York: Macmillan, 1979), p. 430.

[29]Lewis, *Mere Christianity*, p. 101.

[30]Lewis, *God in the Dock*, pp. 317-21.

[31]Walter Hooper, ed., *C. S. Lewis Collected Letters*, vol. 1 (London: HarperCollins, 2000), p. 773 (August 2, 1928).

[32]Lewis, *Mere Christianity*, p. 102.

[33]Ibid., pp. 102-3.

[34]See C. S. Lewis, *The Weight of Glory* (New York: Macmillan, 1980), p. 114.

[35]Lewis, *Four Loves*, p. 148.

[36]Lewis, *Letters of C. S. Lewis*, p. 240 (May 13, 1952).

[37]Though Lewis's change of view was not in line with the official Anglican position of his time, it would seem to be in line with Jesus' words (Mt 19:9) and Paul's counsel (1 Cor 7:15), which seem to allow divorce and remarriage in the case of either adultery or desertion. Clearly, according to the biographies that have been written about Joy and her first husband, he was sexually unfaithful to her and wanted out of the marriage.

[38]Lewis, *A Grief Observed*, p. 20.

[39]Ibid., pp. 55-57.

Chapter Fifteen: Men Are from Mars . . .

[1]Though Lewis talked about Mars as a symbol of masculinity and Venus as a symbol of femininity in *Perelandra*, that is the only thing, so far as I know, that Lewis's and Gray's writing have in common.

[2]C. S. Lewis, *Perelandra* (New York: Macmillan, 1965), p. 200.

[3]Ibid., pp. 199-201.

[4]C. S. Lewis, *That Hideous Strength* (New York: Macmillan, 1974), pp. 315-16.

[5]C. S. Lewis, *God in the Dock*, ed. Walter Hooper (Grand Rapids, Mich.: Eerdmans, 1994), p. 237.

[6]Ibid., p. 234.

[7]Ibid., pp. 235-36.

[8]Ibid., pp. 236-39.

[9]Ibid., p. 239.

[10]C. S. Lewis, *A Preface to Paradise Lost* (New York: Oxford University Press, 1961), pp. 73-74.

[11]C. S. Lewis, *The Weight of Glory* (New York: Macmillan, 1980), p. 114.

[12]Ibid., pp. 114-16.

[13]W. H. Lewis, ed., *Letters of C. S. Lewis* (New York: Harcourt Brace & World, 1966), pp. 117-18 (July 9, 1927).

[14]Ibid., p. 108 (June 5, 1926); p. 110 (February 3, 1927).

[15]Walter Hooper, *C. S. Lewis Companion and Guide* (New York: HarperCollins, 1996), pp. 36-37, 40.

[16]Ibid., pp. 724-26.

[17]Ibid., pp. 720-23.

[18]Lewis, *Letters of C. S. Lewis*, p. 242 (May 28, 1952).

[19]David Graham, ed., *We Remember C. S. Lewis, Essays and Memoirs* (Nashville: Broadman & Holman, 2001), pp. 11-52, 56-58.

[20]To find out more about their relationship read George Sayer, *Jack: A Life of C. S. Lewis* (Wheaton, Ill.: Crossway, 1994), pp. 347-96 and Douglas H. Gresham, *Lenten Lands* (San Francisco: HarperCollins, 1994), pp. 53-95, 102-29.

[21]"Clive Staples Lewis 1898-1963," *The Proceedings of the British Academy* 51 (1965): 12, 19, 419.

[22]For Walter Hooper's response to the charge that Lewis was a misogynist read his address, "C. S. Lewis and C. S. Lewises," in *The Riddle of Joy*, ed. Michael H. Macdonald and Andrew A. Tadie (Grand Rapids, Mich.: Eerdmans, 1989), pp. 38-40.

[23]C. S. Lewis, *The Four Loves* (San Diego: Harcourt Brace Jovanovich, 1960), p. 149.

[24]Lewis, *Letters of C. S. Lewis*, p. 237 (January 10, 1952).

Chapter Sixteen: I Am the King's Man

[1]C. S. Lewis, *That Hideous Strength* (New York: Macmillan, 1974), p. 143.

[2]C. S. Lewis, *Miracles* (New York: Macmillan, 1960), pp. 119-20.

[3]C. S. Lewis, *Present Concerns* (San Diego: Harcourt Brace Jovanovich, 1987), p. 20.

[4]C. S. Lewis, *God in the Dock*, ed. Walter Hooper (Grand Rapids, Mich.: Eerdmans, 1994), p. 64.

[5]C. S. Lewis, *Letters to an American Lady*, ed. Clyde S. Kilby (Grand Rapids, Mich.: Eerdmans, 1967), p. 18 (July 10, 1953).

[6]C. S. Lewis, *The Magician's Nephew* (New York: Macmillan, 1973), pp. 136-40.

[7]C. S. Lewis, *The Horse and His Boy* (New York: HarperCollins, 1994), p. 166.

[8]See also C. S. Lewis, *The Lion, the Witch and the Wardrobe* (New York: HarperCollins, 1994), pp. 133, 181-82.

[9]C. S. Lewis, *The Voyage of the Dawn Treader* (New York: Macmillan, 1973), p. 209.

[10]C. S. Lewis, *The Last Battle* (New York: Macmillan, 1970), p. 31.

[11]C. S. Lewis, *Prince Caspian* (New York: Macmillan, 1973), p. 55.

[12]Lewis, *Horse and His Boy*, p. 151.

[13]Ibid., p. 156.

[14]C. S. Lewis, *The Silver Chair* (New York: Macmillan, 1973), p. 54.

[15]Lewis, *That Hideous Strength*, p. 292.

[16]Unpublished letter to Patricia Hillis, Austin, Texas, March 10, 1959, quoted in Walter Hooper, ed., *C. S. Lewis Companion and Guide* (New York: HarperCollins, 1996), p. 581.

[17]Lewis, *Lion, the Witch and the Wardrobe*, pp. 171-72.

[18]Lewis, *Great Divorce*, p. 107.

Chapter Seventeen: War and Peace

[1]For a fascinating study of Lewis as broadcaster and his relationship with the BBC, see Justin Phillips, *C. S. Lewis at the BBC* (London: HarperCollins, 2002).

[2]C. S. Lewis, *The Weight of Glory* (New York: Macmillan, 1980), p. 24. At the same time, Lewis did not think it appropriate or necessary to inform God in prayer that our wartime cause is righteous. God might have his own opinion on the subject! See W. H. Lewis, ed., *Letters of C. S. Lewis* (New York: Harcourt Brace Jovanovich, 1975), p. 168 (September 10, 1939). For Lewis's thoughts on love of country and patriotism see C. S. Lewis, *The Four Loves* (San Diego: Harcourt Brace Jovanovich, 1960), pp. 39-48. There Lewis says that we must be wary of identifying our cause with God's (p. 48). There is a difference between our cause being right and our being thoroughly righteous (see C. S. Lewis, *Reflections on the Psalms* [San Diego: Harcourt Brace Jovanovich, 1958], p. 17). Lewis also thought it dangerous to identify one's local enemy with the forces of evil. Furthermore, he truly be-

lieved it was a Christian's obligation to pray for one's enemies; see Lewis, *Letters of C. S. Lewis*, p. 183 (April 16, 1940).

[3]See C. S. Lewis, *Surprised by Joy* (New York: Harcourt Brace Jovanovich, 1955), pp. 158-59. Lewis recounts his experiences during the First World War in *Surprised by Joy*, pp. 186-98, and *Collected Letters*, pp. 346-72 (Walter Hooper, ed., *C. S. Lewis Collected Letters*, vol. I [London: HarperCollins, 2000]).

[4]Lewis, *Letters of C. S. Lewis*, p. 166 (May 8, 1939).

[5]See Lewis's war letters in Hooper, *C. S. Lewis Collected Letters*, pp. 347-52.

[6]Lewis, *Surprised by Joy*, p. 196.

[7]See Lewis, *Surprised by Joy*, p. 159.

[8]Lewis, *Weight of Glory*, pp. 29-32.

[9]C. S. Lewis, *The Screwtape Letters* (New York: Macmillan, 1977), p. 89.

[10]Ibid., pp. 25, 33-35.

[11]Ibid., pp. 30-31.

[12]Ibid., p. 26.

[13]Ibid., pp. 28, 70.

[14]Ibid., p. 137.

[15]Lewis, *Letters of C. S. Lewis*, p. 225 (undated).

[16]C. S. Lewis, *God in the Dock*, ed. Walter Hooper (Grand Rapids, Mich.: Eerdmans, 1994), p. 312.

[17]C. S. Lewis, *Present Concerns* (San Diego: Harcourt Brace Jovanovich, 1986), pp. 73-80.

[18]Lewis, *Weight of Glory*, pp. 33-53.

[19]Lewis notes in his sermon, *Learning in War-Time*, that war does not make death more frequent. War puts some deaths earlier, but that makes no real difference because it does not increase or decrease our chances of dying "at peace with God." Nor does war increase the chance of a painful death. The battlefield is the one place where one might hope to die with no pain at all, if killed instantly by a bullet or in a sudden blast. War makes death real to us, and that should be counted as a blessing; see Lewis, *Weight of Glory*, p. 31. Screwtape considered this last effect of war to be disastrous; see Lewis, *Screwtape Letters*, p. 27.

[20]In *Studies in Medieval and Renaissance Literature* (Cambridge: Cambridge University Press, 1996), p. 123, Lewis stated that conquest is an evil that produces almost every other evil in the lives of the conquerors and the victims.

[21]Lewis argues elsewhere (*God in the Dock*, p. 326) that if war is ever lawful, then peace is sometimes sinful.

[22]See also *God in the Dock*, p. 49, where Lewis says that if you can't restrain a violent person by any effort short of killing him or her, then it is the Christian's obligation to do just that.

[23]Lewis believed that "outlawing war" would only make war more like an outlaw without making it less frequent. Getting rid of knights, he asserts, will not alleviate the suffering of peasants. See C. S. Lewis, *English Literature in the Sixteenth Century* (Oxford: Oxford University Press, 1961), p. 153.

[24]Lewis points out in *Mere Christianity* the fact that the sixth commandment does not prohibit all kinds of killing but simply murder. Therefore it can be alright for a Christian judge to sentence someone to death or for a Christian soldier to kill an enemy. In this same place Lewis comments that war is a dreadful thing, but one should not enter into it with a kind of semi-pacifism where one is ashamed of fighting. Lewis concludes that we may kill but not hate and enjoy hating. While we are at war we must earnestly desire the transformation of our enemy from evil to good. See C. S. Lewis, *Mere Christianity* (New York: Macmillan, 1977), pp. 106-8.

[25]Lewis (*God in the Dock*, pp. 325-27) maintained that the determination of whether or not a particular war was just should be delegated to the government. He believed that the witness of Christians would be clearer to the world if all Christians would consent to bear arms and at the same time refuse to obey anti-Christian orders.

[26]Lewis also comments on these same Scriptures in Lewis, *Letters of C. S. Lewis*, p. 248 (November 8, 1952).

[27]Lewis, *Weight of Glory*, p. 53.

Chapter Eighteen: What's Love Got to Do with It?

[1] C. S. Lewis, *The Four Loves* (San Diego: Harcourt Brace Jovanovich, 1960), pp. 11-21.

[2] See also C. S. Lewis, *The Problem of Pain* (New York: Macmillan, 1986), p. 50.

[3] Denis de Rougemont, *Love in the Western World* (Princeton, N.J.: Princeton University Press, 1983), p. 312.

[4] Lewis, *Four Loves*, pp. 25-49.

[5] C. S. Lewis, *Mere Christianity* (New York: Macmillan, 1977), p. 113.

[6] Lewis, *Four Loves*, p. 39.

[7] Ibid., pp. 53-83.

[8] See also C. S. Lewis, *The Great Divorce* (New York: Macmillan, 1979), pp. 96-97.

[9] See W. H. Lewis, ed., *Letters of C. S. Lewis* (New York: Harcourt Brace & World, 1966), p. 274 (February 10, 1957); C. S. Lewis, *The Screwtape Letters* (New York: Macmillan, 1977), p. 18.

[10] Lewis, *Great Divorce*, pp. 90-98.

[11] See also C. S. Lewis, *God in the Dock*, ed. Walter Hooper (Grand Rapids, Mich.: Eerdmans, 1994), p. 285; Lewis, *Screwtape Letters*, p. 123.

[12] Lewis, *Great Divorce*, pp. 92-93.

[13] Lewis, *Four Loves*, pp. 87-127.

[14] See also Walter Hooper, *They Stand Together: The Letters of C. S. Lewis to Arthur Greeves* (New York: Macmillan, 1979), p. 477, where Lewis writes to his friend Arthur Greeves that friendship is the greatest of worldly goods (December 29, 1935).

[15] Lewis, *Four Loves*, p. 116.

[16] See Lewis, *Problem of Pain*, p. 146.

[17] See C. S. Lewis, *Surprised by Joy* (New York: Harcourt Brace Jovanovich, 1955), pp. 130-31, to read of Lewis's first experience of this.

[18] For more on God as Father and Husband see Lewis, *Problem of Pain*, pp. 44-47.

[19] To learn about the differences between true friendship and "The Inner Ring," read C. S. Lewis, *The Weight of Glory* (New York: Macmillan, 1980), pp. 104-5.

[20] Lewis, *Four Loves*, pp. 131-60.

[21] Lewis, *Mere Christianity*, pp. 115-18.

[22] See Lewis, *God in the Dock*, p. 97. Giving alms is a *part* of charity, and the only safe rule in regard to alms is to give more than one can spare; see Lewis, *Mere Christianity*, pp. 81-82.

[23] See Lewis, *God in the Dock*, p. 49; Lewis, *Mere Christianity*, pp. 105, 108.

[24] For more on the will and its relationship to love, see Lewis, *Letters of C. S. Lewis*, pp. 268-69 (undated).

[25] Lewis says in *Problem of Pain* (p. 97) that God accepts us even when we have shown that we prefer everything else to him. What love could be more constant than that? See also Lewis, *Surprised by Joy*, p. 229.

[26] Lewis, *Four Loves*, pp. 163-92.

[27] Ibid., p. 169.

[28] See C. S. Lewis, *Letters to Malcolm: Chiefly on Prayer* (New York: Harcourt Brace Jovanovich, 1964), p. 22.

[29] Lewis, *Four Loves*, p. 176. In *Problem of Pain* (p. 41) Lewis says that God, by loving us, pays us a compliment that is hard to accept. God loves us right where we are, but he loves us too much to leave us where we are; that is his intolerable compliment toward us. See also Lewis, *Problem of Pain*, pp. 46-47, 53; C. S. Lewis, *A Grief Observed* (New York: Bantam, 1976), pp. 49-50; Lewis, *Letters to Malcolm*, pp. 96-97.

[30] C. S. Lewis, *Till We Have Faces* (New York: Harcourt Brace Jovanovich, 1980), pp. 226-308.

[31] For more on agape, see Lewis, *Letters of C. S. Lewis*, pp. 255-56 (February 18, 1954).

[32] Lewis also talks about an "appetite for God" in *Reflections on the Psalms* (San Diego: Harcourt Brace Jovanovich, 1958), p. 51.

[33] As Lewis says in *Miracles* (New York: Macmillan, 1960), p. 52, "Christ did not die for men because they were intrinsically worth dying for, but because He is intrinsically love, and therefore loves infinitely."

[34]Lewis, *Four Loves*, p. 186.

[35]See Lewis, *Great Divorce*, p. 97.

[36]See Lewis, *Letters of C. S. Lewis*, p. 248 (November 8, 1952). And in C. S. Lewis, *Letters to Children*, ed. Lyle W. Dorsett and Marjorie Lamp Mead (New York: Macmillan, 1985), p. 52 (May 6, 1955), Lewis says that the Lord knows how hard it is for us to love him in the way we ought, so he doesn't get angry with us as long as we are trying. Plus, he offers to help us love him more. Lewis also makes clear that while God wants us to love him more, that does not mean he wants us to love others less; see C. S. Lewis, *Letters to an American Lady*, ed. Clyde S. Kilby (Grand Rapids, Mich.: Eerdmans, 1967), p. 58 (August 18, 1956).

[37]Lewis, *God in the Dock*, p. 150.

[38]C. S. Lewis, *Reflections on the Psalms* (San Diego: Harcourt Brace Jovanovich, 1958), p. 97. See also Lewis, *A Grief Observed*, p. 72.

[39]See Brother Lawrence's *Practice of the Presence of God*, ed. Douglas V. Steere (Nashville: Upper Room, 1950).

Chapter Nineteen: The Church

[1]C. S. Lewis, *The Weight of Glory* (New York: Macmillan, 1980), p. 106-7.

[2]See Lewis, *Weight of Glory*, p. 106; W. H. Lewis, ed., *Letters of C. S. Lewis* (New York: Harcourt Brace & World, 1966), p. 224 (December 7, 1950); C. S. Lewis, *Letters to an American Lady*, ed. Clyde S. Kilby (Grand Rapids, Mich.: Eerdmans, 1967), p. 23 (January 1, 1954); p. 36 (February 2, 1955); Heb 10:24-25.

[3]C. S. Lewis, *Surprised by Joy* (New York: Harcourt Brace Jovanovich, 1955), pp. 233-34.

[4]C. S. Lewis, *Mere Christianity* (New York: Macmillan, 1977), p. 51.

[5]Ibid., p. 124.

[6]Ibid., p. 144.

[7]C. S. Lewis, *God in the Dock*, ed. Walter Hooper (Grand Rapids, Mich.: Eerdmans, 1994), pp. 61, 329.

[8]Lewis, *Weight of Glory*, p. 110; Lewis, *Mere Christianity*, p. 159.

[9]Lewis, *Weight of Glory*, p. 112.

[10]C. S. Lewis, *The Problem of Pain* (New York: Macmillan, 1986), pp. 150-51.

[11]C. S. Lewis, *Letters to Malcolm: Chiefly on Prayer* (New York: Harcourt Brace Jovanovich, 1964), p. 10.

[12]Lewis, *Weight of Glory*, p. 113.

[13]Ibid., p. 116.

[14]Lewis, *Mere Christianity*, p. 65; see also Lewis, *Letters of C. S. Lewis*, p. 196 (December 8, 1941).

[15]Lewis, *Mere Christianity*, p. 163.

[16]Ibid., pp. 169-70.

[17]Lewis, *Letters to Malcolm*, p. 43.

[18]Lewis, *Letters of C. S. Lewis*, p. 262 (March 16, 1955). In this same letter Lewis says how strongly he objects to any church making teetotalism a condition of membership, for Jesus turned water into wine, not the other way around. Besides, Lewis says, churches that try to enforce teetotalism are narrow-minded, not recognizing that Christianity grew up in the Mediterranean world, where wine has always been an everyday part of people's diet.

[19]Lewis, *Mere Christianity*, pp. 6-8.

[20]Walter Hooper, ed., *C. S. Lewis Collected Letters*, vol. I (London: HarperCollins, 2000), p. 7 (October 3, 1908).

[21]Lewis, *Surprised by Joy*, p. 33.

[22]Lewis, *Letters to Malcolm*, p. 13.

[23]Lewis, *Letters of C. S. Lewis*, p. 170 (November 8, 1939).

[24]Lewis, *God in the Dock*, p. 336.

[25]Lewis, *Mere Christianity*, p. 9; Lewis, *God in the Dock*, p. 60; Lewis, *Letters to an American Lady*, p. 11 (November 10, 1952).

[26]Lewis, *God in the Dock*, p. 203.

[27]Lewis, *Mere Christianity*, pp. 6-12.

[28]Lewis mentioned in an address to Anglican clergy that to the average layman "church" usually means a sacred building or the clergy. The word *church* does not suggest to them the "company of all faithful people." Lewis felt the term was generally used in a bad sense but that direct defense of the church was the duty of the clergy. However, use of the word *Church*, where there is no time to defend it, alienates sympathy and should be avoided wherever possible. See Lewis, *God in the Dock*, p. 97.

[29]C. S. Lewis, *The Screwtape Letters* (New York: Macmillan, 1977), pp. 12-14.

[30]Ibid., p. 34.

[31]Ibid., p. 75.

[32]Ibid., p. 115.

[33]Ibid., p. 171.

[34]Ibid., pp. 72-73.

[35]Ibid., pp. 73-74.

[36]See Lewis, *Letters of C. S. Lewis*, p. 223 (undated: January 1950); pp. 228-29 (April 23, 1951); p. 230 (undated); C. S. Lewis, *Reflections on the Psalms* (San Diego: Harcourt Brace Jovanovich, 1958), pp. 7-8.

[37]Lewis, *Letters of C. S. Lewis*, p. 243 (undated).

[38]Quoted by Christopher Derrick, *C. S. Lewis and the Church of Rome* (San Francisco: Ignatius Press, 1981), pp. 95-97.

[39]For more on Lewis's position with reference to Roman Catholicism, see George Sayer, *Jack: A Life of C. S. Lewis* (Wheaton, Ill.: Crossway, 1994), pp. 421-22. In connection with this, Sayer once told me that Lewis attended the Roman Catholic Church with him whenever he visited Malvern. Sayer said it was part of Jack's nature to attend whatever church was closest to him without concern for denomination.

[40]Lewis, *Letters of C. S. Lewis*, p. 165 (May 8, 1939).

[41]Ibid., p. 170 (November 8, 1939); see also Rom 14, 15.

[42]Lewis, *God in the Dock*, p. 60.

[43]Martin Moynihan, ed., *The Latin Letters of C. S. Lewis* (South Bend, Ind.: St. Augustine's Press, 1998), pp. 85-87 (August 10, 1953).

[44]Ibid., p. 41 (November 25, 1947).

[45]Lewis, *God in the Dock*, p. 204; see also C. S. Lewis, *Christian Reflections* (London: Geoffrey Bles, 1967), p. vii.

[46]Lewis, *God in the Dock*, pp. 219-20.

[47]Ibid., pp. 89-90.

[48]Ibid., p. 201.

[49]Lewis, *Christian Reflections*, p. 166.

[50]Lewis, *God in the Dock*, pp. 332-33.

[51]Lewis, *Letters to Malcolm*, pp. 4-5.

[52]Ibid., p. 30.

[53]Ibid., pp. 100-101.

[54]Lewis, *God in the Dock*, p. 336.

[55]Lewis, *Letters to Malcolm*, p. 6.

[56]Ibid., p. 8.

[57]Ibid., p. 10.

[58]Lewis, *God in the Dock*, p. 331.

[59]Lewis, *Reflections on the Psalms*, pp. 45-46, 50, 52.

[60]Lewis, *Weight of Glory*, p. 7.

[61]See Lewis, *Surprised by Joy*, pp. 72-74.

[62]Lewis, *Screwtape Letters*, pp. 102-3.

[63]Lewis, *Letters of C. S. Lewis*, pp. 268-69 (undated); see also 1 Cor 13.

[64]Lewis, *God in the Dock*, p. 331; see also Lewis, *Reflections on the Psalms*, p. 94; Lewis, *Christian Reflections*, p. 13.

[65]Lewis, *God in the Dock*, pp. 61-62.

[66]Lewis, *Christian Reflections*, pp. 94-99.

[67]Lewis, *Reflections on the Psalms*, pp. 96-97.

Chapter Twenty: Prayer

[1]C. S. Lewis, *Letters to Malcolm: Chiefly on Prayer* (New York: Harcourt Brace Jovanovich, 1964), pp. 9-13.

[2]Lewis also mentions not needing to use names in prayer. See ibid., p. 18.

[3]Lewis notes that variety in our approach to prayer is helpful from time to time. See W. H. Lewis, ed., *Letters of C. S. Lewis* (New York: Harcourt Brace & World, 1966), p. 245 (October 20, 1952).

[4]See ibid., p. 239 (April 1, 1952).

[5]Lewis, *Letters to Malcolm*, pp. 15-16.

[6]Lewis's one exception to this was praying for his dead wife. Doing so made him halt, bewildered. See C. S. Lewis, *A Grief Observed* (New York: Bantam, 1976), pp. 24-26.

[7]Lewis, *Letters to Malcolm*, p. 107. The one scriptural warrant for praying for the dead that Lewis suggests is Paul's mention of people being baptized for the dead (1 Cor 15:29). If people can be baptized for the dead, why can't they pray for the dead? See Lewis, *Letters of C. S. Lewis*, p. 300 (October 28, 1961). Lewis also mentions 1 Pet 3:19-20. If something can be done for the dead, then why can't we pray for them? See Lewis, *Letters of C. S. Lewis*, p. 302 (December 28, 1961). The Protestant answer is that we can't pray for the dead or ask for their prayers because Scripture does not explicitly instruct us to do so.

[8]See Lewis, *Letters of C. S. Lewis*, p. 256 (July 31, 1954).

[9]Lewis, *Letters to Malcolm*, pp. 16-18.

[10]Ibid., pp. 19-23. Lewis notes how careful we need to be about informing God that our cause is righteous. See Lewis, *Letters of C. S. Lewis*, p. 168 (September 10, 1939). We also need to beware of bargaining with God. See C. S. Lewis, *Reflections on the Psalms* (San Diego: Harcourt Brace Jovanovich, 1958), pp. 97-98.

[11]Lewis, *Letters to Malcolm*, pp. 24-28.

[12]C. S. Lewis, *Mere Christianity* (New York: Macmillan, 1977), p. 161.

[13]For more on this, see C. S. Lewis, *The Screwtape Letters* (New York: Macmillan, 1977), p. 29.

[14]For more on "Give us this day our daily bread," see ibid., p. 126.

[15]See also C. S. Lewis, *Surprised by Joy* (New York: Harcourt Brace Jovanovich, 1955), pp. 77, 211, 231.

[16]Lewis, *Letters to Malcolm*, p. 34.

[17]Ibid., p. 95.

[18]Ibid., pp. 97-99. It should be noted that elsewhere Lewis "rehabilitates" the Puritans as a misunderstood group. See C. S. Lewis, *Selected Literary Essays*, ed. Walter Hooper (Cambridge: Cambridge University Press, 1979), p. 116; C. S. Lewis, *English Literature in the Sixteenth Century* (Oxford: Oxford University Press, 1973), pp. 34-35; C. S. Lewis, *Studies in Medieval and Renaissance Literature* (Cambridge: Cambridge University Press, 1996), pp. 117, 121-22.

[19]We dare not shirk petitionary prayer thinking it is the lowest form of prayer. See Lewis, *Screwtape Letters*, p. 126.

[20]Lewis, *Letters to Malcolm*, p. 35.

[21]C. S. Lewis, *The World's Last Night and Other Essays* (San Diego: Harcourt Brace & Co., 1987), pp. 3-11.

[22]See also Lewis, *A Grief Observed*, p. 34; C. S. Lewis, *Letters to an American Lady*, ed. Clyde S. Kilby (Grand Rapids, Mich.: Eerdmans, 1967), pp. 64-65 (June 18, 1957); George Sayer, *Jack: A Life of C. S. Lewis* (Wheaton, Ill.: Crossway, 1994), p. 368.

[23]See also C. S. Lewis, *Miracles* (New York: Macmillan, 1960), pp. 178-180.

[24]See also Lewis, *World's Last Night*, pp. 26-27; Lewis, *Miracles*, pp. 180-81.

[25]See also Lewis, *Letters of C. S. Lewis*, p. 236 (January 8, 1952); p. 226 (undated).

[26]See also Lewis, *Miracles*, p. 174.

[27]Also quoted in C. S. Lewis, *God in the Dock*, ed. Walter Hooper (Grand Rapids, Mich.: Eerdmans, 1994); see pp. 105-6, 217.

[28]Lewis, *Letters to Malcolm*, p. 50; see also Lewis, *God in the Dock*, pp. 76-79.

[29]Lewis, *Letters to Malcolm*, p. 52.

[30]Ibid., pp. 57-61.

[31]Lewis began wrestling with this issue at least as early as December 8, 1953, when he read his essay "Petitionary Prayer: A Problem Without an Answer" to the Oxford Clerical Society; see C. S. Lewis, *Christian Reflections* (London: Geoffry Bles, 1967), pp. xiii, 142-51. At that time he did not have an answer to the apparent contradiction between Jesus' command in Mk 11:24 and Jesus' practice in the Garden of Gethsemane. But by the time of publishing *Letters to Malcolm*, ten years later, Lewis did have an answer. That answer is presented in what follows.

[32]See Lewis's experience recorded in *Surprised by Joy*, pp. 20-21.

[33]See Lewis, *Letters of C. S. Lewis*, p. 256 (July 31, 1954); Lewis, *Surprised by Joy*, pp. 61-62; Lewis, *Screwtape Letters*, p. 21.

[34]See also Lewis, *Christian Reflections*, p. 150. Lewis also felt that if one were a better Christian one's prayers for others might be more effectual. See Lewis, *Letters to an American Lady*, p. 53 (April 26, 1956).

[35]Lewis, *Letters to Malcolm*, p. 66.

[36]Lewis, *Mere Christianity*, p. 12.

[37]Mt 5:44.

[38]Lewis, *Letters of C. S. Lewis*, p. 226 (undated).

[39]Ibid., p. 183 (April 16, 1940)

[40]Lewis, *Letters to an American Lady*, p. 14 (April 17, 1954).

[41]Ibid., p. 27 (March 10, 1954).

[42]Lewis, *Letters of C. S. Lewis*, p. 226 (undated).

[43]Ibid., p. 247 (November 8, 1952).

[44]Lewis, *Christian Reflections*, pp. 168-69.

[45]C. S. Lewis, *The Four Loves* (San Diego: Harcourt Brace Jovanovich, 1960), pp. 137-38.

[46]Lewis, *Screwtape Letters*, pp. 19-23, 125-29.

[47]Ibid., pp. 125-26.

[48]See C. S. Lewis, *Poems* (San Diego: Harcourt Brace, 1992), pp. 122-23.

[49]See also Lewis, *Letters to an American Lady*, p. 21 (November 6, 1953); Lewis, *Mere Christianity*, pp. 142-43.

[50]Lewis, *Letters to Malcolm*, pp. 67-71.

[51]Lewis, *Mere Christianity*, p. 147.

[52]Lewis, *Letters to Malcolm*, pp. 77-82.

[53]Lewis, *A Grief Observed*, p. 7.

[54]Ibid., pp. 53-54, 71, 80; see also Lewis, *Letters to an American Lady*, p. 89 (September 24, 1960).

[55]Lewis, *Letters to Malcolm*, pp. 83-87.

[56]See Lewis, *A Grief Observed*, pp. 76-78; Lewis, *Screwtape Letters*, p. 22.

[57]Lewis, *Letters to Malcolm*, pp. 88-93.

[58]Ibid., p. 90.

[59]Lewis, *Weight of Glory*, pp. 126-27; see also C. S. Lewis, *The Problem of Pain* (New York: Macmillan, 1986), p. 75.

[60]See Lewis, *Screwtape Letters*, pp. 54-55.

[61]Lewis, *Letters to Malcolm*, pp. 112-17; see also Lewis, *Letters to an American Lady*, pp. 70-71 (March 31, 1958); Lewis, *Screwtape Letters*, p. 39.

Chapter Twenty-One: The Sacraments

[1]C. S. Lewis, *God in the Dock*, ed. Walter Hooper (Grand Rapids, Mich.: Eerdmans, 1994), p. 46.

[2]C. S. Lewis, *The Screwtape Letters* (New York: Macmillan, 1977), p. 35.

[3]Ibid., p. 75.

[4]C. S. Lewis, *Mere Christianity* (New York: Macmillan, 1977), pp. 62-65.

[5]C. S. Lewis, *Reflections on the Psalms* (San Diego: Harcourt Brace Jovanovich, 1958), pp. 48-49.

[6]C. S. Lewis, *Perelandra* (New York: Macmillan, 1965), pp. 143-44.

[7]C. S. Lewis, *The Pilgrim's Regress* (Grand Rapids, Mich.: Eerdmans, 1981), pp. 166-69.

[8]C. S. Lewis, *The Weight of Glory* (New York: Macmillan, 1980), p. 70.

[9]C. S. Lewis, *A Grief Observed* (New York: Bantam, 1976), pp. 75-76.

[10]C. S. Lewis, *Miracles* (New York: Macmillan, 1960), p. 163.

[11]Lewis, *Mere Christianity*, p. 65.

[12]Lewis, *God in the Dock*, p. 241.

[13]Lewis, *Weight of Glory*, p. 112.

[14]Lewis, *Reflections on the Psalms*, p. 52.

[15]Lewis, *Miracles*, p. 125.

[16]W. H. Lewis, *Letters of C. S. Lewis* (New York: Harcourt Brace & World, 1966), p. 239 (March 18, 1952).

[17]C. S. Lewis, *The Voyage of the Dawn Treader* (New York: Macmillan, 1973), pp. 90-91.

[18]C. S. Lewis, *Surprised by Joy* (New York: Harcourt Brace Jovanovich, 1955), p. 181.

[19]Ibid., p. 161.

[20]Walter Hooper, *C. S. Lewis Companion and Guide* (New York: HarperCollins, 1996), p. 32.

[21]Lewis, *Letters of C. S. Lewis*, p. 192 (January 4, 1941).

[22]Ibid., p. 219 (September 6, 1949).

[23]Ibid., pp. 249-50 (April 6-7, 1953).

[24]Roger Lancelyn Green and Walter Hooper, *C. S. Lewis: A Biography* (Glasgow: Collins, 1980), pp. 301-2.

[25]Lewis, *God in the Dock*, p. 61.

[26]Lewis, *Letters of C. S. Lewis*, p. 224 (December 7, 1950).

[27]Lewis, *Weight of Glory*, p. 19.

[28]See Lewis, *Letters of C. S. Lewis*, p. 19.

[29]C. S. Lewis, *Letters to an American Lady*, ed. Clyde S. Kilby (Grand Rapids, Mich.: Eerdmans, 1967), p. 112 (March 19, 1963).

[30]Lewis, *Reflections on the Psalms*, p. 93.

[31]C. S. Lewis, *Letters to Children*, ed. Lyle W. Dorsett and Marjorie Lamp Mead (New York: Macmillan, 1985), p. 26.

[32]Lewis, *Letters to Malcolm*, p. 9.

[33]Ibid., pp. 100-105.

[34]See also Clyde S. Kilby and Marjorie Lamp Mead, eds., *Brothers and Friends: The Diaries of Major Warren Hamilton Lewis* (San Francisco: Harper & Row, 1982), p. 164 (Sunday, December, 1, 1934); p. 171 (Tuesday, January, 14, 1936), for Jack's and Warnie's contrasting views on the sacrament of Holy Communion.

[35]Lewis, *Letters to Malcolm*, p. 103.

[36]Lewis, *Voyage of the Dawn Treader*, pp. 192-202.

[37]See Mt 26:29.

Chapter Twenty-Two: Hell

[1]C. S. Lewis, *Surprised by Joy* (New York: Harcourt Brace Jovanovich, 1955), p. 232.

[2]C. S. Lewis, *Miracles* (New York: Macmillan, 1960), p. 145.

[3]See Ps 6:5; 88:12 for two examples. See also C. S. Lewis, *Reflections on the Psalms* (San Diego: Harcourt Brace Jovanovich, 1958), p. 38.

[4]Lewis, *Reflections on the Psalms*, pp. 36-42; see also C. S. Lewis, *God in the Dock*, ed. Walter Hooper (Grand Rapids, Mich.: Eerdmans, 1994), p. 130.

[5]C. S. Lewis, *The Weight of Glory* (New York: Macmillan, 1980), p. 15.

[6]C. S. Lewis, *The Screwtape Letters* (New York: Macmillan, 1977), p. 54.

[7]C. S. Lewis, *The Problem of Pain* (New York: Macmillan, 1986), p. 54.

[8]Ibid., p. 152.

[9]C. S. Lewis, *The Four Loves* (San Diego: Harcourt Brace Jovanovich, 1960), p. 169.

[10]Lewis, *Problem of Pain*, p. 148.

[11]C. S. Lewis, *Mere Christianity* (New York: Macmillan, 1977), p. 73; see also Lewis, *God in the Dock*, p. 155; C. S. Lewis, *The Great Divorce* (New York: Macmillan, 1979), p. 75.

[12]Lewis, *Mere Christianity*, p. 86.

[13]C. S. Lewis, *Perelandra* (New York: Macmillan, 1965), p. 173.

[14]Lewis's theology of Heaven and hell is rather different from some contemporary "theologies" like those typified in the movie *What Dreams May Come* with Robin Williams. In that movie everything in Heaven is the way you imagine it to be. Imagine anything, dream anything, and it is there. In Lewis's thought this is true of hell but not Heaven. Hell is a state of mind, but Heaven is the one utterly real place, so hard in its reality that the grass of Heaven pierces the feet of ghosts from hell when they first arrive there. See Lewis, *Great Divorce*.

[15]Ibid., pp. 11, 18-23.

[16]Lewis, *Screwtape Letters*, p. ix.

[17]C. S. Lewis, *The Pilgrim's Regress* (Grand Rapids, Mich.: Eerdmans, 1981), p. 180.

[18]See Mt 8:12; 22.13, 25.30 for some examples.

[19]Walter Hooper, *They Stand Together: The Letters of C. S. Lewis to Arthur Greeves* (New York: Macmillan, 1979), p. 508 (May 13, 1946).

[20]C. S. Lewis, *The Last Battle* (New York: Macmillan, 1970), p. 148.

[21]Lewis, *Great Divorce*, p. 69.

[22]Lewis, *Problem of Pain*, pp. 118-28.

[23]This is emphasized throughout Lewis's writings. In *Great Divorce* (p. 72), George MacDonald says that everyone who is in hell chooses to be there. Without human choice there can be no hell. If a person will not choose Heaven, then God will eventually say, "Thy will be done."

[24]Lewis says that if he has spoken too much of hell it is due not to the Puritanism of his Ulster childhood but to the Anglo-Catholicism of the church he attended while at Wynyard School in England. The effect of the teaching about hell there was that it led him seriously to pray, to read his Bible and to attempt to obey his conscience. See Lewis, *Surprised by Joy*, p. 34.

[25]Lewis, *Problem of Pain*, p. 121.

[26]Jn 3:19; 12:48.

[27]In *Dark Tower* Ransom says that people aren't sent to hell; they go there of their own accord. See C. S. Lewis, *The Dark Tower and Other Stories* (New York: Harcourt Brace Jovanovich, 1977), p. 49.

[28]Lewis says in *Surprised by Joy* (p. 77) that divine punishments are also mercies. See also his poem "Divine Justice," in C. S. Lewis, *Poems* (San Diego: Harcourt Brace, 1992), p. 98.

[29]Lewis, *Problem of Pain*, p. 125.

[30]Lewis speculates in *Reflections on the Psalms* (p. 37) whether the fate of unredeemed humanity is to disintegrate in soul as well as in body, to be a witless psychic sediment.

[31]While Lewis suggests here that hell is not in the same time line as Heaven, he expresses his belief, in *Letters to Malcolm: Chiefly on Prayer* (New York: Harcourt Brace Jovanovich, 1964), pp. 109-10, that the blessed dead are in some kind of time. This is supported by Rev 6:10 (NIV), where the souls under the altar in Heaven cry out, "How long, Sovereign Lord, holy and true, until you judge the inhabitants of the earth and avenge our blood?" But, Lewis says, the state of the dead until the resurrection is for him unimaginable. See W. H. Lewis, ed., *Letters of C. S. Lewis* (New York: Harcourt Brace & World, 1966), pp. 294-95 (August 5, 1960); p. 297 (October 16, 1960).

[32]Lewis, *Great Divorce*, pp. 121-23.

[33]Lewis, *Letters of C. S. Lewis*, p. 238 (January 31, 1952).

[34]Lewis, *Great Divorce*, pp. 123-24.

[35]Lewis, *Letters to Malcolm*, p. 76.

[36]Lewis, *Problem of Pain*, p. 128.

Chapter Twenty-Three: Purgatory

[1]C. S. Lewis, *The Problem of Pain* (New York: Macmillan, 1986), p. 124.

[2]C. S. Lewis, *The Screwtape Letters* (New York: Macmillan, 1977), pp. 146-47.

[3]C. S. Lewis, *Mere Christianity* (New York: Macmillan, 1977), p. 172.

[4]C. S. Lewis, *The Great Divorce* (New York: Macmillan, 1979), p. 39.

[5]Ibid., p. 42.

[6]Ibid., p. 67.

[7]Ibid., p. 69.

[8]Ibid., pp. 7-8.

[9]W. H. Lewis, ed., *Letters of C. S. Lewis* (New York: Harcourt Brace & World, 1966), pp. 246-47 (November 8, 1952).

[10]C. S. Lewis, *Letters to An American Lady*, ed. Clyde S. Kilby (Grand Rapids, Mich.: Eerdmans, 1967), p. 81 (July 7, 1959).

[11]Ibid., p. 103 (July 31, 1962).

[12]Lewis, *Letters of C. S. Lewis*, p. 307 (September 17, 1963).

[13]C. S. Lewis, *Reflections on the Psalms* (San Diego: Harcourt Brace Jovanovich, 1958), p. 8.

[14]C. S. Lewis, *A Grief Observed* (New York: Bantam, 1976), pp. 30-31; see also p. 58.

[15]Ibid., pp. 48-49.

[16]For more on More's conception of Purgatory, see C. S. Lewis, *English Literature in the Sixteenth Century* (Oxford: Oxford University Press, 1973), pp. 172-73.

[17]For more on Fisher's conception of Purgatory, see Lewis, *English Literature in the Sixteenth Century*, pp. 163-64.

[18]C. S. Lewis, *Letters to Malcolm: Chiefly on Prayer* (New York: Harcourt Brace Jovanovich, 1964), pp. 108-9. See also *English Literature in the Sixteenth Century*, p. 439, where Lewis mentions Cardinal William Allen's view of Purgatory, a view with which Lewis obviously did not agree.

Chapter Twenty-Four: Heaven

[1]C. S. Lewis, *The Weight of Glory* (New York: Macmillan, 1980), pp. 20-21.

[2]C. S. Lewis, *The Problem of Pain* (New York: Macmillan, 1986), pp. 144-45.

[3]C. S. Lewis, *Letters to Malcolm: Chiefly on Prayer* (New York: Harcourt Brace Jovanovich, 1964), p. 120.

[4]C. S. Lewis, *Christian Reflections* (London: Geoffrey Bles, 1967), pp. 167-68.

[5]C. S. Lewis, *Miracles* (New York: Macmillan, 1960), pp. 157-58.

[6]Lewis, *Problem of Pain*, p. 114.

[7]C. S. Lewis, *The Screwtape Letters* (New York: Macmillan, 1977), p. 133.

[8]Lewis, *Weight of Glory*, pp. 7-8.

[9]Ibid., p. 32.

[10]C. S. Lewis, *Letters to an American Lady*, ed. Clyde S. Kilby (Grand Rapids, Mich.: Eerdmans, 1967), p. 47 (December 6, 1955).

[11]C. S. Lewis, *Mere Christianity* (New York: Macmillan, 1977), p. 121.

[12]Lewis, *Weight of Glory*, p. 9.

[13]Lewis, *Problem of Pain*, p. 153.

[14]Lewis, *Letters to Malcolm*, pp. 92-93.

[15]C. S. Lewis, *The Pilgrim's Regress* (Grand Rapids, Mich.: Eerdmans, 1981), p. 170.'

[16]C. S. Lewis, *The Great Divorce* (New York: Macmillan, 1979), pp. 26-27.

[17]Ibid., pp. 102-3.

[18]Lewis, *Letters to an American Lady*, p. 116 (Friday, June 28, 1963).

[19]Lewis, *Great Divorce*, p. 28.

[20]Ibid., p. 43.

[21]C. S. Lewis, *The Last Battle* (New York: Macmillan, 1970), pp. 169-70.

[22]C. S. Lewis, *Reflections on the Psalms* (San Diego: Harcourt Brace Jovanovich, 1958), p. 42.

[23]Lewis, *Mere Christianity*, p. 118.

[24]Ibid., p. 119; see also Lewis, *Weight of Glory*, pp. 6-7.

[25]Lewis, *Mere Christianity*, p. 120; see also Lewis, *Weight of Glory*, pp. 8-9.

[26]Lewis, *Problem of Pain*, pp. 145-46.

[27]Ibid., pp. 147-48.

[28]Lewis, *Weight of Glory*, p. 6.

[29]W. H. Lewis, ed., *Letters of C. S. Lewis* (New York: Harcourt Brace & World, 1966), p. 289 (November 5, 1959).

[30]Lewis, *Letters to an American Lady*, p. 81 (June 7, 1959).

[31]Lewis, *Weight of Glory*, p. 10.

[32]Ibid., p. 15.

[33]Ibid., p. 17.

[34]Lewis, *Mere Christianity*, pp. 77-70.

[35]Lewis, *Reflections on the Psalms*, pp. 96-97.

[36]Lewis, *Problem of Pain*, p. 91.

[37]Ibid., p. 149; Lewis is quoting *Theologia Germanica*, 51.

[38]C. S. Lewis, *God in the Dock*, ed. Walter Hooper (Grand Rapids, Mich.: Eerdmans, 1994), p. 216.

[39]Lewis, *Great Divorce*, pp. 109-10.

[40]Ibid., p. 30.

[41]Ibid., p. 83.

[42]C. S. Lewis, *Letters to Children*, ed. Lyle W. Dorsett and Marjorie Lamp Mead (New York: Macmillan, 1985), p. 45 (May 29, 1954).

[43]Lewis, *Problem of Pain*, p. 152.

[44]Ibid., p. 126.

[45]Lewis, *Screwtape Letters*, p. 148.

[46]Lewis, *Great Divorce*, p. 61.

[47]Ibid., pp. 61-62.

[48]Lewis, *Problem of Pain*, pp. 61-62.

[49]Lewis, *Miracles*, pp. 159-60.

[50]Lewis, *Weight of Glory*, pp. 67-68.

[51]Ibid., pp. 68-69.

[52]See Lewis, *Weight of Glory*, p. 119; Lewis, *Problem of Pain*, p. 125.

[53]Lewis, *Problem of Pain*, p. 127.

[54]Lewis, *Great Divorce*, p. 118.

[55]Lewis, *Last Battle*, p. 171.

[56]Lewis, *Letters to Malcolm*, pp. 115-16.

[57]Lewis, *Last Battle*, p. 137.

[58]Lewis, *Letters of C. S. Lewis*, p. 248 (November 8, 1952).

[59]C. S. Lewis, *The Four Loves* (San Diego: Harcourt Brace Jovanovich 1960), p. 188.

[60]Ibid., p. 189.

[61]C. S. Lewis, *A Grief Observed* (New York: Bantam, 1976), pp. 28-29.

[62]Lewis, *Last Battle*, p. 177.

[63]Ibid., p. 182.

[64]Lewis, *Letters to an American Lady*, p. 75 (September 30, 1958).

[65]Lewis, *Mere Christianity*, p. 91.

[66]Lewis, *Miracles*, pp. 161-63.

[67]Ibid., p. 159.

[68]Ibid., p. 163.

[69]Ibid., p. 67.

[70]Lewis, *Letters of C. S. Lewis*, p. 288 (September 8, 1959).

[71]Lewis, *Miracles*, p. 151.

[72]Lewis, *Letters to Malcolm*, pp. 121-24.

[73]Lewis, *Weight of Glory*, p. 131.

[74]Lewis, *Great Divorce*, p. 6.

[75]Lewis, *Last Battle*, p. 183.

Chapter Twenty-Five: The World's Last Night

[1]C. S. Lewis, *God in the Dock*, ed. Walter Hooper (Grand Rapids, Mich.: Eerdmans, 1994), p. 336.

[2]Ibid., p. 266.

[3]See 2 Pet 3:9.

[4]C. S. Lewis, *Mere Christianity* (New York: Macmillan, 1977), pp. 65-66.

[5]Compare C. S. Lewis, *The Last Battle* (New York: Macmillan, 1970), pp. 150-51, with Mt 24:29; Is 34:4; 13:10.

[6]Compare ibid., pp. 153-54, with Mt 25:31-46. Lewis says we cannot remove the notion of the final judgment from Jesus' teaching. It is part of the warp and woof of his parables; see C. S. Lewis, *Christian Reflections* (London: Geoffrey Bles, 1967), p. 123.

[7]Compare Lewis, *Last Battle*, p. 155, with 2 Pet 3:10.

[8]Compare ibid., p. 156, with Acts 2:20; Joel 2:31.

[9]Compare ibid., pp. 156-57, with 2 Pet 3:7, 12; Acts 2:19; Joel 2:30.

[10]Compare ibid., p. 157, with Mt 24:29; Is 13:10.

[11]C. S. Lewis, *The World's Last Night and Other Essays* (San Diego: Harcourt Brace, 1987), p. 93.

[12]There are other ways of interpreting Jesus' statement in Mk 13:30 (NIV), that "this generation will certainly not pass away until all these things have happened." There are at least two possible references for "this generation." Jesus may have been talking about the generation that was alive when he made this statement. And indeed that generation saw "the end" that Jesus predicted (Mk 13:1-23). But, according to this interpretation, Jesus was not predicting the end of the world in these verses. He was predicting the end of Jerusalem, as people then knew it, and the destruction of the temple in particular (Mk 13:1-3). This took place in A.D. 70, when Titus sacrificed a pig on the Jewish altar and then leveled the temple. The second reference for "this generation" may be to the generation that would see the sun darkened, the moon not giving its light and the stars falling from the heavens. What Jesus may have been saying was that the generation that would see *these* things would not pass away until they had seen everything accomplished, including his prophesied return (see Mk 13:24–27).

[13]Lewis, *World's Last Night*, pp. 105-6.

[14]Ibid., p. 109.

[15]Ibid., p. 113.

Conclusion

[1]Previously unpublished letter quoted in C. S. Lewis, *Letters to Children*, ed. Lyle W. Dorsett and Marjorie Lamp Mead (New York: Macmillan, 1985), p. 3.

BIBLIOGRAPHY

Athanasius, *The Incarnation of the Word of God: Being the Treatise of St. Athanasius: De Incarnatione Verbi Dei.* Translated by a Religious of C.S.M.V. S. Th. Introduction by C. S. Lewis. London: Bles, The Centenary Press, 1944.

Augustinus, Aurelius. *The Nicene and Post-Nicene Fathers.* Edited by Philip Schaff. Vol. 5: *Saint Augustine: Anti-Pelagian Writings.* Grand Rapids, Mich.: Eerdmans, 1956.

Chesterton, G. K. *Orthodoxy.* Wheaton, Ill.: Harold Shaw Publishers, 1994.

Christensen, Michael J. *C. S. Lewis on Scripture.* Waco, Tex.: Word, 1979.

Como, James, ed. *C. S. Lewis at the Breakfast Table.* New York: Harcourt Brace, 1992.

————— *C S L: The Bulletin of the New York C. S. Lewis Society* vol. 27, no. 9-10 (July-August 1996).

Davidman, Joy. *Smoke on the Mountain.* Foreword by C. S. Lewis. London: Hodder & Stoughton, 1955.

de Rougemont, Denis. *Love in the Western World.* Princeton, N.J.: Princeton University Press, 1983.

Derrick, Christopher. *C. S. Lewis and the Church of Rome.* San Francisco: Ignatius Press, 1981.

Fairweather, Eugene R., ed. *A Scholastic Miscellany: Anselm to Ockham.* Philadelphia: Westminster Press, 1956.

Farrer, Austin. *Lord, I Believe.* 2nd ed. London: The Faith Press, 1958.

————— . *The Glass of Vision.* Glasgow: Dacre Press; Westminster: Robert MacLehose and Co., University Press, 1948.

Goffar, Janine, compiler. *The C. S. Lewis Index.* Wheaton, Ill.: Crossway, 1998.

Graham, David, ed. *We Remember C. S. Lewis: Essays and Memoirs.* Nashville: Broadman & Holman, 2001.

Green, Roger Lancelyn, and Walter Hooper. *C. S. Lewis: A Biography.* Glasgow: Collins, 1980.

Gresham, Douglas H. Lecture on *The Chronicles of Narnia.* Cassette tape in the author's personal library.

————— . *Lenten Lands.* San Francisco: HarperCollins, 1994.

Harvey, Van A. *A Handbook of Theological Terms.* New York: Macmillan, 1964.

Hooper, Walter. *C. S. Lewis Companion and Guide.* New York: HarperCollins, 1996.

————— . *They Stand Together: The Letters of C. S. Lewis to Arthur Greeves.* New York: Macmillan, 1979.

Hooper, Walter, ed. *All My Road Before Me.* Orlando, Fla.: Harcourt Brace Jovanovich, 1991.

————. *C. S. Lewis Collected Letters.* Vol. 1. London: HarperCollins, 2000.

Kelly, J. N. D. *Early Christian Doctrines.* San Francisco: Harper & Row, 1978.

Kilby, Clyde S. *The Christian World of C. S. Lewis.* Grand Rapids, Mich.: Eerdmans, 1964.

————. *Images of Salvation.* Wheaton, Ill.: Harold Shaw Publishers, 1978.

Kilby, Clyde S., and Marjorie Lamp Mead, eds. *Brothers and Friends: The Diaries of Major Warren Hamilton Lewis.* San Francisco: Harper & Row, 1982.

Kreeft, Peter. *C. S. Lewis for the Third Millennium.* San Francisco: Ignatius Press, 1994.

Lane, Tony. *Exploring Christian Thought.* Nashville: Thomas Nelson, 1996.

Lawrence, Brother. *The Practice of the Presence of God.* Edited by Douglas V. Steere. Nashville: Upper Room, 1950.

Lewis, C. S. *The Abolition of Man.* New York: Macmillan, 1978.

————. *The Allegory of Love.* New York: Oxford University Press, 1967.

————. *Christian Reflections.* London: Geoffrey Bles, 1967.

————. *The Dark Tower and Other Stories.* New York: Harcourt Brace Jovanovich, 1977.

————. *English Literature in the Sixteenth Century.* Oxford: Oxford University Press, 1973.

————. *The Four Loves.* San Diego: Harcourt Brace Jovanovich, 1960.

————. *God in the Dock.* Edited by Walter Hooper. Grand Rapids, Mich.: Eerdmans, 1994.

————. *The Great Divorce.* New York: Macmillan, 1979.

————. *A Grief Observed.* New York: Bantam, 1976.

————. *The Horse and His Boy.* New York: HarperCollins, 1994.

————. *The Last Battle.* New York: Macmillan, 1973.

————. *Letters to an American Lady.* Edited by Clyde Kilby. Grand Rapids, Mich.: Eerdmans, 1967.

————. *Letters to Children.* Edited by Lyle W. Dorsett and Marjorie Lamp Mead. New York: Macmillan, 1985.

————. *Letters to Malcolm: Chiefly on Prayer.* New York: Harcourt Brace Jovanovich, 1964.

————. *The Lion, the Witch and the Wardrobe.* New York: Macmillan, 1970.

————. *The Literary Impact of the Authorized Version.* Philadelphia: Fortress, 1967.

————. *The Magician's Nephew.* New York: Macmillan, 1973.

————— . *Mere Christianity.* New York: Macmillan, 1984.

————— . *Miracles.* London: Bles, 1947; reprint, New York: Macmillan, 1978.

————— . *Out of the Silent Planet.* New York: Simon & Schuster, 1996.

————— . *Perelandra.* New York: Macmillan, 1965.

————— . *The Pilgrim's Regress.* Grand Rapids, Mich.: Eerdmans, 1981.

————— . *Poems.* San Diego: Harcourt Brace, 1992.

————— . *A Preface to Paradise Lost.* New York: Oxford University Press, 1961.

————— . *Present Concerns.* San Diego: Harcourt Brace Jovanovich, 1987.

————— . *Prince Caspian.* New York: Macmillan, 1973.

————— . *The Problem of Pain.* New York: Macmillan, 1986.

————— . *Reflections on the Psalms.* San Diego: Harcourt Brace Jovanovich, 1958.

————— . *The Screwtape Letters.* New York: Macmillan, 1977.

————— . *Selected Literary Essays.* Edited by Walter Hooper. Cambridge: Cambridge University Press, 1979.

————— . *The Silver Chair.* New York: Macmillan, 1973.

————— . *Studies in Medieval and Renaissance Literature.* Cambridge: Cambridge University Press, 1996.

————— . *Surprised by Joy.* New York: Harcourt Brace Jovanovich, 1955.

————— . *That Hideous Strength.* New York: Macmillan, 1974.

————— . *Till We Have Faces.* New York: Harcourt Brace Jovanovich, 1980.

————— . *The Voyage of the Dawn Treader.* New York: Macmillan, 1973.

————— . *The Weight of Glory.* New York: Macmillan, 1980.

————— . *The World's Last Night and Other Essays.* San Diego: Harcourt Brace, 1987.

Lewis, W. H., ed. *Letters of C. S. Lewis.* New York: Harcourt Brace & World, 1966.

Lewis, W. H., and Walter Hooper, eds. *Letters of C. S. Lewis.* San Diego: Harcourt Brace, 1993.

Macdonald, Michael H., and Andrew A. Tadie, eds. *The Riddle of Joy.* Grand Rapids, Mich.: Eerdmans, 1989.

Martindale, Wayne, and Jerry Root, eds. *The Quotable Lewis.* Wheaton, Ill.: Tyndale House, 1989.

McDowell, Josh. *More Than a Carpenter.* Wheaton, Ill.: Tyndale House, 1977.

Moynihan, Martin, ed. and trans. *The Latin Letters of C. S. Lewis.* South Bend, Ind.: St. Augustine's Press, 1998.

Myers, Ken. *Mars Hill Tapes.* Interview with Clyde S. Kilby. Vol. 30. January/February 1998.

Nicholi, Armand. *The Question of God.* New York: Free Press, 2002.

Payne, Leanne. *Real Presence: The Holy Spirit in the Works of C. S. Lewis.* Westchester, Ill.:

Cornerstone, 1979.

Phillips, Justin. *C. S. Lewis at the BBC.* London: HarperCollins, 2002.

Sayer, George. *Jack: A Life of C. S. Lewis.* Wheaton, Ill.: Crossway, 1994.

The Book of Common Prayer of the Protestant Episcopal Church. 1945.

The Westminster Confession of Faith. Atlanta: Committee for Christian Education and Publications, 1990.

Vanauken, Sheldon. *Encounter with Light.* Wheaton, Ill.: Marion E. Wade Collection, Wheaton College.

————. *A Severe Mercy.* New York: Bantam. 1979.

Walker, Williston. *A History of the Christian Church.* 4th ed. New York: Charles Scribner's Sons, 1985.

Wilson, A. N. *C. S. Lewis: A Biography.* New York: W. W. Norton, 1990.

Subject Index

Scripture Index

CPSIA information can be obtained at www.ICGtesting.com
Printed in the USA
LVOW08s1237160314

377611LV00001B/153/P